Learn Model Context Protocol with TypeScript

Build agentic systems in TypeScript with the new standard for AI capabilities

Christoffer Noring

‹packt›

Learn Model Context Protocol with TypeScript

Portfolio Director: Ashwin Nair
Relationship Lead: Aaron Lazar
Project Manager: Ruvika Rao
Content Engineer: Runcil Rebello
Technical Editor: Rohit Singh
Copy Editor: Safis Editing
Indexer: Rekha Nair
Proofreader: Runcil Rebello
Production Designer: Shantanu Zagade
Growth Lead: Anamika Singh

First published: November 2025

Production reference: 1211125

Published by Packt Publishing Ltd.
Grosvenor House
11 St Paul's Square
Birmingham
B3 1RB, UK.

ISBN 978-1-80666-139-8
www.packtpub.com

To my wife, without you, I wouldn't be at this point in my life. I owe you everything. Also, to my parents, my biggest fans, your support means the world.

Also, huge thanks to my colleagues at Microsoft for all the help and support, and especially to John Papa and Dan Wahlin for being amazing mentors and friends over the years.

– Christoffer Noring

Foreword

When Christoffer Noring first told me about his idea for a book on the **Model Context Protocol** (**MCP**), I was immediately intrigued. The concept of bringing clarity to such a rapidly evolving area of AI felt both timely and necessary. Christoffer has always had a gift for explaining complex technical systems in a way that makes them accessible without oversimplifying. In this book, he channels that clarity into a complete guide to understanding and building AI systems with MCP.

What stands out most to me is the way Christoffer approaches the subject. He doesn't just document how MCP works; he places it in the context of real challenges and walks you through different options to consider. The material is practical, thoughtfully organized, and written with the same curiosity and care that Chris brings to his talks and tutorials.

The range of topics, which includes sampling, elicitation, security, server design, and more, shows how MCP supports building AI systems that are both adaptive and reliable. The examples are grounded in real-world use, depicting how design directly impacts the performance and behavior of AI as it interacts with MCP servers and tools.

This book is a practical map for anyone developing AI systems that rely on strong architectural foundations. I'm confident readers will come away not only understanding MCP but also with a deeper appreciation for how thoughtful MCP protocol and tool planning and design can significantly enhance your custom AI systems and impact the way you interact with AI assistants.

Dan Wahlin

Principal Content Engineer, Microsoft

Contributors

About the author

Christoffer Noring is a passionate developer and educator who specializes in modern web technologies and AI integrations and works as an engineer at Microsoft. He's also a tutor at the University of Oxford and is a published author on Angular, RxJS, generative AI, and now MCP. Christoffer has almost two decades of experience in software development and is a frequent speaker at tech conferences worldwide. According to his manager, his best quality is being able to break down complex technical concepts into simple, understandable terms. He hopes you agree! ;)

When not coding or writing, Christoffer is probably growing another user community, mentoring developers, or spending time with his family.

About the reviewers

Mark McDonagh is a seasoned technology executive and information security specialist with over 25 years of experience in enterprise software development, cloud transformation, and cybersecurity governance. He has led high-performing cloud engineering teams in the telecom, contact-center, and airline industries, delivering secure, scalable platforms and overseeing compliance programs. Mark holds a Bachelor's degree in Computer Systems, a Master's in Cybersecurity and Computer Forensics, and a Postgraduate Diploma in Executive Management, and is currently pursing a Postgraduate in AI/ML.

Outside of work, Mark actively contributes to standards development and cybersecurity education through volunteer roles with standards organizations, most recently with the Cloud Security Alliance's **Customer Communications Management** (**CCM**) and AI initiatives. Mark currently leads Governance and Information Security at Verodat, where he helps shape resilient, AI-driven data platforms and contributes to emerging protocols like the MCP. In his spare time Mark also volunteers to help people in need through his work for the Legion of Mary.

Tejul Pandit is a Senior Staff Machine Learning Engineer with over seven years of experience in the field. She holds a Master's degree in Artificial Intelligence from Northwestern University and is the author of multiple research papers and patents. Her expertise lies in designing and implementing ML-based architectures, including leading the company's first large-scale deployment of a machine learning model that significantly reduced human effort while maintaining high efficacy. Tejul is actively involved in LLM-based **Retrieval-Augmented Generation** (**RAG**) research, focusing on building efficient RAG systems and effective prompting strategies, and has been invited to present at AI and ML conferences on topics such as building efficient RAG pipelines and enterprise AI applications.

Maxim Salnikov is a leader at the intersection of cloud, web, and artificial intelligence. With over two decades of software engineering experience, he has dedicated his career to empowering developers and shaping the future of technology.

As a Senior Solution Engineer at Microsoft, Maxim is on the front lines of the AI revolution, focusing on next-generation AI-native developer tools and platforms. His influence extends globally through his work as an international speaker and a key organizer for Norway's largest developer communities. A true pioneer in the Generative AI space, he founded the world's first Prompt Engineering Conference, establishing a global platform for innovation in this critical new field.

Table of Contents

Chapter 5: Creating MCP Servers for Web Consumption with Streamable HTTP   91

Chapter 6: Maintaining Clean Architecture with an Advanced Server Approach   121

Chapter 7: Consuming Servers by Building Bespoke Clients/Agents   155

Chapter 11: Securing Your Application 233

Chapter 12: Bringing MCP Apps to Production 261

Preface

The **Model Context Protocol (MCP)** represents a revolutionary approach to building **artificial intelligence (AI)** applications that can efficiently distribute resources, standardize capabilities, and facilitate seamless communication between different components in complex systems. As AI continues to evolve and integrate into every aspect of our digital lives, the need for standardized, scalable, and secure protocols becomes increasingly critical.

MCP addresses fundamental challenges that developers face when building AI applications: resource distribution bottlenecks, lack of standardization across different components, complexity in building and testing distributed systems, and the intricate process of developing clients that can effectively interact with servers and **large language models (LLMs)**. By providing a structured framework, MCP enables developers to create more efficient, maintainable, and scalable AI applications.

Among all the protocols and frameworks available for AI application development, MCP stands out because it offers several key advantages:

- It provides a standardized way to describe and communicate capabilities between different system components
- It enables efficient resource distribution across multiple servers, improving performance and scalability
- It offers comprehensive guidelines for building, testing, and deploying both servers and clients
- It supports multiple communication methods, including **standard input/output (STDIO)** and **server-sent events (SSE)**
- It facilitates integration with modern development tools and platforms

In this comprehensive book, we will first explore the foundational concepts of the MCP, understanding its architecture, components, and the problems it solves in modern AI application development.

Once you understand the core protocol concepts, we will dive deep into practical implementation, covering how to build and test MCP servers using various approaches, including STDIO and SSE-based servers. We will also explore advanced server development techniques and patterns that will help you create robust, production-ready applications.

The book then progresses to client development, showing you how to build effective clients both with and without LLM integration, and how to consume MCP servers using popular tools such as Claude Desktop and Virtual Studio Code (VS Code) agent mode. We will also cover advanced topics such as sampling and elicitation techniques that can enhance your AI applications.

Finally, we will address critical production concerns, including security best practices, deployment strategies, and scaling considerations that are essential for running MCP applications in real-world environments.

This book will guide you through numerous practical examples and exercises, demonstrating best practices for building MCP applications and providing hands-on experience with real-world scenarios. The examples and code samples are designed to be immediately applicable to your own projects, whether you're building simple proofs of concept or complex enterprise applications.

The author acknowledges the use of cutting-edge AI, in this case GitHub Copilot, with the sole aim of enhancing the language and clarity within the book, thereby ensuring a smooth reading experience for readers. It's important to note that the content itself has been crafted by the author and edited by a professional publishing team.

Who this book is for

This book is for developers, AI engineers, and software architects looking to build sophisticated AI applications using the MCP. Whether you're a backend developer wanting to create efficient AI servers, a frontend developer looking to integrate AI capabilities into your applications, or an AI researcher exploring new ways to structure AI systems, this book provides the knowledge and practical skills you need.

Basic programming experience in TypeScript is recommended, along with familiarity with web development concepts, API design, and fundamental AI/ML concepts. Experience with modern development tools and practices will help you get the most out of this book.

What this book covers

Chapter 1, Introducing the Model Context Protocol, introduces the Model Context Protocol, its historical background, and the fundamental problems it solves in AI application development. You'll understand why MCP is essential for modern AI systems.

Chapter 2, Explaining the Model Context Protocol, provides a comprehensive deep dive into the MCP protocol itself, covering its architecture, key components (hosts, clients, servers), communication methods (STDIO and SSE), and the standard capabilities framework.

Chapter 3, Building and Testing Servers, focuses on practical server development using STDIO communication, covering server architecture, resource and tool implementation, and comprehensive testing strategies using inspector tools.

Chapter 4, Building SSE Servers, explores SSE-based server development, showing you how to build real-time, streaming MCP servers for more dynamic applications.

Chapter 5, Creating MCP Servers for Web Consumption with Streamable HTTP, covers advanced Streamable HTTP techniques for MCP servers, enabling you to build highly scalable and efficient server implementations.

Chapter 6, Maintaining Clean Architecture with an Advanced Server Approach, delves into sophisticated server patterns, advanced resource management, complex tool implementations, and production-ready server architectures.

Chapter 7, Consuming Servers by Building Bespoke Clients/Agents, teaches you how to develop MCP clients, both standalone applications and those integrated with LLMs, covering client architecture and best practices.

Chapter 8, Consuming Servers Using an IDE, demonstrates how to effectively use MCP servers through various clients and tools, including Claude Desktop, VS Code agent mode, and custom client implementations.

Chapter 9, Delegating Tasks with Sampling, explores advanced sampling techniques for AI applications, showing how to leverage MCP's capabilities for sophisticated AI interactions and content generation.

Chapter 10, Improving Interactive Workflows with Elicitation, covers techniques for effective information elicitation in AI applications, demonstrating how to design systems that can intelligently gather and process information.

Chapter 11, Securing Your Application, addresses comprehensive security considerations for MCP applications, including authentication, authorization, data protection, and secure communication patterns.

Chapter 12, Bringing MCP Apps to Production, provides practical guidance on deploying MCP applications to production environments, covering scaling strategies, monitoring, and maintenance best practices.

To get the most out of this book

To follow along with the examples and exercises in this book, you'll need the following:

- TypeScript installed on your system
- A code editor or IDE (VS Code is recommended)
- Basic familiarity with command-line interfaces
- An understanding of HTTP, JSON, and basic networking concepts
- Access to modern AI tools such as Claude or ChatGPT for testing examples

All the code examples are designed to run on Windows, macOS, and Linux. The book includes specific installation instructions and setup guidance for each major platform.

Download the example code files

The code bundle for the book is hosted on GitHub at https://github.com/PacktPublishing/Learn-Model-Context-Protocol-with-TypeScript. We also have other code bundles from our rich catalog of books and videos available at https://github.com/PacktPublishing. Check them out!

Download the color images

We also provide a PDF file that has color images of the screenshots/diagrams used in this book. You can download it here: https://packt.link/gbp/9781806661398.

Conventions used

There are a number of text conventions used throughout this book.

CodeInText: Indicates code words in text, database table names, folder names, filenames, file extensions, pathnames, dummy URLs, user input, and Twitter handles. For example: "The server.js file is executed via the node command."

A block of code is set as follows:

```
interface Transport {
  // Start processing messages
  start(): Promise<void>;

  // Send a JSON-RPC message
  send(message: JSONRPCMessage): Promise<void>;

  // Close the connection
  close(): Promise<void>;

  // Callbacks
  onclose?: () => void;
  onerror?: (error: Error) => void;
  onmessage?: (message: JSONRPCMessage) => void;
}
```

Any command-line input or output is written as follows:

```
npx @modelcontextprotocol/inspector node ./build/index.js
```

Bold: Indicates a new term, an important word, or words that you see on the screen. For instance, words in menus or dialog boxes appear in the text like this. For example: "In short, **JavaScript Object Notation-Remote Procedure Call (JSON-RPC)** messages are exchanged between the client and the server."

Warnings or important notes appear like this.

Tips and tricks appear like this.

Get in touch

Feedback from our readers is always welcome.

General feedback: If you have questions about any aspect of this book or have any general feedback, please email us at customercare@packt.com and mention the book's title in the subject of your message.

Errata: Although we have taken every care to ensure the accuracy of our content, mistakes do happen. If you have found a mistake in this book, we would be grateful if you reported this to us. Please visit http://www.packt.com/submit-errata, click **Submit Errata**, and fill in the form.

Piracy: If you come across any illegal copies of our works in any form on the internet, we would be grateful if you would provide us with the location address or website name. Please contact us at copyright@packt.com with a link to the material.

If you are interested in becoming an author: If there is a topic that you have expertise in and you are interested in either writing or contributing to a book, please visit http://authors.packt.com/.

Share your thoughts

Once you've read *Learn Model Context Protocol with TypeScript*, we'd love to hear your thoughts! Scan the QR code below to go straight to the Amazon review page for this book and share your feedback.

https://packt.link/r/180666139X

Your review is important to us and the tech community and will help us make sure we're delivering excellent quality content.

Free Benefits with Your Book

This book comes with free benefits to support your learning. Activate them now for instant access (see the "*How to Unlock*" section for instructions).

Here's a quick overview of what you can instantly unlock with your purchase:

PDF and ePub Copies

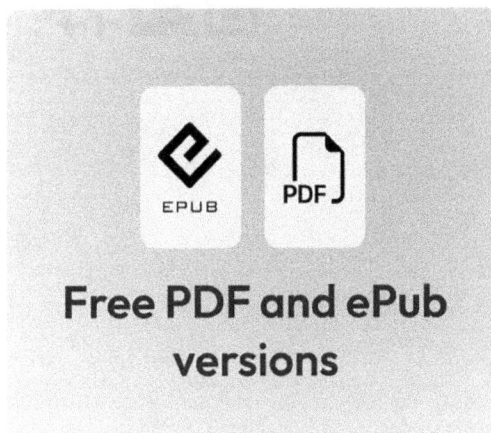

Free PDF and ePub versions

Next-Gen Web-Based Reader

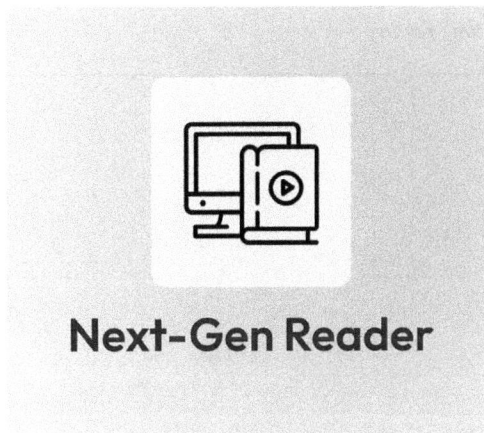

Next-Gen Reader

Access a DRM-free PDF copy of this book to read anywhere, on any device.

Use a DRM-free ePub version with your favorite e-reader.

Multi-device progress sync: Pick up where you left off, on any device.

Highlighting and notetaking: Capture ideas and turn reading into lasting knowledge.

Bookmarking: Save and revisit key sections whenever you need them.

Dark mode: Reduce eye strain by switching to dark or sepia themes.

How to Unlock

UNLOCK NOW

Scan the QR code (or go to packtpub.com/unlock). Search for this book by name, confirm the edition, and then follow the steps on the page.

Note: Keep your invoice handy. Purchases made directly from Packt don't require one.

1

Introducing the Model Context Protocol

Generative AI has rapidly become a force in today's technological landscape, reshaping industries and redefining how we approach problem-solving. From natural language processing to image generation, the integration of generative AI into various domains has opened up new possibilities for innovation and efficiency.

For us developers, integrating generative AI into app development workflows is not without its complexities. We must carefully evaluate factors such as model accuracy, ethical considerations, and computational efficiency.

It's in the process of building applications that we need to consider how we standardize the way we build our AI applications. Standardization means that everything looks the same, which should mean easier integration and collaboration across different teams and tools.

This is where the **Model Context Protocol** (**MCP**) comes in, to standardize how we ensure that AI-powered applications can easily find what they need from tools, content, and prompts; more on that shortly.

The chapter covers the following topics:

- How we got here, from SOAP to REST to GraphQL to gRPC to MCP
- The need for a standard
- Endless possibilities: know how to prompt, and a world of MCP servers is your oyster
- What is the MCP?

Free Benefits with Your Book

Your purchase includes a free PDF copy of this book along with other exclusive benefits. Check the *Free Benefits with Your Book* section in the *Preface* to unlock them instantly and maximize your learning experience.

How we got here, from SOAP to REST to GraphQL to gRPC to MCP

Before we dive into the details of the MCP, let's take a step back and look at how we got here.

One of my early memories of using web requests involved using XML to send and receive data. This was back in the days of **Simple Object Access Protocol (SOAP)**, which was a protocol for exchanging structured information in the implementation of web services. It was great, but it was also very complex and felt heavy.

Then came **Representational State Transfer (REST)**, which was a simpler way to build web services. It used HTTP and JSON, which made it easier to work with. REST was, and is, great.

There's nothing inherently wrong with REST, but you could argue that if you had a backend team and a frontend team, the frontend team would often be waiting for the backend team to finish their work before they could start building the frontend. This is where **GraphQL** came in, which allowed you to query only the data you needed and made it easier to work with APIs. Of course, that creates other problems, such as over-fetching and under-fetching data and what's known as the **N+1 problem**. The N+1 problem is a common performance issue in GraphQL APIs where multiple requests are made to fetch related data, leading to inefficiencies and increased latency.

There's also **Google Remote Procedure Call (gRPC)**, which is a high-performance RPC framework that uses HTTP/2 and Protocol Buffers. gRPC is great for microservices and allows you to define your APIs in a more structured way, but it can be complex to set up and use.

The need for a standard

All of these formats are great in their own right, but they all have their own problems. Also, the problem isn't often of this nature, but rather a string of questions that we need to ask ourselves when building applications:

- **What does this app/API do?** How do we easily expose the capabilities of our applications in a way that is easy to understand and use? Of course, no one has really agreed on a standard for this yet, until now.

- **How do we build apps if prompts are the new way to interact?** Add to that that users are becoming accustomed to using prompts to interact with applications, and you start wondering what part is the generative AI part, and what part is the capabilities of the application itself?

- **Should large language model (LLM) and other capabilities be kept separate?** Also, do I really need the generative AI part and the capabilities of the application to all be in the same place?

- **If they were kept separate, what could we gain?** If we could separate the two, in a client and server part, then maybe we could easily consume servers built by others – *Hello agentic era.*

These are some good questions to ask yourself. But this doesn't answer why we need a standard. Let's look at that further:

- **We, as developers, are too good at programming**: Here's the problem: as developers, we're almost too good at programming, meaning that we're used to gluing different things together. We can build applications that use multiple AI models, and we can make applications talk to each other that use different protocols and formats. This is not always easy, but we can do it.

- **We can do it, but at what cost?** As mentioned, just because we can *glue* virtually anything together doesn't mean we should. Yes, we can wrap anything into a REST API and make it talk to anything else. But how much time and effort does that take?

- **The solution, a standard**: Now, you see the need for a standard, hopefully. The great news is that there is a standard that is being developed to solve this problem. It's called the MCP. This enables you to not only describe your resources and capabilities in a standardized way, but also describe how to interact with them.

That means that you can literally throw the MCP on top of any app and suddenly any client that talks MCP can interact with it. Imagine the following scenario: you have a client, and that client can talk to a number of MCP servers that run both locally and remotely. All of this is made possible because you listed these servers in an mcp.json file.

Suddenly, you have access to tools to access anything you can imagine, from databases to cloud providers to any other service that exposes an MCP server. You're becoming *agentic* with little to no effort. Imagine the possibilities!

Let's talk about some of the possibilities that the MCP opens up for us.

Endless possibilities: know how to prompt, and a world of MCP servers is your oyster

Endless is a big word, so what do we mean? Imagine this: there are skills that you may not have today. In a world with MCP servers, that's no longer a problem, because with APIs wrapped by the MCP, an agent will allow you to prompt to get what you need done.

Take the creation and management of 3D models, for example. **Blender** is a common tool for creating 3D models. To use it, you need 3D modeling skills. So, you will spend hours learning how to use the app, and I'm sure it's a skill worth having.

Due to Blender's MCP server, knowledge of 3D modeling is no longer needed as much. You can instead state what you want done through a prompt. It's like the movie *The Matrix*, where the protagonist, Neo, says, "*I know Kung Fu*" after having information uploaded directly into his brain. The future is here. If you know how to prompt, you're Neo.

Here's the link to the Blender MCP server and the capabilities exposed: `https://github.com/ahujasid/blender-mcp`.

Any client now, with its own LLM and speaking MCP, will be able to call any MCP server, because Blender isn't the only example; other major companies are leaning into MCP as well. Here are some examples:

- GitHub MCP
- Playwright MCP
- Google Maps

For a list of MCP servers, check out the following link: `https://github.com/modelcontextprotocol/servers`.

There are many more servers out there, and more are being added every day, so roll up your sleeves and start building your own MCP servers and use what's out there as well!

You're probably thinking what I'm thinking: we all get our own Jarvis, the AI assistant from the movie *Iron Man*, capable of doing anything. All we need to do is leverage existing MCP servers and build the ones that are missing; just use MCP.

Imagine having a personal assistant that can help you with anything you need, from scheduling appointments to managing your finances. With MCP, this is now possible.

The future is knocking on your door, loud and clear. Are you ready to answer?

What is the MCP?

Here's what the official MCP website has to say about it:

> *The Model Context Protocol, MCP is an open protocol designed to standardize how applications provide context to* **large language models (LLMs)**. *Think of it like a USB-C port for AI applications, providing a standardized way to connect AI models to various data sources and tools.*

What does that mean for app developers?

It means the way we build our applications is changing and becoming more standardized. By learning and using MCP, all your apps will be able to communicate with each other and share data in a standardized way. That means you will spend less time worrying about how to connect or *glue* your app to other apps and more time building the features that matter.

We'll dive more into the details of these concepts in the next chapter, but for now, we understand at a mile-high level what the MCP is and how it works, and what major components are involved.

Summary and next steps: now what?

We understand the problem, the solution, and the possibilities, which are endless, and we even know some core concepts of the MCP. But we probably need to know a bit more about it before we can start building our own MCP servers. We'll look at that in the next chapter.

Get This Book's PDF Version and Exclusive Extras

UNLOCK NOW

Scan the QR code (or go to packtpub.com/unlock). Search for this book by name, confirm the edition, and then follow the steps on the page.

Note: Keep your invoice handy. Purchases made directly from Packt don't require an invoice.

2

Explaining the Model Context Protocol

The MCP consists of many parts. In short, **JavaScript Object Notation-Remote Procedure Call (JSON-RPC)** messages are exchanged between the client and the server. A JSON-RPC message is a message following the JSON-RPC specification, which means it has the jsonrpc, id, method, and params fields, and the data type is JSON. An example could look like so:

```
{
  "jsonrpc": "2.0",
  "id": 1,
  "method": "doSomething",
  "params": {
    "foo": "bar"
  }
}
```

To make it easier to understand, and more interesting, this chapter attempts to explain the protocol by taking you through an implementation of it. For that reason, we hope this chapter is an easier read (not just architecture diagrams) and a glimpse into *how things work*. If you're keen on getting started with building MCP servers, then jump straight to *Chapter 3*, but if you want to understand the MCP protocol a bit more, then keep reading. You can also return to this chapter later.

In this chapter, you will learn about the following:

- The most common message flows in MCP and their message types
- How the underlying SDK implementation roughly works

The chapter covers the following topics:

- Learning about the protocol by implementing it
- Transports in MCP

Learning about the protocol by implementing it

Instead of making this a *dry* chapter about a protocol and its different messages, let's make it enjoyable by actually talking about the processes and messages while implementing them. As part of explaining the process and its flows, you will be shown both the flows as diagrams and also implemented as code. Let's begin.

Transports in MCP

The idea with transports in MCP is that they define how clients and servers communicate. MCP is transport agnostic, meaning it can work over HTTP, WebSockets, STDIO, and more. The transport is the layer that handles the underlying message exchange. It exchanges messages of type JSON-RPC.

MCP has a set of transports it supports from STDIO (for servers running locally) to streamable transports such as WebSockets and **Server-Sent-Events** (**SSEs**), and finally request/response transports such as HTTP.

Each transport uses the same type of interface, looking like so:

```
interface Transport {
  // Start processing messages
  start(): Promise<void>;

  // Send a JSON-RPC message
  send(message: JSONRPCMessage): Promise<void>;

  // Close the connection
  close(): Promise<void>;

  // Callbacks
  onclose?: () => void;
  onerror?: (error: Error) => void;
  onmessage?: (message: JSONRPCMessage) => void;
}
```

The idea with such an interface is to have the implementation adhere to a certain behavior – namely, how to do the following:

- Start processing messages
- Send messages
- Close the connection
- Handle various events, such as connections being closed, an error being raised, or a message being sent

STDIO transport

Okay, let's start our journey understanding and implementing the message flow in MCP. We will use the STDIO transport as an example for this exercise. Let's go!

I'm sure you're familiar with seeing messages in the console or even typing into the console – that's **standard input and output**, or **STDIO** for short. But how can we leverage these *streams* for a program? Well, let's start thinking in terms of a server and a client. A client would write a message to a server, and a server would respond with something. Let's look at a very simple server implementation for STDIO:

The `readline` library will help us listen to input and output streams. Additionally, the server needs to listen to the `line` event for incoming messages from the client.

Let's create the server code:

```
// server.js

import readline from 'readline';

const rl = readline.createInterface({
  input: process.stdin,
  output: process.stdout,
  terminal: false
});

rl.on('line', (line) => {
  if (line.includes('exit')) {
    console.log('EXIT received: Server closing down...');
    process.exit(0);
  } else {
```

```
      console.log("line received: (Server data):", line);
      }
});
```

The server code consists of the following:

- A call to `readline` that takes `stdin` and `stdout` and produces `r1`, a reference we can work with to listen to messages.

- A message handler on the on event that checks for data containing `exit`, in which case we will exit, or otherwise just acknowledge a message being received.

Creating a client

So, how can we create a client for this? Well, a client should be sending messages and be able to receive server messages. A way to achieve this is by creating the server as a child process with the client being the parent process sending messages to the server. Then, we can communicate with it via standard input and output.

Here's what an implementation can look like:

To create the server, we can use the `spawn` method from the `child_process` module. Here's code that creates a child process:

```
import { spawn } from 'child_process';
const child = spawn('node', ['server.js']);
```

In the preceding code, the `server.js` file is executed via the `node` command. Because it is run with the `spawn` function, it's now a child process.

To then send messages to the server, we can write to its `stdin` and read from its `stdout`. This code will send a message that the server can listen to:

```
child.stdin.write("data 1\n");
```

To listen to the server, you need to listen for incoming messages on the child process's `stdout` like so:

```
child.stdout.on('data', (data) => {
  console.log(`Client::ondata> (FROM SERVER): ${data}`);
});
```

With this knowledge, let's now write a client:

```javascript
// client.js

import { spawn } from 'child_process';

const child = spawn('node', ['server.js']);

// Listen for data from the child
child.stdout.on('data', (data) => {
  console.log(`Client::ondata> (FROM SERVER): ${data}`);
});

// sending data to the server
console.log("Client sending data to server...");
child.stdin.write("data 1\n");
child.stdin.write("exit\n");

// Optionally handle errors
child.stderr.on('data', (data) => {
  console.error(`Client::onerror> (FROM SERVER): ${data}`);
});
// Handle child process exit
child.on('exit', (code) => {
  console.log(`Client::onexit> (FROM SERVER): SERVER exited with code
    ${code}`);
});
```

Let's break down the client code:

- The spawn method calls node `server.js`. This will start up the server so we can communicate via a reference `child`.

- A message listens to `on("data")`. This will be called when the server sends something back to the client.

- Data is sent via placing a message on `stdin`:

  ```javascript
  child.stdin.write("data 1\n");
  child.stdin.write("exit\n");
  ```

The second line will have the server call `process.exit(0)`, which will close the connection and trigger the `exit` event on the client.

- Handled errors on `stderr.on("data")` and how to exit even `on("exit")`.

If we run `client.js`, we should see an output like so:

```
Client sending data to server...
Client::ondata> (FROM SERVER): line received: (Server data): data 1
EXIT received: Server closing down...

Client::onexit> (FROM SERVER): SERVER exited with code 0
```

This code is a great start to build on to start implementing MCP and the STDIO transport. In fact, this is pretty much what happens, except for the fact that MCP communicates with JSON-RPC messages, so let's make it more like MCP next.

MCP and STDIO transport

Our code in the previous section pretty much acted like the STDIO transport does for MCP. For that to be fully true, though, we need the client and server to exchange JSON-RPC messages. So, what are those?

Let's have a look at an example `jsonrpc` message:

```
const listTools = {
    "jsonrpc": "2.0",
    "id": 1,
    "method": "tools/list",
    "params": {}
};
```

Here, we have a JSON-RPC message, and what makes it one is, first, it's in JSON format, and secondly, it has an attribute called `jsonrpc`. Furthermore, it should have an `id` attribute, `method`, and `params`. The preceding `tools/list` message is something a client would send to a server, and the server should respond with its available tools, as this command is used to figure out what tools a server has.

So, what's our first step when building an MCP server? Well, it's the initialization process, also known as a **handshake**, so let's work on that next.

See a running example of this code in the solution folder – check `https://github.com/PacktPublishing/Learn-Model-Context-Protocol-with-TypeScript/blob/main/Chapter02/solutions/README.md`.

The initialization process in MCP

Next, now that we have simple client and server code working, we should focus on the initialization process in MCP, sometimes referred to as a handshake.

Here's what initialization looks like at the mile-high level:

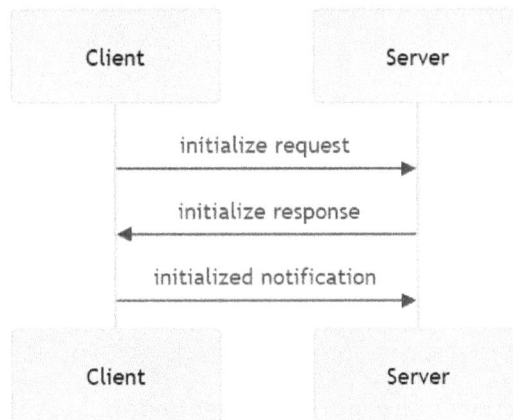

Figure 2.1 – Initialization process

What happens in the preceding process is this:

- First, the client sends an *initialize* request, meaning it wants to know from the server what its capabilities are.
- Then, the server responds with its capabilities – that is, what features it has.
- Lastly, the client lets the server know it's ready to perform operations by sending an *initialized* notification. Before the mentioned notification, any other types of messages, such as listing or running tools, should produce an error response as the *handshake* hasn't fully taken place.

Let's look at the message for each step:

1. **Client sends initialize request**: Here's what the client sends to the server:

```json
{
  "jsonrpc": "2.0",
  "id": 1,
  "method": "initialize",
  "params": {
    "protocolVersion": "2024-11-05",
    "capabilities": {
      "roots": {
        "listChanged": true
      },
      "sampling": {}
    },
    "clientInfo": {
      "name": "ExampleClient",
      "version": "1.0.0"
    }
  }
}
```

This is an *initialize* message, which you can see from `method` with the value `initialize`. The client must also send its `capabilities`, which includes `roots` and `sampling` in this case. Here's a closer look at the capabilities of the client:

```json
"capabilities": {
    "roots": {
        "listChanged": true
    },
    "sampling": {}
}
```

2. **Server initializes response**: The server, on the other hand, must answer with a similar message of its capabilities – that is, whether it supports tools, resources, prompts, notifications, and so on. Here's what a typical server response looks like:

```json
{
  "jsonrpc": "2.0",
```

```
    "id": 1,
    "result": {
      "protocolVersion": "2024-11-05",
      "capabilities": {
        "logging": {},
        "prompts": {
          "listChanged": true
        },
        "resources": {
          "subscribe": true,
          "listChanged": true
        },
        "tools": {
          "listChanged": true
        }
      },
      "serverInfo": {
        "name": "ExampleServer",
        "version": "1.0.0"
      }
    }
  }
}
```

Observe the `capabilities` attribute in the response, containing things such as logging, prompts, resources, and tools. **Logging** is the ability of the server to send log messages to the client. We will show an example of logging notifications in *Chapter 5*. The other capabilities – prompts, resources, and tools – are the basic features that a server can have – more on those in *Chapter 3*.

This answer will help the client determine what it can and can't use. It also provides information on protocol version and server info.

Let's have a look at the *initialized* message coming from the client, and then we'll try implementing the preceding message flow.

3. **Concluding the handshake**: As the final step, the client sends an *initialized* message. This is the final message of the *handshake*. Once received, the server is ready to take on any type of JSON-RPC message from the client on tools, resources, or prompts. This message from the client should not produce a response from the server. However, the server should remember it's been initialized. Once initialized, *normal* operations can take place, such as calling tools, prompts, and more. Here's the *initialized* message in detail – as you can see, it doesn't carry much information but is crucial for the client and server to operate normally. Before this notification has been sent, you can't do much.

```
{
  "jsonrpc": "2.0",
  "method": "notifications/initialized"
}
```

How can we implement this? Let us look at that next.

Implementing initialization

There were a few messages exchanged back and forth. In reality, the client can just send `initialized` to the server and you're done, but it's considered good practice to exchange capabilities first via `initialize`.

The client code in the previous subsection was just sending text messages and JSON-RPC messages, but it wasn't really following the flow of the initialization process. To address this, we need to change the client so that it properly handles the initialization sequence. After said sequence is complete, then the client can send other types of messages such as listing tools and so on.

Let's see if we can organize the client code to support initialization. First, let's get a high-level idea of how things should work with the following code:

```
async function main() {
    await connect();
    // After connection, you can start sending messages
    listTools();
}
```

In the preceding `main` function, we call `connect`, which, once done, has carried out a handshake that involves sending an *initialize* message, waited for the server's response, and finally, sent out an *initialized* notification. Secondly, we call `listTools`, which should send off a request to the server asking it to list its tools.

For one, the connect method needs to wait for the stream to return a message from the server. The way we listen to such a message is via a callback pattern that looks like so:

```
stream("on", (data) => {
  // Handle incoming messages from the server
});
```

We don't know when the message on the stream will arrive. The way we set up our main method earlier is by calling connect, followed by listTools, to get our code to behave in a synchronized way. We can achieve that synchronous-looking behavior by wrapping the stream's callback in a promise, and instead of listening to the on event, we can use once, which means the first time we get data, it stops listening. That means our connect method needs to be async, and it needs to return a Promise that wraps the stream. So, it needs to look something like so:

```
async function connect(){
  return new Promise((resolve, reject) => {
    // wrap any event from the stream
  })
}
```

With all that in mind, here's what we need to do: send our message, get a response from the stream (the server), and then stop listening to ensure that no new messages are processed until the handshake is complete. After that, we need to set up new listeners for any future actions, such as listing tools and more. Which means if we try to pseudo-code the connect method with this added context, it needs to look something like so:

```
initialized = false;

async function connect() {
  sendMessage(initializationMessage);
  return new Promise((resolve, reject) => {
    stream.once("data", (data) => {
      // 1. is json-rpc initialize response, then resolve promise
      // and stop listening to the stream
      if (isInitializeResponseMessage(data)) {
        // 2. setup new listeners
        setupListeners();

        // 3. set initialized flag
```

```
        initialized = true;

        // 4. we're done, let's resolve the promise
        resolve();

      } else {
        reject(new Error("Unexpected message received during
          initialization."));
      }
    });
  });
}
```

We also call listTools within that main function. Just like connect, it needs to be async and wait for the server's response. It also needs to stop listening to the stream once it gets a server response. So listTools can look like so, we're using pseudo code here as well:

```
async function listTools() {
  sendMessage(listToolsMessage);
  return new Promise((resolve,reject) => {
    stream.once("data", data => {
      if(isListToolsResponseMessage(data)) {
        resolve(data);
      } else {
        reject(new Error("Unexpected message received during list tools."));
      }
    })


  })
}
```

Let's try to build out the client with our idea for how the connect and listTools methods should work.

```
// client.ts

import { spawn } from 'child_process';

import { fileURLToPath } from 'url';
```

```
import { dirname, join } from 'path';
import { initializeMessage, initializedMessage, listToolsMessage }
  from "./utils/messages.js";
import { isJsonRpcMessage, getRpcMessage, isInitializeResponseMessage }
  from "./utils/helpers.js";


const __filename = fileURLToPath(import.meta.url);
const __dirname = dirname(__filename);


let serverPath = join(__dirname, 'server.js');
console.log("DEBUG Client starting server at:", serverPath);



const child = spawn('node', [serverPath]);


let initialized = false;

// Listen for data from the child

function handleRpcMessage(data) {
    console.log("handleRpcMessage");

    let message = getRpcMessage(data.toString().trim());
    if (!message) {
        console.error("Invalid JSON RPC message received:", data);
        return;
    }

    console.log(message.result);
}

function listTools() {
    console.log("DEBUG Client asks for tools list...");
    child.stdin.write(JSON.stringify(listToolsMessage) + "\n");
}
```

```
async function connect(): Promise<void> {
  // sending data to the server
  console.log("DEBUG Client sending data to server...");
  child.stdin.write(JSON.stringify(initializeMessage) + "\n");

  // constructs a promise wrapping a child process so we can
  // wait for a response
    return new Promise((resolve, reject) => {
        child.stdout.once('data', (data) => {
            const message = data.toString().trim();
            if (isJsonRpcMessage(message)) {
                const json = getRpcMessage(message);
                if (isInitializeResponseMessage(json)) {
                    console.log("DEBUG Client received initialize
                        response:", json.result);

                    // sends an initialized notification to signal the
                    // "handshake" being completed
                    child.stdin.write(JSON.stringify(initializedMessage) +
                        "\n");
                    console.log("DEBUG Client connected and
                        initialized:");
                    initialized = true;

                    // setting up listeners that can be used by
                    // notifications
                    setupListeners();
                    resolve();
                } else {
                    reject(new Error("Unexpected message received
                        during initialization."));
                }
            } else {
                reject(new Error("Invalid JSON RPC message received
                    during initialization."));
            }
        });
```

```javascript
    });
}


function setupListeners() {
    child.stdout.resume(); // kick it back into action
    console.log("DEBUG CLIENT, Setting up listeners for child
        process...");
    child.stdout.on('data', (data) => {

        if(isJsonRpcMessage(data.toString().trim())) {
            handleRpcMessage(data);
        } else {
            console.log(`CLIENT::ondata> (FROM SERVER): Unrecognized
                message: ${data.toString().trim()}`);
        }
    });

    // Optionally handle errors
    child.stderr.on('data', (data) => {
      console.error(`Client::onerror> (FROM SERVER): ${data}`);
    });

    // Handle child process exit
    child.on('exit', (code) => {
      console.log(`Client::onexit> (FROM SERVER): SERVER exited
        with code ${code}`);
    });
}

async function main() {
    await connect();
    // After connection, you can start sending messages
    listTools();
}

main();
```

What's happening now is that we've done the following:

- Created a `connect()` function that connects to the server. Thereafter, we set up listeners to the process stream.

- Defined a `main()` function where we connect and add a call to `listTools` just to show `main` is the place where you want to define client behavior.

- Improved the code by creating a `utils` folder with helper functions and messages.

What we can see from the preceding implementation is that we followed our design principles when we pseudo-coded the `connect` and `listTools` functions. However, we're only dispatching the list tools message and not listening to a response, so we need to fix that later in the chapter.

Let's work on the server part:

Let's work on the server implementation. It needs to check whether it's initialized; if so, it can work on producing a response. A construct like the following can do the check for this:

```
if(initialized) {
  if(isJsonRpcMessage(line)) {
    let message = getJsonRpcMessage(line);
    switch(message.method) {
        case "tools/list":
            console.log(JSON.stringify(listToolsResponse));
            break;
        default:
            console.log(JSON.stringify(errorResponse));
            break;
    }
  } else {
    console.log(JSON.stringify(errorResponse));
  }
```

If it's not initialized, we need to check the message and ensure it says `initialize` or `notifications/initialized`. If neither of those is present, we can respond with an error message.

```
else { // not initialized
  if(isJsonRpcMessage(line)) {
    let message = getJsonRpcMessage(line);
    switch(message.method) {
      case "initialize":
```

```
            console.log(JSON.stringify(initializeResponse));
            break;
        case "notifications/initialized":
          initialized = true;
          break;
        default:
          console.log("Server not initialized, only initialize or
            notifications/initialized methods are supported at this
              point: ", message.method);
    }
  } else {
    console.error("Invalid JSON-RPC message received:", line);
  }
}
```

Let's assemble the server based on understanding the two preceding cases to handle – initialized and not initialized states. Here's the complete server:

```
// server.ts

import readline from 'readline';
import { getJsonRpcMessage, isJsonRpcMessage } from './utils/helpers.js';
import { initializeResponse, listToolsResponse, errorResponse } from
  './utils/messages.js';

let initialized = false;

const rl = readline.createInterface({
  input: process.stdin,
  output: process.stdout,
  terminal: false
});

rl.on('line', (line) => {
  if (line.includes('exit')) {
    console.log('EXIT received: Server closing down...');
    process.exit(0);
  } else {
```

```
    if(initialized) {
      if(isJsonRpcMessage(line)) {
        let message = getJsonRpcMessage(line);
        switch(message.method) {
            case "tools/list":
                console.log(JSON.stringify(listToolsResponse));
                break;
            default:
                console.log(JSON.stringify(errorResponse));
                break;
        }
      } else {
        console.log(JSON.stringify(errorResponse));
      }
    } else { // not initialized
        if(isJsonRpcMessage(line)) {
          let message = getJsonRpcMessage(line);
          switch(message.method) {
            case "initialize":
              console.log(JSON.stringify(initializeResponse));
              break;
            case "notifications/initialized":
              initialized = true;
              break;
            default:
              console.log("Server not initialized, only initialize
                or notifications/initialized methods are supported
                  at this point: ", message.method);
          }
        } else {
          console.error("Invalid JSON-RPC message received:", line);
        }
    }
  }
});
```

Here, we're dealing with the following:

- If we're *not* initialized, then we make sure we only deal with initialize and notifications/ initialized as valid event types. For the latter, we will set initialized to true.

- If we are initialized, then we figure out which message type it is. At present, we only support tools/list but will add more in a future section of this chapter.

- server.ts also uses the utils folder for messages and helper methods.

See a running example of this code in the solution folder. Check *Initialization* (https://github.com/ PacktPublishing/Learn-Model-Context-Protocol-with-TypeScript/blob/main/Chapter02/ solutions/README.md).

Supporting features

Now that we have code that's looking more robust, let's support features such as tools, resources, and prompts.

You've already seen how connect is a method we call to handshake with the server. Thereafter, we want to call a tool, a resource, and a prompt, and wait for it to respond before carrying on with the next action. So, for that behavior to be possible, we need to do the following:

1. Place the message on the stream.
2. Wait for the response to arrive.
3. If we get a normal response back, show it, if it's a notification, then ignore it. Notifications from the server are usually a special message or a progress update, and we'll implement support for that in the next section.

Great, we have a plan. Let's revisit our main method to see what we have.

Let's start out with our main function in the client. It should call connect to set up the connection to the server, and it should list the tools. Here's the code we have so far:

```
// client.ts

// code omitted for brevity

async function main() {
    await connect();
    // After connection, you can start sending messages
    listTools();
}
```

We call connect, and we also call `listTools`, but we don't wait for the response, so if we wanted to do something such as calling a tool based on listing the tools first, then we would need to change the implementation. Let's see what an updated implementation could look like:

```
async function main() {
    await connect();
    // After connection, you can start sending messages
    let tools = await listTools();
    callTool(tool[0], args);
}
```

Now, we first list the tools via `listTools`, then we store the result in the `tools` variable. Then we call a tool via the `callTool` method. Great, but we do need to change the code so it actually works.

Let's start thinking about how we need to modify `listTools`. Let's change its signature first:

```
async listTools(): Promise<void> {
  // TODO: send a tools/call message to server
}
```

Okay, we got a signature we like – that is, it responds with a `Promise`, so we can call it like so: `await listTools()`. We're dealing with streams from a process, which means we can push messages to the stream via `client.stdin.write(message)` and listen to responses via `client.stdout.on("message")`. We need to figure out how to make events from a process and a `Promise` construct work together. We've already set up handlers that listen to messages, but how can we make that work within the context of a `Promise`? The answer is that we can't. To solve this, we will set up specific listeners only used for the `Promise` and stop subscribing to said listeners once done.

Here's how:

```
function listTools(): Promise<void> {
    child.stdin.write(JSON.stringify(listToolsMessage) + "\n");

    return new Promise((resolve, reject) => {
        // we need to tell it to resolve when we get the response

        function handleMessage(data) {
            const message = data.toString().trim();
            if (!isNotificationMessage(message)) {
                const json = getRpcMessage(message);
```

```
                    // show response
                    // console.log(json.result);
                    resolve(json.result);

                    child.stdout.removeListener('data', handleMessage);
                    // remove listener after handling the message

            } else {
                    // Notification do nothing, let other handlers take care
                    // of it
                    // keep listener here as we got a notification and
                    // we're still waiting for the response        }
                }
            }


        child.stdout.on('data',handleMessage);
    });
}
```

The listTools function consists of the following:

- Promise, which resolves once we get a response back from the server.
- A handler method, handleMessage, within the promise structure that checks whether something is a normal response. If so, it stops subscribing; if not, then we do nothing and let other process event handlers take care of notifications. More on notifications later in this chapter.

Let's update the main() method to this code:

```
async function main() {
    await connect();
    // After connection, you can start sending messages
    let toolResponse = await listTools();
    console.log("Tools response:", toolResponse);
}
```

Running this code would now get you an output like so:

```
DEBUG Client starting server at: /workspaces/mcp-book/02 - mcp protocol/
solutions/typescript/2-features/build/server.js
DEBUG Client sending data to server...
DEBUG Client received initialize response: {
  protocolVersion: '2024-11-05',
  capabilities: {
    logging: {},
    prompts: { listChanged: true },
    resources: { subscribe: true, listChanged: true },
    tools: { listChanged: true }
  },
  serverInfo: { name: 'ExampleServer', version: '1.0.0' }
}
DEBUG Client connected and initialized:
DEBUG CLIENT, Setting up listeners for child process...
Tools response: {
  tools: [
    {
      name: 'ExampleTool',
      version: '1.0.0',
      description: 'An example tool for demonstration purposes.'
    }
  ]
}
```

Okay, so we solved listing tools, as we can now capture the response.

Next, let's focus on supporting calling a tool. For this, we will first tackle the server part. What we need is a new case where we support the tools/call method, like so:

```
// server.ts
// code omitted for brevity

case "tools/call":
  let toolResponse = `Called tool ${message.params.name} with
    arguments ${JSON.stringify(message.params.args)}`;
```

```
let callToolResponse = {
    "jsonrpc": "2.0",
    "id": message.id,
    "result": {
        "properties": {
            "content": {
                "description": "description of the content",
                "items": [
                    { "type": "text", "text": toolResponse }
                ]
            }
        }
    }
}


console.log(JSON.stringify(callToolResponse));
break;
```

Here, we create a response that responds with a structure where the interesting part of the response is coded into the items attribute. The items attribute contains an array of text blocks. In this case, we only return one such text block containing the name of the tool and the arguments that were passed.

Let's look at what we need to do to support calling a tool on the client.

First, we need the callTool method:

```
// client.ts

// code omitted for brevity

function callTool(toolName: string, args: any[]): Promise<any> {
    // defined a JSON-RPC message
    let toolMessage = {
        "jsonrpc": "2.0",
        "method": "tools/call",
        "params": {
            "name": toolName,
            "args": args
```

```
        },
        "id": 1
    };


    // sent the message to the server
    child.stdin.write(JSON.stringify(toolMessage) + "\n");


    // wrapping the child process in a Promise to handle the response
    return new Promise((resolve, reject) => {
        function handleMessage(data) {
            const message = data.toString().trim();
            if (!isNotificationMessage(message)) {
                const json = getRpcMessage(message);
                resolve(json.result);

                child.stdout.removeListener('data', handleMessage);
            }
        }

        child.stdout.on('data', handleMessage);
    });
}
```

Here's what we did:

- Created a `callTool` in a way that resembled `listTools` in that it first constructs a JSON-RPC message followed by dispatching the message
- Created a `Promise` that, when resolved, takes the result from the server
- Removed the listener once we were done listening for the response from the server

Here's what we're changing the main method to, so we include a call to a tool and print its response:

```
// client.ts


async function main() {
    await connect();
    // After connection, you can start sending messages
    let toolResponse = await listTools();
    console.log("Tools response:", toolResponse);
```

```
    let callToolResponse = await callTool("exampleTool",
        ["arg1", "arg2"]);
    console.log("Call tool response:", callToolResponse);
    let items = callToolResponse.properties.content.items;
    for (let item of items) {
        console.log("Item:", item.text);
    }
}
```

The updated `main` method now does the following:

- Calls `callTool` and saves the response to `callToolResponse`.
- Prints the response by navigating into the response structure and the `items` property.

Should we run the program at this point, we would see an output like so:

```
DEBUG Client starting server at: /workspaces/mcp-book/02 - mcp protocol/
solutions/typescript/2-features/build/server.js
DEBUG Client sending data to server...
DEBUG Client received initialize response: {
  protocolVersion: '2024-11-05',
  capabilities: {
    logging: {},
    prompts: { listChanged: true },
    resources: { subscribe: true, listChanged: true },
    tools: { listChanged: true }
  },
  serverInfo: { name: 'ExampleServer', version: '1.0.0' }
}
DEBUG Client connected and initialized:
DEBUG CLIENT, Setting up listeners for child process...
Tools response: {
  tools: [
    {
      name: 'ExampleTool',
      version: '1.0.0',
      description: 'An example tool for demonstration purposes.'
    }
  ]
```

```
}
Call tool response: {
  properties: {
    content: { description: 'description of the content', items: [Array] }
  }
}
Item: Called tool exampleTool with arguments ["arg1","arg2"]
```

Note the part of the response that now incorporates calling the tool and printing the response from that:

```
Call tool response: {
  properties: {
    content: { description: 'description of the content', items: [Array] }
  }
}
Item: Called tool exampleTool with arguments ["arg1","arg2"]
```

Let's move on to notifications next. Notifications can be sent in both directions, from server to client as well as from client to server.

See a running example of this code in the solution folder – check *Features* (https://github.com/PacktPublishing/Learn-Model-Context-Protocol-with-TypeScript/blob/main/Chapter02/solutions/README.md).

Notifications, report progress, and important updates

Notifications are something both the client and the server can send to each other. Usually, they want to tell each party something important happened – for example, a long-running tool response might report progress, or a server may send a message to report on a change in its capabilities. So, how can we support notifications? Well, there are two aspects of it:

- **Sending a notification-type message** from either client or server. This looks like so:

```
{
  "jsonrpc": "2.0",
  "method": "notifications/[type]",
  "params": {}
}
```

[type] is usually cancelled or progress. For a full specification of types, check https://github.com/modelcontextprotocol/modelcontextprotocol/blob/main/schema/2025-03-26/schema.ts.

- **The role of the client.** For a client, a notification is seen as an extra thing, and something you should show, for example, in a user interface to improve the user's experience. A notification from a client to a server, though, tends to be different. For example, a client sends a notification to the server to set the state to initialized.

How can we implement this, then?

Let's tackle implementing notifications. Here's the plan for how the implementation will happen:

- onnotification is a variable you can assign a function if you want to display notifications
- Add logic to the main message handler to call onnotification

We've already added logic to listTools, which is very general and can be used for any type of ask, such as calling a tool, listing resources, and so on, so let's do some refactoring as well.

First, let's address onnotification:

```typescript
// client.ts

let onnotification: Function | null = null;

// .. code omitted for brevity

async function main() {
    onnotification = (message) => {
        console.log("NOTIFICATION RECEIVED:", message);
    };

    await connect();
    // After connection, you can start sending messages
    let toolResponse = await listTools();
    console.log("Tools response:", toolResponse);
}
```

We've done the following:

- Defined onnotification, which will be used to store a reference to a function

- Added an implementation to onnotification, like so:

```
onnotification = (message) => {
   console.log("NOTIFICATION RECEIVED:", message);
};
```

Now that we run the app, we will see the following output:

```
DEBUG Client starting server at: /path/server.js
DEBUG Client sending data to server...
DEBUG Client received initialize response: {
  protocolVersion: '2024-11-05',
  capabilities: {
    logging: {},
    prompts: { listChanged: true },
    resources: { subscribe: true, listChanged: true },
    tools: { listChanged: true }
  },
  serverInfo: { name: 'ExampleServer', version: '1.0.0' }
}
DEBUG Client connected and initialized:
DEBUG CLIENT, Setting up listeners for child process...
NOTIFICATION RECEIVED: {
  jsonrpc: '2.0',
  method: 'notifications/progress',
  params: { message: 'Working on it...' }
}
Tools response: {
  tools: [
    {
      name: 'ExampleTool',
      version: '1.0.0',
      description: 'An example tool for demonstration purposes.'
    }
  ]
}
```

You can clearly see how it says NOTIFICATION RECEIVED, which means, we're able to capture notifications from the server.

We promised to clean up the message handler a bit, as it can be used to list or call any feature. A good way to accomplish that is by breaking out the message handler functionality for listTools into its own function, like so:

```
function _handleMessageResponse(): Promise<void> {
    return new Promise((resolve, reject) => {
        // we need to tell it to resolve when we get the response

        function handleMessage(data) {
            const message = data.toString().trim();
            if (!isNotificationMessage(message)) {
                const json = getRpcMessage(message);

                // show response
                // console.log(json.result);
                resolve(json.result);

                child.stdout.removeListener('data', handleMessage);
// remove listener after handling the message

            } else {
                // Notification do nothing, let other handlers take care
                // of it
                // keep listener here as we got a notification and we're
                // still waiting for the response       }
            }
        }

        child.stdout.on('data',handleMessage);
    });
}
```

This then means `listTools` looks a lot simpler:

```
function listTools(): Promise<void> {
    child.stdin.write(JSON.stringify(listToolsMessage) + "\n");

    return _handleMessageResponse();
}
```

Let's do one more improvement to this code. `child.stdin.write(JSON.stringify(listToolsMessage) + "\n");` can be improved. Let's create the following methods:

```
function _makeRequest(message: any) {
    child.stdin.write(_serializeMessage(message));
}


function _serializeMessage(message: any): string {
    return JSON.stringify(message) + "\n";
}


function listTools(): Promise<void> {
    _makeRequest(listToolsMessage);

    return _handleMessageResponse();
}
```

See how we've done the following:

- Created `_makeRequest` to write to the stream
- Defined `_serializeMessage` to stringify the message
- Replaced the code in `listTools` so it uses `_makeRequest`

Great – we've managed to implement notifications and did some nice refactoring. Let's look at sampling next.

See a running example of this code in the solution folder – check *Notifications* (`https://github.com/PacktPublishing/Learn-Model-Context-Protocol-with-TypeScript/blob/main/Chapter02/solutions/README.md`).

Sampling – help the server complete a request

Sampling is an interesting feature. What it means is that the server is telling the client, *I don't know how to do this*, or *You do it better – can you please help me complete this request?*. More specifically, the server asks the client to complete the request using the client's **large language model (LLM)**.

Okay, so we established that the server sometimes needs the client to help it complete a request. The way the client helps is by asking its LLM for the response, which it then passes back to the server.

What is the starting point, though? Well, it could be a client that calls a tool on the server, and then the tool generates a sampling request. Then the flow could look like so:

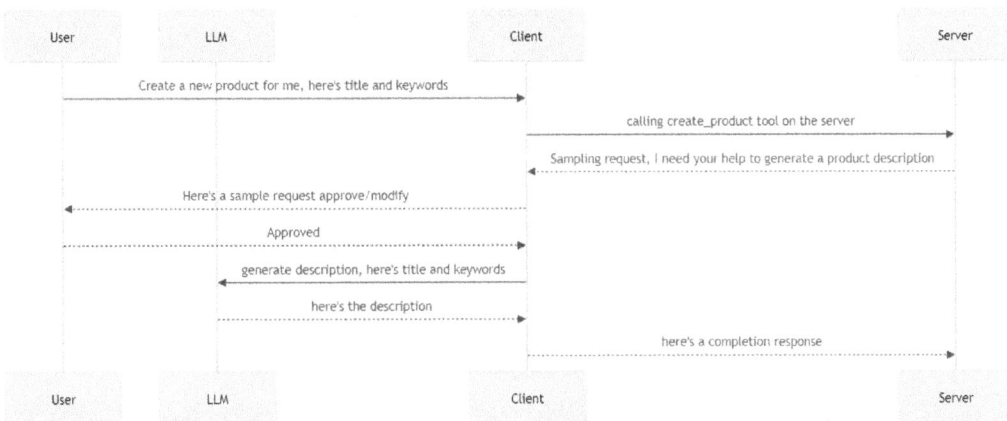

Figure 2.2 – Sampling flow, scenario 1

Or, it could be an external service that generates an event that the server listens to. Here's the flow for that scenario:

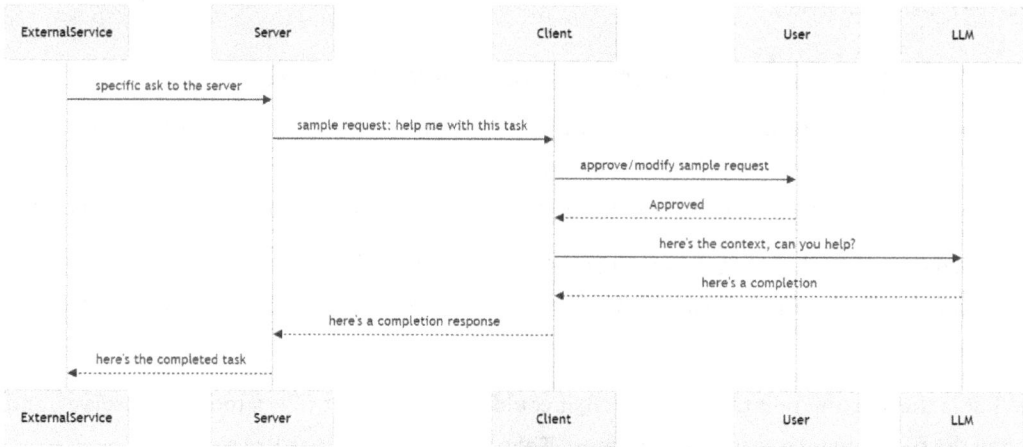

Figure 2.3 – Sampling flow, scenario 2

From a message standpoint, here's what the server is sending to the client:

```
{
  messages: [
    {
      role: "user" | "assistant",
      content: {
        type: "text" | "image",

        // For text:
        text?: string,

        // For images:
        data?: string,               // base64 encoded
        mimeType?: string
      }
    }
  ],
  modelPreferences?: {
    hints?: [{
      name?: string                  // Suggested model name/family
    }],
```

```
        costPriority?: number,         // 0-1, importance of minimizing cost
        speedPriority?: number,        // 0-1, importance of low latency
        intelligencePriority?: number  // 0-1, importance of capabilities
    },
    systemPrompt?: string,
    includeContext?: "none" | "thisServer" | "allServers",
    temperature?: number,
    maxTokens: number,
    stopSequences?: string[],
    metadata?: Record<string, unknown>
}
```

Here's some of the information included in the preceding request:

- `messages` is a chat conversation between an assistant and a user, and provides the required context for the request
- `modelPreferences`: Here, the server can specify things such as the preferred model name and decide the prioritization of cost, speed, and capabilities

There's also model configuration data being sent on temperature, the number of tokens to use, and more. It's worth calling out that these are recommendations that the client can choose to accept or modify.

The client should then respond with a completion message, like so:

```
{
  model: string,   // Name of the model used
  stopReason?: "endTurn" | "stopSequence" | "maxTokens" | string,
  role: "user" | "assistant",
  content: {
    type: "text" | "image",
    text?: string,
    data?: string,
    mimeType?: string
  }
}
```

In the preceding response, the following information is covered:

- `model` is the model used. It doesn't have to be the same as what the server asked for.
- `stopReason` – it's good to know whether you got a full response or whether it stopped for some other reason.
- `content` is the content response.

Introducing a scenario: e-commerce

When does this happen, though? Well, the server could be listening to events that it should react to. For example, let's say you have an e-commerce scenario and there are new products being registered by a system somewhere. However, before these products can be sold, they need a proper description. This description is something a client and its LLM can help with.

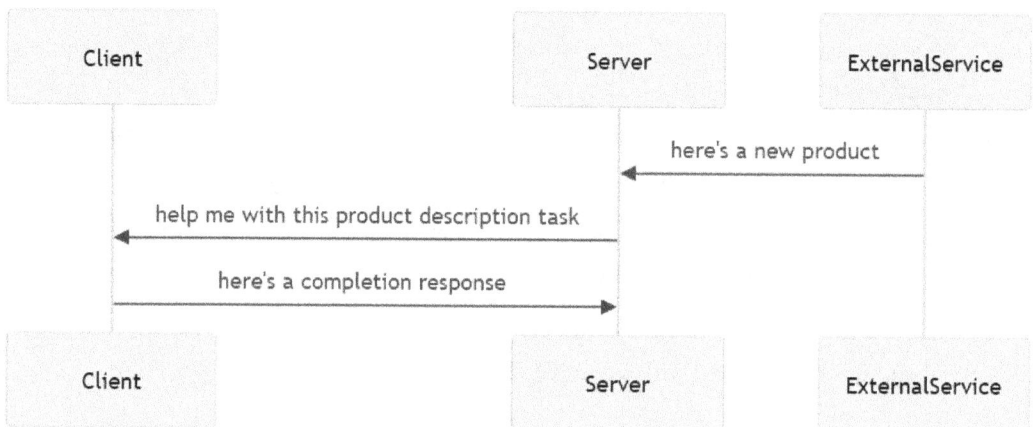

Figure 2.4 – E-commerce scenario flow

In the final step, the server logs, stores, and possibly caches the response.

Let's look at a request in this context. Here's an example request from a server:

```
{
  "method": "sampling/createMessage",
  "params": {
    "messages": [
      {
        "role": "user",
        "content": {
          "type": "text",
```

```
            "text": "Create a selling product description for
              this sweater, keywoards autumn, cozy, knitted"
         }
       }
    ],
    "systemPrompt": "You are a helpful assistant assisting with
      product descriptions",
    "includeContext": "thisServer",
    "maxTokens": 300
  }
}
```

As you can see, we settled on only providing it with context and omitted any recommendations on the model to use or configuration, but we could add that if we wanted.

It's now up to the client how to interpret this request and respond.

Implementing sampling

Let's implement sampling in our code, and we'll use the product description scenario so you can see how it can be used. Here's what we need:

- **External service:** This service should produce a new product in need of a product description. This product has been registered by someone else in another system and shows up in this server as a message payload as a result of listening to an event. This is scenario-specific code.

- **Server – sample request:** We just need the capability to send a json-rpc request.

- **Client response:** We need to listen to this specific message type, call the LLM using the message's payload, and return a response to the server.

Let's start with the external service. This isn't really part of MCP, but it will hopefully give you a sense of how you can integrate an external component that produces a message that you're interested in:

```
class Product {
    id: number;
    name: string;
    price: number;
    keywords: string[];
```

```typescript
    constructor(id: number, name: string, price: number,
        keywords: string[]) {
        this.id = id;
        this.name = name;
        this.price = price;
        this.keywords = keywords;
    }
}


class ExternalService {
    map: { [key: string]: Function[] } = {}
    currentIndex = 0;

    products: Product[] = [
        new Product(1, 'Cable, 3M', 100, ['electronics', 'gadgets']),
        new Product(2, 'Stereo', 150, ['home', 'appliances']),
        new Product(3, 'Jacket', 200, ['outdoors', 'sports']),
    ];
    constructor() {
        // Simulate some external service that emits events
        let id = setInterval(() => {
            if(this.currentIndex < this.products.length) {
                this.emit('new-product',
                    this.products[this.currentIndex]);
                this.currentIndex++;
            } else {
                clearTimeout(id);
            }
        }, 1000);
    }


    emit(event: string, data) {
        if (this.map[event]) {
            this.map[event].forEach(listener => listener(data));
        }
    }
}
```

```
    addListener(event, listener: Function) {
        if (!this.map[event]) {
            this.map[event] = [];
        }
        this.map[event].push(listener);
    }

    removeListener(event, listener) {
        if (this.map[event]) {
            this.map[event] = this.map[event].filter(l => l !== listener);
        }
    }
}
```

In the preceding code, we've done the following:

- Defined a Product class that is what we will ask the LLM to work with on the client side.

- Created an ExternalService class that will emit any products in need of wanting their product description updating. The class handles subscriptions and emitting messages to specific events and listeners.

So, what about the MCP-specific parts?

Well, here we need to realize that it starts with the server, and the server is listening to ExternalService. Once there's a message showing up there, we should send this message to the client.

Therefore, we need a function that can listen to ExternalService and dispatch a message:

```
function listenToExternalService() {
    const externalService = new ExternalService();
    externalService.addListener('new-product', (product: Product) => {
        // create the sampling message
        let samplingMessage = {
            "jsonrpc": "2.0",
            "id": 1,
            "method": "sampling/createMessage",
```

```
        "params": {
            "messages": [{
                "role": "system",
                "content": {
                    "type": "text",
                    "text": `New product available: ${product.name}
                        (ID: ${product.id}, Price: ${product.price}).
                            Keywords: ${product.keywords.join(', ')}`
                }
            }],
            "systemPrompt": "You are a helpful assistant assisting
                with product descriptions",
            "includeContext": "thisServer",
            "maxTokens": 300
        }
    };
    // send the sampling message to the console
    console.log(JSON.stringify(samplingMessage));
    });
}
```

Here, you see the following:

- A listener being added and a function that dispatches a sampling message to the client
- The sampling message contains a chat conversation including the product information, so the LLM will have context of what to generate a response to

Let's move on to the client and see what we need to do.

In the client, we need to deal with this incoming message type, invoke an LLM, and then create a response. The `handleRpcMessage` needs to be updated to handle this case:

```
// client.ts

function handleRpcMessage(data) {
    let message = getRpcMessage(data.toString().trim());
    if (message.method && message.method.startsWith("sampling/")) {
        onsampling?.(message);
```

```
            return;
    } else if(message.result) {
        onmessage?.(message.result);
        // If the message has a result, it is a response to a request

    } else if (message.method &&
        message.method.startsWith("notifications/")) {
        onnotification?.(message);
    } else {
        console.log(`CLIENT::ondata> (FROM SERVER): Unrecognized message:
          ${data.toString().trim()}`);
    }
}
```

This is the code that specifically handles the sampling: if (message.method && message.method. startsWith("sampling/")). It calls onnotification?.(message). This means that we need to define onsampling next:

```
// client.ts

async function main() {
    onsampling = (message) => {
        console.log("SAMPLING RECEIVED:", message);
        console.log(message.params.messages[0].content.text);
        // call your LLM, product response back to server
        createSampleResponse(message.params.messages[0].content.text);
    };

    // omitted for brevity
```

Here, you see how we set up a handler to onsampling and we call createSampleResponse, so let's look at the latter here:

```
async function createSampleResponse(message: string) {
    const llmResponse = await callLLM(message);
    // make copy sampleResponse to avoid mutating the original
    const copy = { ...sampleResponse };
    copy.content.text = llmResponse;
```

```
    _makeRequest(sampleResponse);
}

async function callLLM(message: string): Promise<string> {
    return Promise.resolve(`LLM response to: ${message}`);
}
```

There are two things defined here:

- `createSampleResponse`: This function creates a sample response and dispatches it back to the server. It uses `callLLM` to produce the response.

- `callLLM`: This is just a mock implementation that you need to replace with an actual call to an LLM.

That's it – that's how sampling works. It originates in the server as the result of an event, and then it asks the client for help, and the client responds. It should be emphasized that the client doesn't have to do exactly what the server wants it to do – that is, use a specific mode or configuration. You should present the server request in front of an equal user so they have a chance to respond and configure what the client sends back – that is, *human in the loop*.

See a running example of this code in the solution folder – check *Sampling* (`https://github.com/PacktPublishing/Learn-Model-Context-Protocol-with-TypeScript/blob/main/Chapter02/solutions/README.md`).

SSE transport

At this point, we've gone through large parts of the MCP. So, what's the difference between SSE and STDIO? The main difference is how messages flow. In STDIO, messages are passed on your local machine between `stdin` and `stdout` streams; for SSE, messages flow over the web using HTTP. That means all the major motions, such as handshake, initialization, tool calling, and so on, need to be rethought as web requests from the client and web requests to the server.

Conceptually, SSE transport is implemented as a web server with the `/messages` and `/sse` routes. The former handles incoming MCP messages, while the latter is used to establish a connection for streaming events.

Here's what that looks like from a high level:

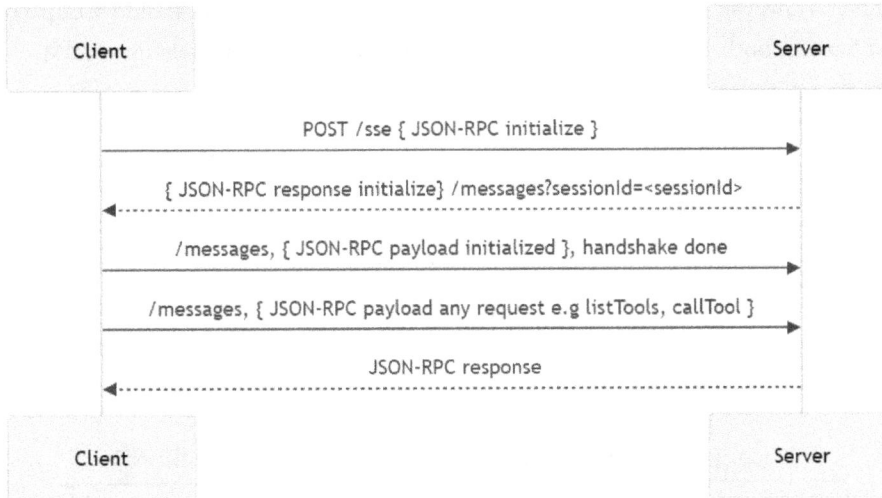

Figure 2.5 – SSE transport flow

We will cover SSE in more detail in *Chapter 4*, but now we have a good understanding at a mile-high level of what the difference is compared to STDIO.

Streamable HTTP

Streamable HTTP is just like SSE in the sense that MCP servers using Streamable HTTP can be reached via a URL on the web. There are some differences and similarities. Let's make that a bit clearer:

- Both SSE and Streamable HTTP need the client to accept text/event-stream. For Streamable HTTP, the client also needs to accept application/json, as the server can choose whether to stream responses or send them as JSON. For SSE, the server always sends content as text/event-stream.

- SSE connections are usually long-lived GET requests, where Streamable HTTP is typically POST.

From an implementation standpoint, it's very similar to that of SSE – that is, it's implemented as a web server. However, for Streamable HTTP, in the context of MCP, you should set up a route, / mcp, that handles both connections and messages, and it should also be set up as POST.

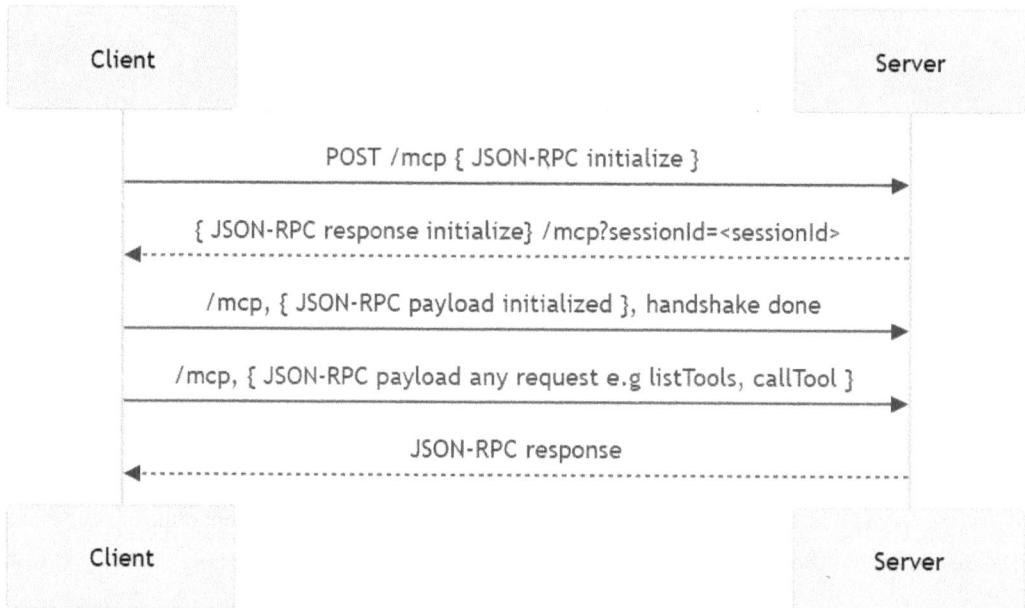

Figure 2.6 – Streamable HTTP flow

Therefore, implementing Streamable HTTP is a bit easier than SSE as you only need to keep track of one endpoint, /mcp. There's more on Streamable HTTP in *Chapter 5*.

Summary

In this chapter, we covered quite a bit of information. The most important takeaway is that client and server communication needs to be initialized before further action can take place. Fortunately, most SDKs take care of the initialization part, and you can usually start the client-server communication by calling and listing tools and more. Hopefully, this was a good read for both those who find diagrams clarifying and those who like to see how code looks. The code *works*, but could surely be improved for performance, maintainability, and more. Do give the code a try – check the solutions folder.

In the next chapter, we will learn how to build and test our first server. The chapter will serve as a good introduction to getting hands-on with MCP.

Assignment

Try running the code provided in `https://github.com/PacktPublishing/Learn-Model-Context-Protocol-with-TypeScript/blob/main/Chapter02/solutions/README.md` to see how things work. The code should do the following:

- Initialize a connection
- Send an initialized notification
- List tools
- Call a tool and produce notifications
- Produce sample messages

The code is built up in steps, so it's worth going through all the subfolders for your chosen runtime.

Solution

You can access the solution at `https://github.com/PacktPublishing/Learn-Model-Context-Protocol-with-TypeScript/blob/main/Chapter02/solutions/README.md`.

Quiz

What needs to happen before a *handshake* between a server and a client can be considered complete?

- A: The client needs to first send *initialize*, wait for the server response, and then send *initialized*.
- B: The client and server can call, for example, list tools right away.
- C: The client needs to send *initialized* to the server.

You can access the solution at `https://github.com/PacktPublishing/Learn-Model-Context-Protocol-with-TypeScript/blob/main/Chapter02/solutions/solution-quiz.md`.

Get This Book's PDF Version and Exclusive Extras

3

Building and Testing Servers

In this chapter, we will cover the basics of building and testing servers. We will start with a simple server that uses the STDIO transport. The STDIO transport is a simple way to communicate with the server using standard input and output streams. Building STDIO servers is a great way to get started with the **Model Context Protocol (MCP)** and understand how it works. It should also be added that the STDIO transport is the most common way to communicate with the server, and it's meant for servers running on your machine.

As part of the chapter, we will also cover different ways of testing the server. It's important that what we build works as expected. We will cover different tools that can be used visually, in the CLI, and in code.

In this chapter, you will learn how to do the following:

- Build a simple server using the STDIO transport
- Describe the core concepts of the server
- Test the server using different tools

The chapter covers the following topics:

- A STDIO server
- Concepts
- Runtimes
- Testing the server
- First server

A STDIO server

Using STDIO transport means that the server communicates with the client through standard input and output streams. This means that the server can read input from the client via **standard input (stdin)** and send output back to the client via **standard output (stdout)**. Okay, that sounds simple, but how does it work?

MCP uses JSON-RPC 2.0 as its wire format. Thereby, it needs to convert stream messages into JSON-RPC format for transmission and convert received JSON-RPC messages back into stream messages. Imagine the following example in the terminal:

```
>> hello world
```

To be used in a STDIO server, the preceding message would be converted into JSON-RPC format, and it would look like this:

```
{
  "jsonrpc": "2.0",
  "method": "sendMessage",
  "params": {
    "message": "hello world"
  },
  "id": 1
}
```

That's an interesting example, but what really matters to you as a developer is two things:

- How to build a STDIO server. We'll show this shortly in an upcoming section.
- Why it matters, and what it means that your server is a STDIO server. It means that your server is running on your local machine and is communicating with the client through standard input and output streams. In *Chapter 4* and *Chapter 5*, we'll show you how to build a server that can communicate with servers over the internet.

Concepts

Let's take a look at the core concepts (features, if you will) that the server can offer.

Resources

These are the data and context that the server can provide to the client. The way MCP is meant to be used is by the client having an LLM when they communicate with the server. Resources in this use case serve as context that could be added to the LLM at the time of the prompt. Imagine the following scenario playing out:

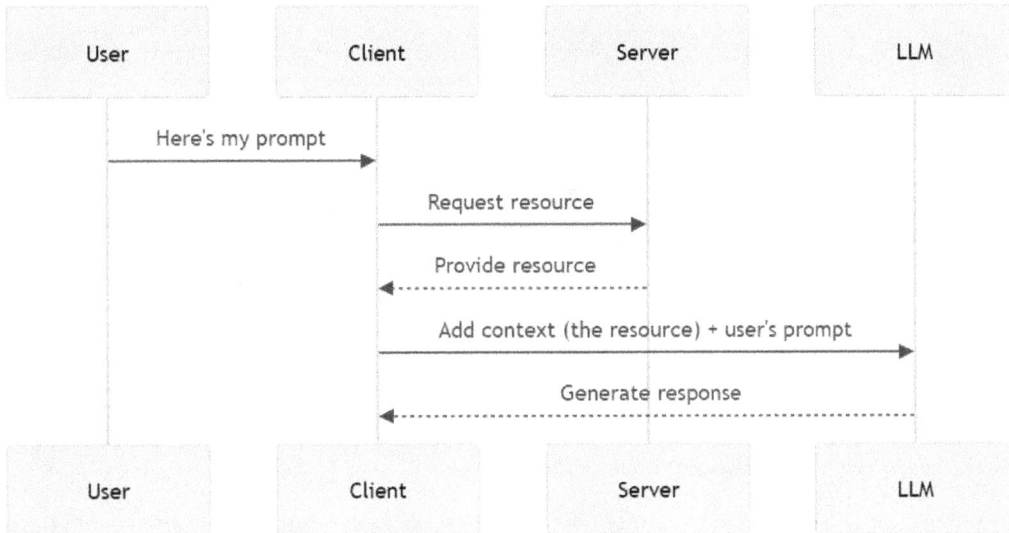

Figure 3.1 – Resources scenario

In this scenario, the context ensures that the end user gets a better result as the server's context is paired with the user's prompt, like a simplified **retrieval-augmented generation (RAG)** pattern. That is, you pair the user's prompt with your data to get a better response.

A specific example implementing this way of thinking could be where the user asks for products like so:

Prompt

```
User: I'm looking for a new laptop
```

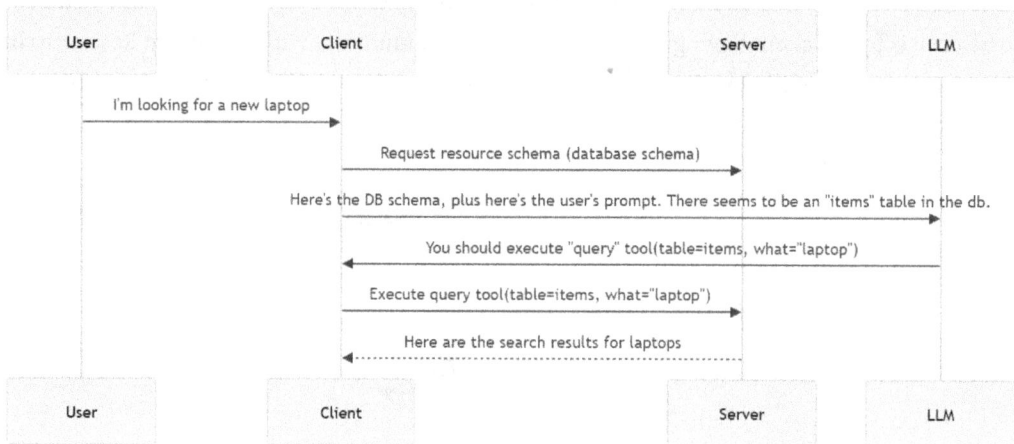

Figure 3.2 – Example of a resource interaction

In this specific product query, we call resources first to learn what table to query, and then we let the LLM identify which tool to call. Thanks to calling the resource, we gain extra knowledge on what tools to select and what parameters to use.

Resources can also be used in a manner where the LLM isn't used, but the way you should think about your server is that it's here to empower a client's LLM. That means the tools, resources, and prompts you provide should be helpful.

Now that we understand when resources are used, let's talk more about the nature of them. Resources are static and can be anything that the server can access and share with the client. What's important to know is that you can ask for a resource either with or without a template. If there's only one file or one app setting configuration, it makes sense to create that with a set name such as config:

```
server.resource(
  "config",
  "config://app",
  async (uri) => ({
```

```
    contents: [{
      uri: uri.href,
      text: "App configuration here"
    }]
  })
);
```

Here, we are returning the same type of information each time.

However, if there are many types of settings, such as user settings, calendar settings, and so on, it might make sense to create a more templated version such as settings://{type}:

```
server.resource(
  "settings",
  new ResourceTemplate("settings://{type}", { list: undefined }),
  async (uri, { type }) => ({
    // read content from file
    contents: [{
      uri: uri.href,
      text: `Settings from file ${type}`
    }]
  })
);
```

The settings are still non-changing, but there are many of them, so we choose to group them under one namespace.

Tools

Tools are the functions or capabilities that the server can perform. Examples of tools include data processing functions, tools that call an API to fetch data, and more. For tools, we need to define the input and output by providing a schema. How this is done looks different depending on the used runtime, but the idea is that it should be clear to the consumer of the tool what the input and output are. For example, if we have a tool that takes two numbers and returns their product, we can define it like this:

```
server.tool(
  "multiply",
  { first: z.number(), second: z.number() },
```

```
  async ({ first, second }) => ({
    content: [{ type: "text", text: String(first * second) }]
  })
);
```

In this example, we define a tool called `multiply`; the schema for the input is defined using **Zod**, a TypeScript-first schema declaration and validation library. The input is two numbers, `first` and `second`, and the output is a string that contains the product of the two numbers. The output has a default output schema defined by the SDK, but you can also define your own output schema.

Prompts

Prompts are the templated messages or workflows that guide the interactions between the client and server. A good example of a prompt is a template that helps the client write a product description or slogan in the context of an e-commerce application. Just like resources and tools, prompts can take input. Here's an example of a prompt that takes a product name and returns a product description:

```
server.prompt(
  "product-description",
  "Write a product description for a product",
  async ({ product }) => ({
    content: [{ type: "text", text: `Product description for ${product}`
      }]
  })
);
```

In this example, we define a prompt called `product-description` that takes a product name as input and returns a product description. The prompt is defined using a template that contains the {product} placeholder.

Now that we know what our server can contain, what else do we need to know?

Runtimes

The officially supported runtimes at present for MCP are Typescript, Python, .NET, Java and Kotlin, Rust, and Go. More are being added all the time. For an updated list of runtimes, please refer to the MCP documentation here: `https://modelcontextprotocol.io/docs/sdk`. Each of these runtimes has its own SDK you can use. The implementation of the runtimes is similar, but there are some differences. Excited? Let's get started!

Testing the server

There are many tools at your disposal to test the server. Why we test is that we want to ensure that the server is working as expected. The tools we will cover in this chapter are as follows.

Inspector

This is a CLI tool that can present both a UI and a CLI interface. The latter is meant for scripting and automation.

The UI is meant for manual testing and debugging. In this example command, we run the inspector tool. Ensure that you stand in the same directory as the server file when you run the following commands.

Running the inspector tool with TypeScript entails running it using npx like so:

```
npx @modelcontextprotocol/inspector node ./build/index.js
```

Here, we're running the inspector tool using npx. You can also add the ./build/index.js to npx @modelcontextprotocol/inspector executable path, but that's optional. At the latest, you need to fill in this information on the web page.

Ensure you then fill in the following fields:

- **Transport Type: STDIO**
- **Command:** node
- **Arguments:** ./build/index.js

The arguments field specifies the path to the built JavaScript file that will be executed by the inspector tool.

By running this tool, we can test the server in visual mode. Here's a screenshot of the inspector tool:

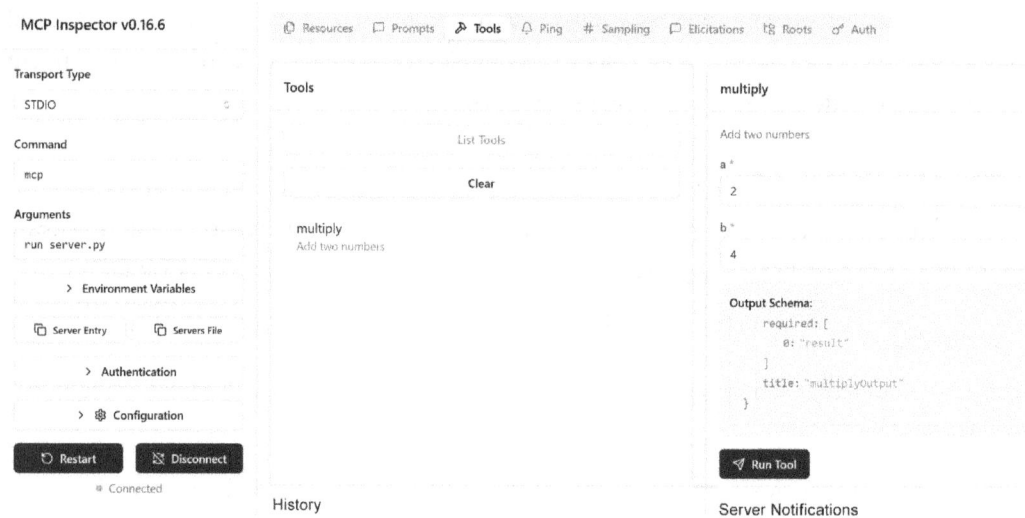

Figure 3.3 – Inspector tool

Ensure that the visual tool specifies the following fields:

- **Transport Type: STDIO**
- **Command:** mcp
- **Arguments:** run server.py

You can also run the inspector tool in CLI mode. This is useful for scripting and automation. You type almost the same command as earlier, but you add the --cli flag:

```
npx @modelcontextprotocol/inspector --cli mcp run server.py --method
tools/list
```

Here, we are adding the --method command followed by the tools/list argument, which says we want to list all tools on the server.

cURL

A standard command-line tool such as cURL can be used to send requests to the server. This is normally used to test servers using SSE or Streamable HTTP as transport. Other tools capable of making web requests can be used as well. A `curl` command will only work if the server is running on the internet, which is the case with SSE servers. For STDIO servers, you need to use the inspector or a custom client to send requests to the server. Let's see a typical `curl` command:

```
curl -X POST -H "Content-Type: application/json" -d '{"method": "tools/
list", "params": {}, "id": 1}' http://localhost:3000/sse
```

In the preceding command, we are sending a `POST` request to the server with the `tools/list` method. The server will respond with a list of tools available on the server. This is a good alternative to using the inspector in CLI mode.

Tests

It's possible to write unit tests for the server. This is a good practice in addition to using the inspector. The tests can be run in a CI/CD pipeline and are useful to ensure that the server is working as expected. You can use any testing framework you like, and you can add resources, tools, and prompts to the server and then test them. Let's see an example of a test:

```
@pytest.mark.anyio
async def test_add_tool_decorator(self):
    mcp = FastMCP()

    @mcp.tool()
    def add(x: int, y: int) -> int:
        return x + y

    assert len(mcp._tool_manager.list_tools()) == 1
```

In the preceding example, we do the following:

- Use the pytest framework to test the server
- Create a new server instance and add a tool called add
- Test that the tool is added to the server and that the number of tools is equal to 1

This is a simple test, but it shows how you can use pytest to test the server.

Now, we have a good grasp of the concepts and features of the server; let's write down the plan for how we will go about building our first server.

First server

To build our first server, let's first go through the steps to build a simple server:

1. **Create a new project**: We will create a new project with the needed dependencies and set up any environment specifics. You're highly encouraged to create a virtual environment to ensure you don't install libraries globally. By using a virtual environment, each project is isolated from other projects and you don't have to worry about conflicting library versions that might otherwise occur.

2. **Install dependencies**: Here, we will list and install dependencies for the project, which differ, of course, depending on the runtime you are using.

3. **Add server code**: This is where we will add the server's features. As part of this, we will discuss the feature, its input and output, and schemas.

4. **Test the server with inspector**: Inspector is a tool that helps you ensure new features work okay. The tool allows you to run it in both CLI mode and a visual mode, where it shows a web browser UI:

   - The CLI mode is appropriate for CI/CD scenarios, as it responds with JSON in a terminal

   - The visual mode is more appropriate when you, as a developer, try to ensure that the server is working as it should

Let's write some code!

Step 1: Create a new project

Before we write any code, we need a project. This will set us up for success. The project will contain everything we need to write our server and define tests and scripts for testing and running the server:

1. Create the following folder structure:

   ```
   ├── src/
   |---- server.ts
   ```

   This structure sets us up nicely for organizing our server code.

2.   Run the following command to initialize a new Node.js project:

```
npm init -y
```

This creates a package.json file, which we can use to manage our project dependencies and scripts.

3.   Let's configure package.json; it should look like the following:

```
{
    "type": "module",
    "bin": {
      "mcp-example": "./build/index.js"
    },
    "scripts": {
      "start": "node ./build/index.js",
      "build": "tsc"
    },
    "files": [
      "build"
    ],
    "dependencies": {
        "@modelcontextprotocol/sdk": "^1.8.0",
        "type": "^2.7.3",
        "zod": "^3.24.2"
    },
    "devDependencies": {
        "@types/node": "^20.11.24",
        "typescript": "^5.3.3"
    }
}
```

What we did was this:

- **Scripts**: We added some useful scripts to the package.json file, namely, start and build. The latter is used to compile the TypeScript code into JavaScript, and the former is used to run the compiled JavaScript code, which is our server.

- **Defined binary name**: We added a bin field to specify the command that will be run when the package is executed. So, if we wanted to run our server, we could use the npx mcp-example command. This sets us up nicely if we decide to distribute our package via npm, for example.

- **Dependencies**: We also specified the dependencies that our project needs to run. This includes the MCP SDK and Zod and development dependencies such as Type-Script and the Node.js type definitions.

Great! We're now set up for our next phase to install dependencies. Let's do that next.

Step 2: Install dependencies

We've got everything we need specified in the package.json file. Now, we need to install the dependencies:

1. Run the following command in the terminal:

```
npm install
```

2. Let's configure TypeScript. To do so, we need a tsconfig.json file, which we can create with the tsc init command.

3. Change the just-created tsconfig.json file to the following:

```json
{
  "compilerOptions": {
    "target": "ES2022",
    "module": "Node16",
    "moduleResolution": "Node16",
    "outDir": "./build",
    "rootDir": "./src",
    "strict": true,
    "esModuleInterop": true,
    "skipLibCheck": true,
    "forceConsistentCasingInFileNames": true
  },
  "include": ["src/**/*"],
  "exclude": ["node_modules"]
}
```

Here, we set target to ES2022, which means that the TypeScript code will be compiled to JavaScript that is compatible with the ES2022 version of JavaScript. We also changed the module system to Node16, which is the latest version of the Node.js module system.

Great, now we have everything we need to start writing our server.

Step 3: Add server code

1. Let's start by adding imports and code that will create a server instance:

```
import { McpServer, ResourceTemplate } from
   "@modelcontextprotocol/sdk/server/mcp.js";
import { STDIOServerTransport } from
   "@modelcontextprotocol/sdk/server/STDIO.js";
import { z } from "zod";

// Create an MCP server
const server = new McpServer({
  name: "Demo",
  version: "1.0.0"
});
```

This will create a server instance with the name Demo and version 1.0.0. The server instance is created using the McpServer class from the SDK.

2. Next, let's add our first tool:

```
server.tool("multiply",
    { first: z.number(), second: z.number() },
    async ({ first, second }) => ({
      content: [{ type: "text", text: String(first * second) }]
    })
);
```

3. Let's add a resource:

```
server.resource("get_greeting", new ResourceTemplate("greeting://
{name}", { list: () => {
    return {
      resources: [
          {
              "name": "get_greeting",
              "description": "Get a personalized greeting",
              "mimeType": "text/plain",
              "uri": "greeting://{name}"
          }
      ]
```

```
    };
  } }), async (uri, { name }) => ({
    contents: [{
            uri: uri.href,
            text: `Hello: ${name}`
        }]
  }));
```

4. Add a prompt with the following code:

```
server.prompt(
  "review-code",
  { code: z.string() },
  ({ code }) => ({
    messages: [{
      role: "user",
      content: {
        type: "text",
        text: `Please review this code:\n\n${code}`
      }
    }]
  })
);
```

The preceding code does the following:

- It creates a prompt called review-code that takes a code snippet as input and returns a review of the code
- The prompt is defined using a template that contains the {code} placeholder

5. Finally, let's add the code that will start the server:

```
async function main() {
    const transport = new STDIOServerTransport();
    await server.connect(transport);
    console.error("MCPServer started on stdin/stdout");
}
main().catch((error) => {
    console.error("Fatal error: ", error);
    process.exit(1);
});
```

Here's the full code for the server:

```
import { McpServer, ResourceTemplate } from
  "@modelcontextprotocol/sdk/server/mcp.js";
import { STDIOServerTransport } from
  "@modelcontextprotocol/sdk/server/STDIO.js";
import { z } from "zod";

// Create an MCP server
const server = new McpServer({
    name: "Demo",
    version: "1.0.0"
});


server.tool("multiply",
{
    first: z.number(),
    second: z.number()
},
async ({ first, second }) => ({
    content: [{
        type: "text",
        text: String(first * second)
    }]
})
);

server.resource("get_greeting", new ResourceTemplate("greeting://{name}",
  { list: () => {
    return {
        resources: [
            {
                "name": "get_greeting",
                "description": "Get a personalized greeting",
                "mimeType": "text/plain",
                "uri": "greeting://{name}"
            }
```

```
        ]
    };
    } }), async (uri, { name }) => ({
    contents: [{
            uri: uri.href,
            text: `Hello: ${name}`
        }]
}));

async function main() {
    const transport = new STDIOServerTransport();
    await server.connect(transport);
    console.error("MCPServer started on stdin/stdout");
}
main().catch((error) => {
    console.error("Fatal error: ", error);
    process.exit(1);
});
```

Step 4: Test the server with the inspector

Here, we will use the inspector to test the server. The inspector is a CLI tool that can present both a UI and a CLI interface. The latter is meant for scripting and automation. The UI is meant for manual testing and debugging:

1. Add the following entry to the package.json file and the scripts section:

   ```
   "inspector": "npx @modelcontextprotocol/inspector node build/index.js"
   ```

2. Run the following command in the terminal:

   ```
   npm run inspector
   ```

   This should start a web server with a visual interface, allowing you to test the sample:

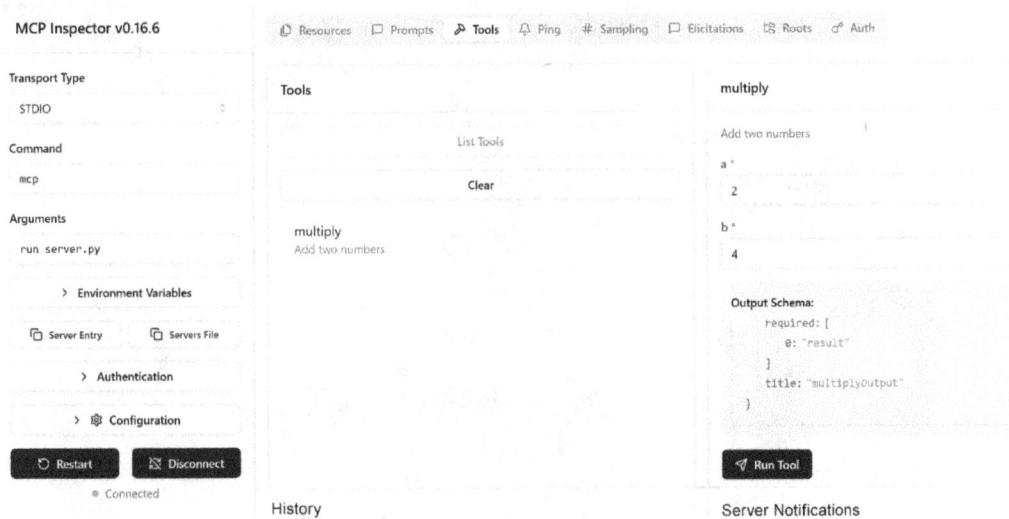

Figure 3.4 – Inspector tool

In the preceding figure, we've already filled out the **Command** field. Adjust this field to fit your chosen runtime. Click **Connect** to connect to the server.

Step 5: Test the server with the inspector in CLI mode

In this subsection, we will run the inspector directly in CLI mode. The inspector is a Node.js app, and mcp dev is a wrapper around it.

At the time of this writing, mcp dev does not support all the features made available in the inspector. We will therefore show how to run the inspector directly as a Node.js app as that's what it's been written in.

Let's show some useful commands you can run in the inspector:

- **List tools:** Run the following command in the terminal:

```
npx @modelcontextprotocol/inspector --cli mcp run server.py --method
tools/list
```

This will list all the tools available on the server, and you should see the following output:

```
{
  "tools": [
    {
      "name": "multiply",
      "description": "Multiply two numbers",
```

```
      "inputSchema": {
        "type": "object",
        "properties": {
          "first": {
            "title": "First",
            "type": "integer"
          },
          "second": {
            "title": "Second",
            "type": "integer"
          }
        },
        "required": [
          "first",
          "second"
        ],
        "title": "multiplyArguments"
      },
      "outputSchema": {
        "type": "object",
        "properties": {
          "result": {
            "title": "Result",
            "type": "integer"
          }
        },
        "required": [
          "result"
        ],
        "title": "multiplyOutput"
      }
    }
  ]
}
```

Here, you see all the tools on the server in JSON format. We only have one tool, `multiply`, but we can see that it has an `inputSchema` with `first` and `second` parameters.

- **Call a tool**: Run the following command in the terminal:

```
npx @modelcontextprotocol/inspector --cli mcp run server.py --method
tools/call --tool-name multiply --tool-arg first=2 --tool-arg
second=4
```

You should see a response like this:

```
{
  "content": [
    {
      "type": "text",
      "text": "8"
    }
  ],
  "structuredContent": {
    "result": "8"
  },
  "isError": false
}
```

- **List resources**: Run the following command in the terminal:

```
npx @modelcontextprotocol/inspector --cli mcp run server.py --method
resources/list
```

This will list all the resources available in the server, and you should see the following output:

```
{
  "resources": []
}
```

Empty? The reason is that there's a difference between a resource and a templated resource. Here's how you can list the templated resources:

```
npx @modelcontextprotocol/inspector --cli mcp run server.py --method
resources/templates/list
```

You should get a response like this:

```
{
  "resourceTemplates": [
    {
      "uriTemplate": "greeting://{name}",
      "name": "get_greeting",
      "description": "Get a personalized greeting"
    }
  ]
}
```

- Let's call our templated resource:

```
npx @modelcontextprotocol/inspector --cli mcp run server.py --method
resources/read --uri greeting://chris
```

You should see a response like this:

```
{
  "contents": [
    {
      "uri": "greeting://chris",
      "mimeType": "text/plain",
      "text": "Hello, chris!"
    }
  ]
}
```

- Let's list prompts next with the following command:

```
npx @modelcontextprotocol/inspector --cli mcp run server.py --method
prompts/list
```

You should see an output similar to the following:

```
{
  "prompts": [
    {
      "name": "review_code",
      "description": "",
      "arguments": [
```

```
        {
            "name": "code",
            "required": true
        }
      ]
    }
  ]
}
```

- To call a prompt, we would type the name of the prompt and prompts/get, like so:

```
npx @modelcontextprotocol/inspector --cli mcp run server.py
--method prompts/get --prompt-name review_code --prompt-args
code="print('Hello World')"
```

You should see a response like this:

```
{
  "messages": [
    {
      "role": "user",
      "content": {
        "type": "text",
        "text": "Please review this code:\n\nprint('Hello World')"
      }
    }
  ]
}
```

Summary

In this chapter, we covered how to build your first server. For our first server, we used the STDIO transport to create a server meant to be run on our machine. We also looked into various ways of testing out the server features using a tool called the inspector. The inspector tool has two different modalities, CLI mode and visual mode. The former mode is used for CI/CD scenarios, and the latter for you as a developer quickly trying out features.

In our upcoming chapter, we'll describe the SSE transport, which you can use if you want the server to be consumed via a URL address.

Assignment — an e-commerce STDIO server

For this MCP server, we will add capabilities that can be used in the context of an e-commerce application. Therefore, the server will need the following features.

It will need these tools:

- `get-orders`: This tool will return a list of orders. The optional input is a customer ID, and the output is a list of orders. Each order should contain the following fields: ID, customer ID, quantity, total price, and status.

- `get-order`: This tool will return a specific order. The input is the order ID, and the output is an order. The order should contain the following fields: ID, customer ID, quantity, total price, and status.

- `place-order`: This tool will place an order. The input is the customer ID and the cart ID.

- `get-cart`: This tool will return a cart.

- `get-cart-items`: This tool will return a list of items in the cart. The input is the cart ID, and the output is a list of items. Each item should contain the following fields: ID, name, description, price, quantity, and product ID.

- `add-to-cart`: This tool will add an item to the cart. The input is the cart ID, product ID, and quantity. The output is a success message. If the cart ID is not provided, the tool should create a new cart and add the item to the new cart. The output should be a success message and the cart ID.

- `products`: This tool will return a list of products. The optional input is a category, and the output is a list of products. The product should contain the following fields: ID, name, description, price, and category. The output should be in JSON format.

- `product`: This tool should return a specific product. The input is the product ID, and the output is a product. The product should contain the following fields: name, description, price, category, and ID. The output should be in JSON format.

- `categories`: This tool will return a list of categories. The output should be in JSON format. The categories should contain the following fields: ID, name, and description. The output should be in JSON format.

- `get-customers`: This tool will return a list of customers. The output should be in JSON format. It should contain the following fields: ID, name, and email.

It will need this resource:

- `product_catalog`: This resource will return a list of products in the catalog. The optional input is a category, and the output is a list of products. Each product should contain the following fields: name, description, and category. The idea is that the resource will return a list of products in the catalog, in case potential customers want to see them.

As you can see, this will support a simple e-commerce application and a customer trying to either put items in a cart or place an order.

> You can keep state within memory data structures.

Solution

You can find the solution at `https://github.com/PacktPublishing/Learn-Model-Context-Protocol-with-TypeScript/blob/main/Chapter03/solutions/README.md`.

Quiz

What of the following is something a server can expose?

- A: Tools, prompts, and services
- B: Tools and prompts
- C: Prompts, tools, and resources

You can find the solution at `https://github.com/PacktPublishing/Learn-Model-Context-Protocol-with-TypeScript/blob/main/Chapter03/solutions/solution-quiz.md`.

References

- **Inspector tool:** `https://github.com/modelcontextprotocol/inspector`
- **Model Context Protocol:** `https://github.com/modelcontextprotocol/`
- **TypeScript SDK:** `https://github.com/modelcontextprotocol/typescript-sdk`

Get This Book's PDF Version and Exclusive Extras

UNLOCK NOW

Scan the QR code (or go to packtpub.com/unlock). Search for this book by name, confirm the edition, and then follow the steps on the page.

Note: Keep your invoice handy. Purchases made directly from Packt don't require an invoice.

4

Building SSE Servers

So far, you've seen how you can build MCP servers using STDIO as transport. That's a great choice of transport for servers meant to run locally. However, if you want to connect to servers remotely via HTTP or if you want responses from LLMs streamed, then there's another transport called **Server-Sent Events (SSE)** better suited to this scenario.

> SSE transport has been deprecated in favor of Streamable HTTP transport per May 2025. However, there are still more than 2000+ MCP servers built using SSE transport, so it's important to keep that in mind should you encounter such servers in the wild and need to integrate or maintain them.

In this chapter, we'll focus on building and testing MCP servers using SSE as transport.

The chapter covers the following topics:

- SSE concepts
- Creating an SSE server as a web app
- Testing with SSE
- Creating an SSE server

Let's dive into the details of SSE and how to build a server using it.

SSE concepts

There are some concepts we need to understand before we can start building our server. First off, a server using SSE as transport is a server that can be accessed via HTTP. That means, even if it can run locally, it can also be accessed remotely. The implications of this are that this is a server that we need to expose using a web server.

SSE is a standard for unidirectional communication from server to client over a single, long-lived HTTP connection. It allows servers to push real-time updates to clients without requiring the client to poll for changes. Here are some more details:

- **Protocol**: SSE uses standard HTTP with the MIME type text/event-stream
- **Client API**: The browser uses the EventSource API to receive events
- **Format**: Messages are sent as plain text with fields such as event, data, and id, each terminated by two endlines

It's typically used for dashboard-like applications where real-time updates are crucial.

In MCP, SSE is split up into two parts: the part where we connect to the server and perform initialization (e.g., *handshake*), and a message part where we apply messages to the server that ends up reading or writing data. So, we need to implement the following endpoints:

- **SSE endpoint**: This endpoint is used as a way to handshake the connection between the client and the server. By sending a request to this endpoint, the client will receive a response that will keep the connection open.
- **Message endpoint**: This endpoint is what's used to route messages to the MCP server and its features.

It should be said that, depending on the chosen runtime and SDK, you may need to implement these endpoints yourself, but for some runtimes, it happens under the hood. Regardless, it's good to know how it works and what the endpoints are doing.

Creating an SSE server as a web app

The big difference compared to using the STDIO transport is that we need to expose an SSE server as a web application. Depending on whether we use Python or TypeScript, that means we need to implement the necessary HTTP endpoints.

In TypeScript, we can use any web framework we want in combination with the MCP SDK to build and host our app. As we stated before, we just need to respond to an SSE endpoint for initialization and a message endpoint for sending messages. This degree of freedom is a good thing, as you might have different preferences for frameworks and libraries. Here's what such an implementation might look like if using the Express framework:

```
// using Express as framework

app.get('/sse', async (req, res) => {
  // Create SSE transport for legacy clients
  const transport = new SSEServerTransport('/messages', res);
  transports.sse[transport.sessionId] = transport;

  res.on("close", () => {
    delete transports.sse[transport.sessionId];
  });

  await server.connect(transport);
});

// Legacy message endpoint for older clients
app.post('/messages', async (req, res) => {
  const sessionId = req.query.sessionId as string;
  const transport = transports.sse[sessionId];
  if (transport) {
    await transport.handlePostMessage(req, res, req.body);
  } else {
    res.status(400).send('No transport found for sessionId');
  }
});
```

In this code, we create two HTTP endpoints: one for the SSE connection and one for sending messages. The SSE endpoint is responsible for initializing the connection and keeping it open, while the message endpoint is used for routing messages to the appropriate transport. The important code here is in the '/messages' endpoint, where we handle incoming messages from clients and route them to the SSE transport, like so: transport.handlePostMessage.

This is code you write once, and you need to write similar code if you choose a framework other than Express.

Testing with SSE

There are differences, though, when it comes to how testing tools using SSE work. Let's list the differences:

- **Inspector tool**: The inspector tool is a command-line tool that allows you to test your server using both a visual interface and a command-line interface. The difference between STDIO and SSE is that you need to specify **Transport Type** as SSE and **URL** as `http://<address>:<port>/sse`. This is something you need to do when using the visual interface.

  For the CLI mode, you need to specify a URL instead of how to run the server. So, the following command will work, provided you have the server running at `localhost:8000`:

  ```
  npx @modelcontextprotocol/inspector --cli http:localhost:8000/sse
  --method tools/list
  ```

  Let's see the difference in the visual interface:

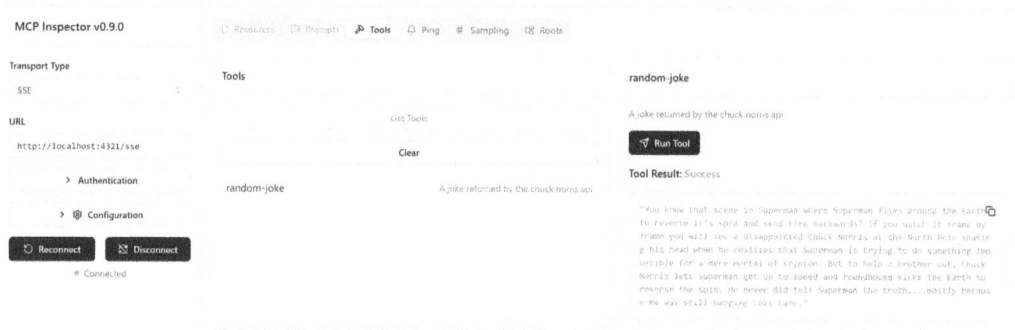

Figure 4.1 – Inspector tool, visual mode, SSE

  Note how **Transport Type** is set to SSE and **URL** is set to `http://localhost:8000/sse`. Remember with STDIO how we didn't have a **URL** field and rather a field to specify how to run the server? This is the difference between STDIO and SSE when it comes to the inspector tool.

- **Web client**: Because the SSE server is running on HTTP, you can use any HTTP client to test it. This includes tools such as Postman, cURL, or even your web browser. To use cURL, you can use the following command:

  1. Get the session ID:

     ```
     export MCP_SERVER="http://0.0.0.0:8000"
     curl "${MCP_SERVER}/sse"
     ```

     This will produce a response like this:

     ```
     ```text
     event: endpoint
     data: http://localhost:5001/messages?session_id=<my session
     id>
     ```
     ```

  2. Use the session ID to send a message to the server on the message endpoint.

     > Ensure you send this in another terminal instance. The answer to this request will appear in the first terminal though.

     ```
     export MCP_ENDPOINT="http://localhost:8000/messages?session_
     id=<my session id>"
     ```

  3. Send a message to the server, such as listing tools, in a separate terminal from the one that you sent the initialize request to.

     ```
     curl -X POST "${MCP_ENDPOINT}" -H "Content-Type: application/
     json" -d '{
       "jsonrpc": "2.0",
       "id": 1,
       "method": "tools/list"
     }'
     ```

So, yes, it's possible to do this using curl, but it's a bit cumbersome, which makes the inspector tool a great choice for testing your server – also for SSE.

Creating an SSE server

Okay, so we understand the concepts of SSE and how to build a server, and even how our testing tools work and are different from STDIO. Now it's time to build our own SSE server. We'll learn how to do the following:

1. Set up a project

2. Add the server code

3. Test the server

Create the project

Let's create a new project like so:

1. Create a new directory, src, for your project with the following structure:

    ```
    src/
    ├── index.ts
    package.json
    tsconfig.json
    ```

2. Add the following code to package.json:

    ```json
    {
        "type": "module",
        "bin": {
            "weather": "./build/index.js"
        },
        "scripts": {
            "build": "tsc",
            "inspector": "npx @modelcontextprotocol/inspector",
            "start": "node ./build/index.js"
        },
        "files": [
            "build"
        ],
        "dependencies": {
            "@modelcontextprotocol/sdk": "^1.8.0",
            "type": "^2.7.3",
    ```

```
          "uuid": "^11.1.0",
          "zod": "^3.24.2",
          "express": ""
      },
      "devDependencies": {
          "@types/node": "^20.11.24",
          "@types/uuid": "^10.0.0",
          "typescript": "^5.3.3"
      }
  }
```

3. Add the following code to `tsconfig.json`:

```
{
    "compilerOptions": {
      "target": "ES2022",
      "module": "Node16",
      "moduleResolution": "Node16",
      "outDir": "./build",
      "rootDir": "./src",
      "strict": true,
      "esModuleInterop": true,
      "skipLibCheck": true,
      "forceConsistentCasingInFileNames": true,
      "noImplicitAny": false
    },
    "include": ["src/**/*"],
    "exclude": ["node_modules"]
}
```

4. Install the dependencies:

```
npm install
```

There, you should be all set up to start building your SSE server.

Add the server code

Now add the following code to your project:

In index.ts, add the following code:

```typescript
import express from "express";
import { McpServer } from "@modelcontextprotocol/sdk/server/mcp.js";
import { StreamableHTTPServerTransport } from
  "@modelcontextprotocol/sdk/server/streamableHttp.js";
import { SSEServerTransport } from
  "@modelcontextprotocol/sdk/server/sse.js";
import { z } from "zod";

const server = new McpServer({
  name: "SSE Server",
  version: "1.0.0"
});

const app = express();
app.use(express.json());

// Store transports for each session type
const transports = {
  sse: {} as Record<string, SSEServerTransport>
};

app.get('/sse', async (req, res) => {
  // Create SSE transport for legacy clients
  const transport = new SSEServerTransport('/messages', res);
  transports.sse[transport.sessionId] = transport;

  res.on("close", () => {
    delete transports.sse[transport.sessionId];
  });

  await server.connect(transport);
});
```

```
// Legacy message endpoint for older clients
app.post('/messages', async (req, res) => {
  const sessionId = req.query.sessionId as string;
  const transport = transports.sse[sessionId];
  if (transport) {
    await transport.handlePostMessage(req, res, req.body);
  } else {
    res.status(400).send('No transport found for sessionId');
  }
});

app.listen(3000, () => {
    console.log("Server is running on http://localhost:3000");
    console.log("SSE endpoint: http://localhost:3000/sse");
    console.log("Legacy message endpoint: http://localhost:3000/messages");
});
```

In the preceding code, we've done the following:

- Imported the necessary modules from Express and MCP
- Created an instance of McpServer with the name of the application
- Instantiated an Express app and mounted the SSE server to the existing Express server
- Instructed the server to use SSE as transport
- Created endpoints for /sse and /messages, which will be used to handle the SSE hand-shake and message routing
- Finally, we started listening on port 3000

Add features

The next step is about adding features to your server. As mentioned, there's no difference between STDIO and SSE when it comes to features. You can use the same decorators and methods to create features.

Now, let's add features to our server:

```
// Add a tool
server.tool(
  "add",
```

```
  "add two numbers",
  {
    a: z.number(),
    b: z.number()
  },
  async ({ a, b }) => {
    console.log("Server: ", a, b);
    return {
      content: [{ type: "text", text: `Result: ${a + b}` }]
    };
  }
);
```

In the preceding code, we've defined a tool called add that takes two numbers as input and returns their sum.

You'll get the chance to add more features later in the assignment, but for now, you have a working server with a feature that adds two numbers.

Run it

The next step is to run the server.

Start the server using the command line:

```
npm run start
```

You should see the following output:

```
Server is running on http://localhost:3000
SSE endpoint: http://localhost:3000/sse
Legacy message endpoint: http://localhost:3000/messages
```

Test it

We will test our server in three different ways:

- **Inspector tool, as a visual interface**: This is a good way to test your server and see how it works

- **Inspector tool with the cli option**: The CLI option provides a response directly in the command line. This is a good way to test your servers in, for example, CI/CD pipelines.

- **Using a client**: Here, we'll use cURL to test that our server responds to requests. This is a good way to quickly test your server.

Inspector tool

Let's try the Inspector tool using the visual interface.

Start the Inspector tool using the command line:

```
npm run inspector
```

Set the following fields in the UI:

- **Transport Type:** sse:
- **URL:** http://localhost:3000/sse:
- **Method:** add:
- **Input fields:**
    - **a:** 5
    - **b:** 10

Run it.

You should see the following output:

```
Result: 15
```

Inspector tool as a cli option

For this option, we'll use the Inspector tool like before, but with the added --cli option to run it in CLI mode. Remember, we will get the response directly in the command line as opposed to the UI.

```
npx @modelcontextprotocol/inspector --cli http://localhost:3000/sse
--method tools/call --tool-name add --tool-arg a=5 --tool-arg b=10
```

You should see the following output:

```
{
  "content": [
    {
      "type": "text",
      "text": "15"
    }
  ],
  "structuredContent": {
    "result": 15
  },
```

```
    "isError": false
}
```

curl command

To test with cURL, there are three calls we need to make:

1. A call to `/sse`. This should give us a session ID back:

    ```
    curl http://127.0.0.1:3000/sse
    ```

    You should see an output similar to the following:

    ```
    event: endpoint
    data: /messages/?session_id=53ddee76d5ec4b4aaa9420f24462210a
    ```

2. A call to `/messages` with the session ID also containing the initialized MCP message.

    In a *separate terminal*, run the following command:

    ```
    curl -X POST "http://127.0.0.1:3000/messages/?session_
    id=53ddee76d5ec4b4aaa9420f24462210a" -H "Content-Type: application/
    json" -d '{
        "jsonrpc": "2.0",
        "method": "notifications/initialized"
    }'
    ```

    This will tell the server we're ready to communicate.

3. **Feature ask**: the following `curl` command is asking to list tools on the MCP Server.

    The following command should be run in the *same terminal as the previous command*:

    ```
    curl -X POST "http://127.0.0.1:3000/
    messages/?sessionId=53ddee76d5ec4b4aaa9420f24462210a" -H "Content-
    Type: application/json" -d '{
      "jsonrpc": "2.0",
      "id": 1,
      "method": "tools/list",
      "params": {}
    }'
    ```

You should now see a response in the *first terminal* you used when you initialized the connection. It should look similar to the following:

```
event:message
data: {"result":{"tools":[{"name":"products","description":
"get products by category","inputSchema":{"type":"object",
"properties":{"category":{"type":"string"}},"additionalProperties"
:false,"$schema":"http://json-schema.org/draft-07/schema#"}},
{"name":"cart-list","description":"get products in
cart","inputSchema":{"type":"object","properties":{},
"additionalProperties":false,"$schema":"http://json-schema.org/
draft-07/schema#"}},{"name":"cart-add","description":"Adding
products to cart","inputSchema":{"type":"object","properties":
{"title":{"type":"string"}},"additionalProperties":false,
"$schema":"http://json-schema.org/draft-07/schema#"}},{"name"
:"add","inputSchema":{"type":"object","properties":{"a":
{"type":"number"},"b":{"type":"number"}},"required":["a","b"],
"additionalProperties":false,"$schema":"http://json-schema.org/
draft-07/schema#"}}]},"jsonrpc":"2.0","id":1}
```

As a recommendation, I prefer to use the Inspector tool as it provides a better experience and is easier to use. The `curl` command is more of a low-level approach and could be nice to use to get an initial session ID. It does tell you how the underlying protocol works, which can be helpful for debugging.

Summary

In this chapter, we learned about SSE and how to build a server using it.

We also learned about the differences between STDIO and SSE when it comes to testing tools and how to use the Inspector tool with SSE. The difference is that STDIO listens to stdin and stdout while SSE listens to HTTP requests. SSE can also be used to stream responses from LLMs.

Finally, we built our own SSE server and tested it using the Inspector tool and cURL.

In the next chapter, we will look into another transport called Streamable HTTP, which is the preferred transport to use when exposing a server via a URL.

Assignment — SSE server

In this assignment, you will build out an SSE server with some features to support the following use cases:

- List products by category
- Add products to cart
- List products in cart

You can use the code provided in this chapter as a starting point.

Solution

You can access the solution at https://github.com/PacktPublishing/Learn-Model-Context-Protocol-with-TypeScript/blob/main/Chapter04/solutions/README.md.

Quiz

1. What is the SSE transport used for?

    - A: To expose a server via HTTP
    - B: To expose a server via STDIO
    - C: To enable streaming of responses from LLMs

2. Which routes are used for SSE?

    - A: /mcp
    - B: /sse
    - C: /messages

You can access the solution at https://github.com/PacktPublishing/Learn-Model-Context-Protocol-with-TypeScript/blob/main/Chapter04/solutions/solution-quiz.md.

References

- **Lifecycle:** https://modelcontextprotocol.info/specification/draft/basic/lifecycle/
- **Starlette:** https://www.starlette.io/
- **Transports:** https://modelcontextprotocol.io/docs/concepts/transports

Get This Book's PDF Version and Exclusive Extras

UNLOCK NOW

Scan the QR code (or go to packtpub.com/unlock). Search for this book by name, confirm the edition, and then follow the steps on the page.

Note: Keep your invoice handy. Purchases made directly from Packt don't require an invoice.

5

Creating MCP Servers for Web Consumption with Streamable HTTP

In *Chapter 4*, we discussed building MCP servers with the **Server-Sent Events (SSE)** transport. In that chapter, you learned that if you want users to access your MCP server on the web, you can't use stdio, but instead you need to use a transport such as SSE or, as described in this chapter, Streamable HTTP.

So, in this chapter, you will learn about the following:

- The Streamable HTTP transport
- Why this transport should be used over SSE
- How to work with concepts such as notifications and resumability

The chapter covers the following topics:

- Streamable HTTP versus SSE, and why it is the new standard
- Streamable HTTP in MCP
- Resumability
- Notifications
- Creating and testing a server with Streamable HTTP
- Testing the server
- Testing resumability

Streamable HTTP versus SSE, and why it is the new standard

The differences between SSE and Streamable HTTP are important to understand when choosing the right technology for your application.

There are some key distinctions. The first reason is that SSE in MCP is considered **deprecated**; you should be using Streamable HTTP instead.

So, why is there a chapter called *SSE* in this book? The reason is that this book is written for you as both a developer of MCP servers and also as a consumer of servers, where you might be writing a client toward an existing server that might be using SSE. In short, you should know how to deal with both types of transport due to there being legacy code that you might be asked to work with. In fact, the article at `https://github.com/modelcontextprotocol/modelcontextprotocol/discussions/308` states that 20 reference servers, over 50 official integrations, and 186 community-developed servers and clients were using SSE when it was announced that it was deprecated. This means when you develop for MCP, ensure you keep in mind that you need to handle both SSE and Streamable HTTP, even if you develop new servers in Streamable HTTP.

Okay, but why the deprecation decision? Well, there are several reasons why Streamable HTTP is a better choice:

- **Single endpoint simplicity**: Clients and servers communicate via a single endpoint (e.g., `/mcp`), supporting both `POST` and `GET` methods. This simplifies implementation and reduces connection overhead.
- **Resumability support**: Streamable HTTP supports resumable sessions using headers such as `Last-Event-ID` and `Mcp-Session-ID`, allowing clients to reconnect and resume streams reliably. This is a powerful feature where, when clients lose connection, they can resume connection and start receiving data from where they were before the disconnect rather than starting from the beginning.

- **Better compatibility**: It works seamlessly with modern HTTP infrastructure—load balancers, proxies, and API gateways—where SSE often fails or requires workarounds.

- **Bidirectional communication**: While SSE is unidirectional, Streamable HTTP can be upgraded to support bidirectional flows, making it more versatile for agent-to-agent or client-server interactions.

- **Future-proofing**: Streamable HTTP aligns with evolving MCP standards and community best practices. It's modular, extensible, and designed for stateless or session-based models. Stateless servers are more lightweight and easier to construct, and being able to choose the right model for the right scenario is a compelling argument.

Streamable HTTP in MCP

Okay, so normally when we're talking about streaming, some of you might think of how you divide up files in chunks or how you have AI models return their response in smaller parts. However, in the context of MCP, streaming is more about how we transmit data over HTTP while following the *streamable* standard, meaning that clients using Streamable HTTP typically send the following Accept header: `Accept: application/json, text/event-stream`.

This tells the server the client can handle both batch JSON responses and streamed events (via SSE). The server can choose the appropriate response mode based on the request type and context.

Is that it, streaming that just sends simple responses? There's a bit more to it, namely, resumability.

Resumability

Resumability is a concept that means that, if a client loses connection with a server while data is being transferred, upon reconnecting with the server, it can resume the data exchange where it was, rather than starting from the beginning. For long-running operations, this can be a game-changer. Technically, resumability can be achieved by both SSE and Streamable HTTP, but within the context of the MCP protocol, it's only supported for Streamable HTTP.

Let's illustrate it with a diagram:

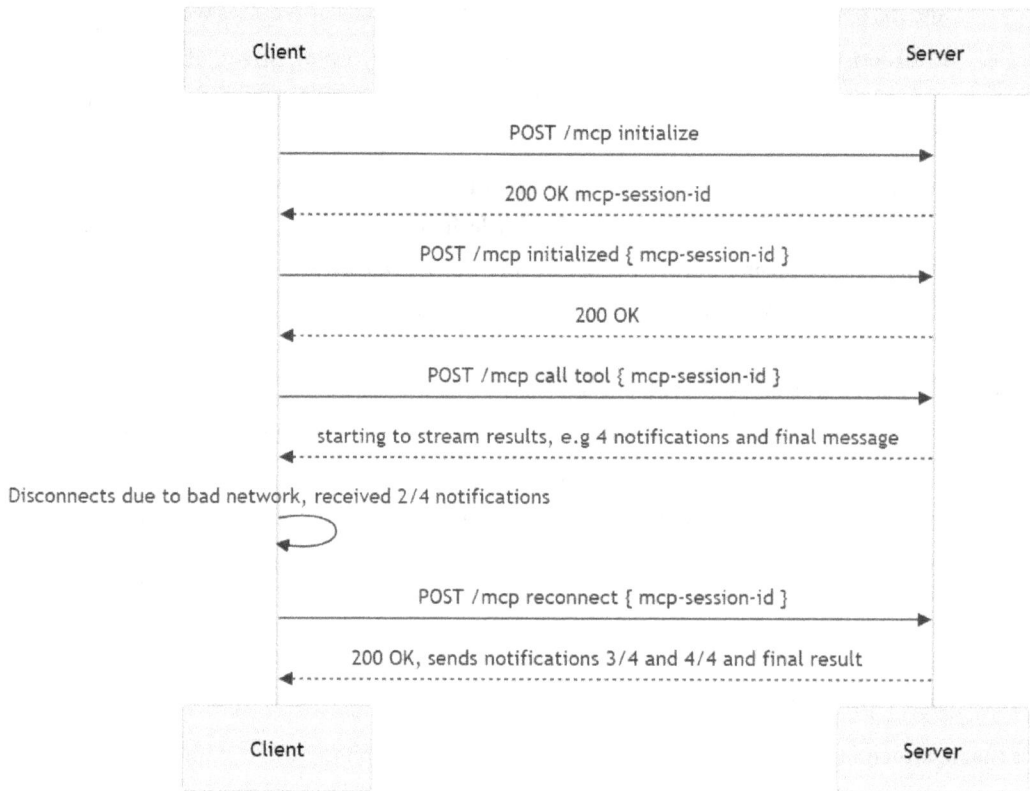

Figure 5.1 – Resumability

As you can see from the preceding diagram, the client doesn't have to restart from the beginning but can resume where they were. This works because the client, upon reconnecting, sends Mcp-Session-Id and Last-Event-Id headers. It's important to note that upon disconnecting, the client needs to do so gracefully, so it stores these two headers for later use.

What needs to be done on the server side to support this, though? Well, the server needs to do the following for resumability to work:

1. Create a session store, which is where produced messages are placed.
2. Set up a middleware that handles incoming requests and outgoing responses to ensure messages are properly stored and can be retrieved for resuming sessions. Exactly how this happens differs between frameworks.

Here's the code:

```typescript
// define post handler
function mcpPostHandler(req: Request, res: Response) {
  const { method, params } = req.body;

  // code omitted for brevity

  if (!sessionId && isInitializeRequest(req.body)) {

    // 1. Create an in-memory store
    const eventStore = new InMemoryEventStore();

    // 2. Create the transport and pass store to it
    transport = new StreamableHTTPServerTransport({
      sessionIdGenerator: () => randomUUID(),
      eventStore, // Enable resumability
      onsessioninitialized: (sessionId) => {
        // Store the transport by session ID when session is initialized
        // This avoids race conditions where requests might come in
        // before the session is stored
        console.log(`Session initialized with ID: ${sessionId}`);
        transports[sessionId] = transport;
      }
    });
  }
}

// 4. Set up post handler
app.post('/mcp', authMiddleware, mcpPostHandler);
```

In this code, we do the following:

1. Create an in-memory store.

2. Create the transport and pass the store to it.

3. Set up the session initialization handler.

4. Set up a post handler.

Okay, now that we understand a bit more about how resumability can really improve the user experience, as the client can get messages where they were when the disconnect happened, let's talk about another concept, namely, notifications.

Notifications

Notifications are not a concept unique to Streamable HTTP but can also be used in SSE. However, paired with resumability, they suddenly become very powerful. Let's describe what they are first and then discuss how they relate to resumability.

Notifications come in many different forms to communicate that something important has happened. They are real-time updates and, for the sake of the SDK, are handled as a separate thing. That means the SDK provides a special way to listen to notifications by implementing a handler for them, as you will soon see.

Here are some scenarios where notifications make sense:

- Status updates
- Progress notifications
- Error messages
- Informational messages

For example, the final message sent from the client to the server is a notification called `notifications/initialized` and signals that the client and the server can exchange non-handshake messages and more normal operations such as listing tools, reading a resource, and so on. The following is the JSON-RPC shape of the `notifications/initialized` message:

```
{
  "jsonrpc": "2.0",
  "method": "notifications/initialized"
}
```

Producing a notification

How do we produce a notification? Well, a notification is nothing more than a JSON-RPC message, and your SDK usually has a dedicated method to make it easier to send notifications. As there are different types of notifications, it's more a matter of using the right method with the appropriate parameters.

The server has a convenient method called sendNotification, which makes it easy to send notifications. It takes two parameters, namely, method, which specifies which type of notification to send, and params, which contains the data for the notification:

```
Server.tool(
    "process-files",
    { message: z.string() },
    // 1. Destructure the input object to get a reference to
    // sendNotification
    async ({ message }, { sendNotification }) => {

        // 2. Send notification
        await sendNotification({
            method: "notifications/message",
            params: { level: "info", data: `some notification` }
        });

        // 3. Return final result
        return {
            content: [{ type: "text", text: `Final result` }]
        };
    });
```

Let's explain the code:

1. The callback function takes both input parameters and the context object. From the context object, we can dig out the sendNotification method that we use for sending notifications.

2. The sendNotification method is called to send a notification with the specified method and parameters.

3. The tool returns a final result.

Handling a notification

When you consume notifications as a client, they show up in a different place than where you would normally expect them. Instead of being part of the regular message flow, they are handled separately with their own callbacks.

```
// 1. Import the necessary schemas

import { LoggingMessageNotificationSchema,
} from '@modelcontextprotocol/sdk/types.js';



// 2. Set up a notification handler capable of handling notifications
client.setNotificationHandler(LoggingMessageNotificationSchema,
  (notification) => {
    console.log(`\nNotification: ${notification.params.level} -
      ${notification.params.data}`);

});
```

In this code, we do the following:

1. Import the necessary schema, called `LoggingMessageNotificationSchema`.
2. Set up a notification handler capable of handling notifications.

That's it, that's all we need to do to handle notifications in our client.

Notifications in the Inspector tool

Great, now that we have a sense for how to set up sending notifications and receiving them, let's see how notifications appear in our Inspector tool, as we need to learn to look for them in the right place.

If you start the Inspector tool in a visual mode, you will see a screen like this:

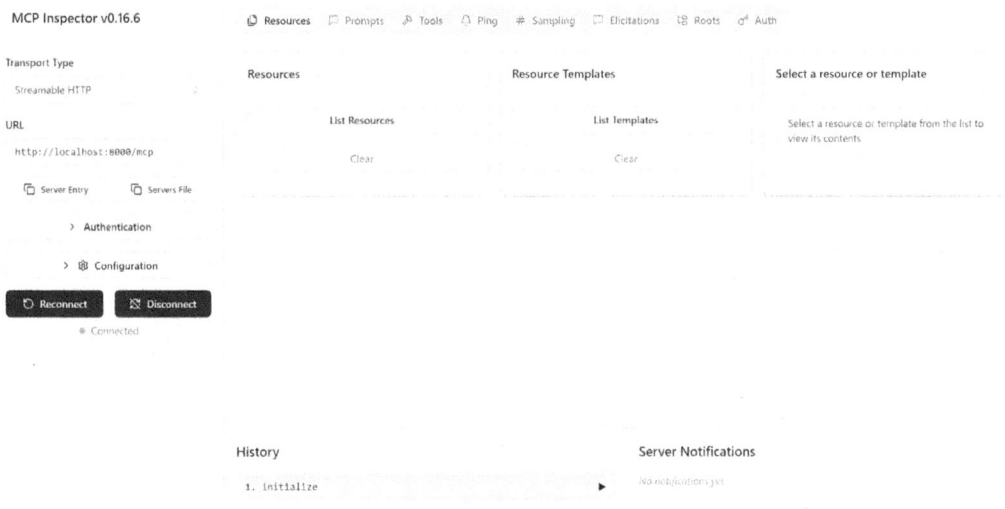

Figure 5.2 – Inspector tool

Now, if you run a tool, you will see the tool result, and you will see an area below it showing notifications, like so:

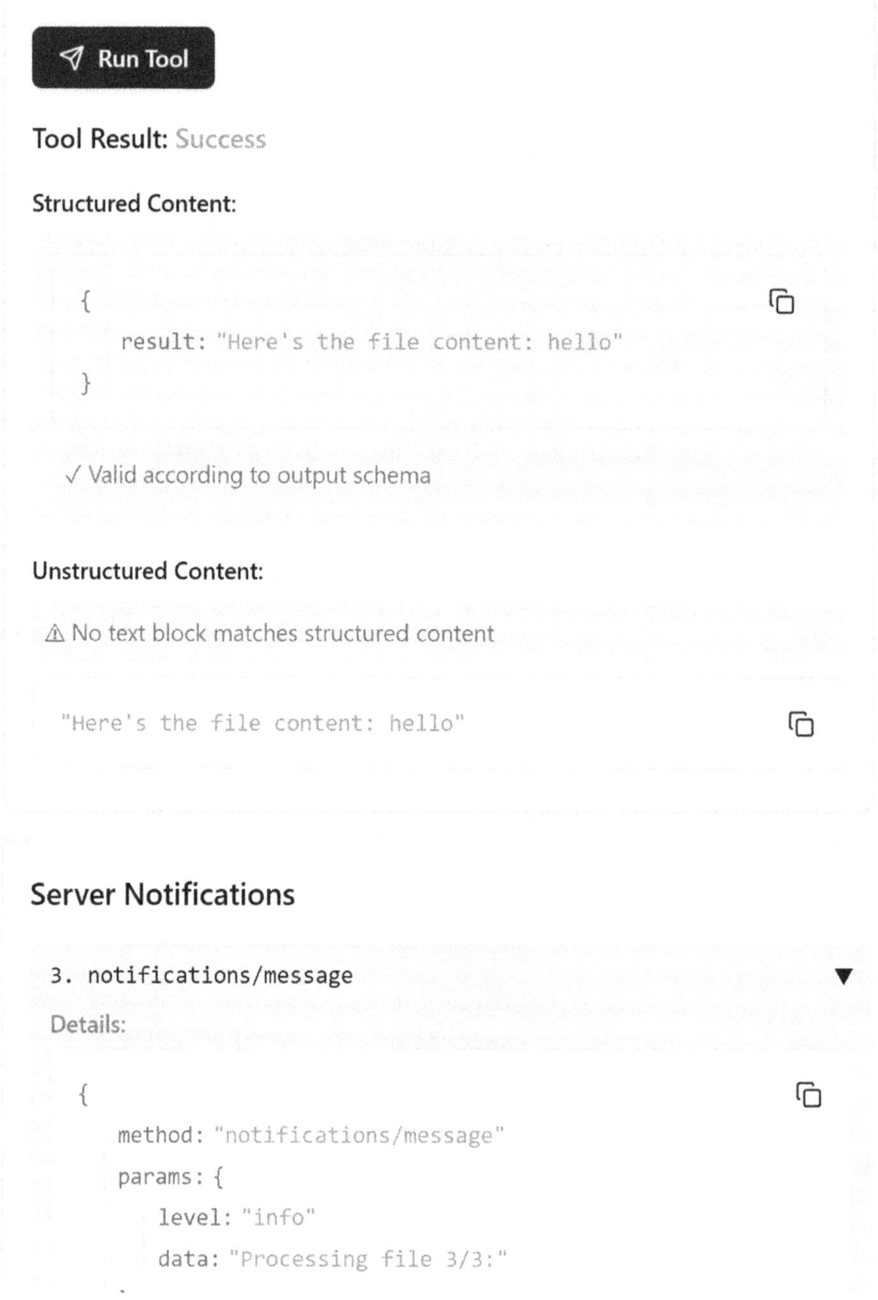

◁ Run Tool

Tool Result: Success

Structured Content:

```
{
    result: "Here's the file content: hello"
}
```

✓ Valid according to output schema

Unstructured Content:

⚠ No text block matches structured content

```
"Here's the file content: hello"
```

Server Notifications

```
3. notifications/message                                    ▼
```
Details:

```
{
    method: "notifications/message"
    params: {
        level: "info"
        data: "Processing file 3/3:"
```

Figure 5.3 – Notifications

Notifications with resumability

As we said before, notifications can be sent with SSE and Streamable HTTP, but with the latter, it becomes extra important. Imagine you have a client that disconnects a number of times due to a spotty internet connection, but thanks to logic in the client performing reconnects and resumability support in the server, the end user still has a good experience, as they won't miss out on either notifications or normal messages, such as a tool response, for example.

Now, let's move on to creating a server.

Creating and testing a server with Streamable HTTP

Let's create a server, and in doing so, we'll also integrate notifications. After the server is built, in the next section, we'll try testing it out with the different tools we have at our disposal, such as writing our own client, using the Inspector tool, and testing with cURL.

To get the server to use streaming, you need to do the following:

- Create a POST /mcp route that will be used to connect to the MCP server. Calling said route should produce a sessionId that can be used to connect to the server if you're a client. Using the client SDK, you don't need to worry about passing the sessionId, but if you write your own client, you need to pass it.
- Create an instance of the StreamableHTTPServerTransport transport type and pass it to the MCP server.
- Define a GET request to /mcp that returns the sessionId and a DELETE request to /mcp that closes the session.
- Define what features the MCP server should have that look normal, in terms of adding tools, resources, and prompts.

Here's what the code might look like:

```
import express from "express";
import { randomUUID } from "node:crypto";
import { McpServer } from "@modelcontextprotocol/sdk/server/mcp.js";
import { StreamableHTTPServerTransport } from
  "@modelcontextprotocol/sdk/server/streamableHttp.js";
import { isInitializeRequest } from "@modelcontextprotocol/sdk/types.js"
import z from "zod";
```

```javascript
const port = 8000;

const app = express();
app.use(express.json());

// Map to store transports by session ID
const transports: { [sessionId: string]: StreamableHTTPServerTransport }
  = {};

// Handle POST requests for client-to-server communication
app.post('/mcp', async (req, res) => {
  // Check for existing session ID
  const sessionId = req.headers['mcp-session-id'] as string | undefined;
  let transport: StreamableHTTPServerTransport;

  if (sessionId && transports[sessionId]) {
    // Reuse existing transport
    transport = transports[sessionId];
  } else if (!sessionId && isInitializeRequest(req.body)) {
    // New initialization request
    transport = new StreamableHTTPServerTransport({
      sessionIdGenerator: () => randomUUID(),
      onsessioninitialized: (sessionId) => {
        // Store the transport by session ID
        transports[sessionId] = transport;
      }
    });

    // Clean up transport when closed
    transport.onclose = () => {
      if (transport.sessionId) {
        delete transports[transport.sessionId];
      }
    };
    const server = new McpServer({
      name: "example-server",
      version: "1.0.0"
```

```
    },{
      capabilities: { logging: {} }
    });

    server.tool(
        "process-files",
        { message: z.string() },
        async ({ message }, { sendNotification }) => {

            // Simulate processing files

            return {
                content: [{ type: "text", text: `All files processed:
                    ${message}` }]
            };
        }
    );

    // ... set up server resources, tools, and prompts ...

    // Connect to the MCP server
    await server.connect(transport);
  } else {
    // Invalid request
    res.status(400).json({
      jsonrpc: '2.0',
      error: {
        code: -32000,
        message: 'Bad Request: No valid session ID provided',
      },
      id: null,
    });
    return;
  }

  // Handle the request
  await transport.handleRequest(req, res, req.body);
```

```
  });

  // Reusable handler for GET and DELETE requests
  const handleSessionRequest = async (req: express.Request, res:
    express.Response) => {
    const sessionId = req.headers['mcp-session-id'] as string | undefined;
    if (!sessionId || !transports[sessionId]) {
      res.status(400).send('Invalid or missing session ID');
      return;
    }

    const transport = transports[sessionId];
    await transport.handleRequest(req, res);
  };

  // Handle GET requests for server-to-client notifications via SSE
  app.get('/mcp', handleSessionRequest);

  // Handle DELETE requests for session termination
  app.delete('/mcp', handleSessionRequest);

  app.listen(port, () => {
      console.log(`MCP server listening on port ${port}`);
  });
```

In the preceding code, we did the following:

- Created an Express server that listens on port 8000
- Defined a POST /mcp route that initializes a new session or reuses an existing one based on the session ID provided in the request headers
- Used StreamableHTTPServerTransport to handle streaming requests and responses
- Implemented a tool called process-files that simulates processing files and returns a message
- Defined GET and DELETE routes for managing sessions, allowing clients to connect and disconnect from the server

Here's our plan for implementing a Streamable HTTP server:

1. Set up the server to handle Streamable HTTP type requests.
2. Instruct the server to have logging capabilities, as this is what the server needs to be able to produce notifications.
3. Implement a tool that simulates processing files.
4. Update the tool to send notifications using the Context object.

For our first step, we need to add an /mcp endpoint, which needs to have logic to recognize whether this is a new connection or not. If it's a new connection, it should produce a session ID; if not, it should reuse an old transport. Here's the code setting all that up:

```
app.post('/mcp', async (req, res) => {
  // Check for existing session ID
  const sessionId = req.headers['mcp-session-id'] as string | undefined;
  let transport: StreamableHTTPServerTransport;

  if (sessionId && transports[sessionId]) {
    // Reuse existing transport
    transport = transports[sessionId];
  } else if (!sessionId && isInitializeRequest(req.body)) {
    // New initialization request
    // 1. Set up the transport as streamable HTTP.
    transport = new StreamableHTTPServerTransport({
      sessionIdGenerator: () => randomUUID(),
      onsessioninitialized: (sessionId) => {
        // Store the transport by session ID
        transports[sessionId] = transport;
      }
    });

    // Clean up transport when closed
    transport.onclose = () => {
      if (transport.sessionId) {
        delete transports[transport.sessionId];
      }
    };

    // TODO create the mcp server
```

Note how this code creates an instance of `StreamableHTTPServerTransport` if it's a new connection; this means it will use Streamable HTTP.

What's missing is creating the MCP server instance and ensuring that it supports logging capabilities that need to be allowed to send notifications. Let's add logging capabilities to the MCP server with this code:

```
const server = new McpServer({
  name: "example-server",
  version: "1.0.0"
},{
  // 2. Add logging capabilities
  capabilities: { logging: {} }
});
```

Note the second object we pass to the `McpServer` constructor. This object contains the server capabilities, and we enable the logging capability by adding `capabilities: { logging: {} }`.

Next, let's ensure that our tool can send notifications by destructuring `sendNotification` from the `Context` object passed as the second parameter in the tool's callback handler:

```
// 3. Adding a tool
server.tool(
    "process-files",
    { message: z.string() },
    async (
      { message }) => {
        return {
            content: [{ type: "text", text: `Files processed: ${message}`
                }]
        };
    })
```

Finally, we need to ensure that we can send notifications and actually add a line of code in the tool that sends a notification by changing the tool to this code:

```
server.tool(
    "process-files",
    { message: z.string() },
    async (
```

```
        { message },
        // 4a. Destructure sendNotification from context
        { sendNotification }) => {

        let counter = 0;

        for(let file of filesToProcess) {
            if (file.processed) {
                continue; // Skip already processed files
            }
            counter++;
            // 4b. Send notification for each processed file
            await sendNotification({
                method: "notifications/message",
                params: { level: "info", data: `${file.name} processed` }
            });
            file.processed = true;
        }

        return {
            content: [{ type: "text", text: `Files processed: ${counter}`
                }]
        };
    }
);
```

Note the comments in the code that say 4a and 4b. The first one destructures sendNotification from the Context object, allowing us to use it within the tool's callback handler. The other comment indicates where we send a notification for each processed file by calling await sendNotification() with the appropriate method and parameters.

Great, that's all we need to create a server using the Streamable HTTP transport and logging capabilities that enable us to send notifications.

Let's look at testing our server next.

Testing the server

As always, we have different choices to try out the server functionality:

- Creating a client
- Using the Inspector tool
- Testing with cURL

Let's try out each of these options.

Using the Inspector tool

We covered the Inspector tool earlier in this chapter, but let's quickly remind ourselves how it works with our newly created server. We can call the Inspector tool like so to start up a web server. Select the following fields:

- **Transport Type: http**
- **Server URL**: http://localhost:8000/mcp (adjust the port if necessary)

Click the **Connect** button to connect to the server so you can use its features and then enter the following:

```
npx @modelcontextprotocol/inspector
```

As you can see, it's very similar to testing SSE servers; just change the transport type and make sure your URL has /mcp at the end instead of /sse.

Testing with cURL

We introduced cURL in the previous chapter; we can use it here as well. To get a session ID, you will need to send an initialize message. The message should contain what capabilities you support, such as tools, for example.

Here's the message you need to send:

```
curl -X POST "http://127.0.0.1:8000/mcp" -H "Accept: text/event-stream,
application/json" -H "Content-Type: application/json" -d '{
  "jsonrpc": "2.0",
  "id": 1,
  "method": "initialize",
  "params": { "protocolVersion": "2025-03-26", "capabilities": { "tools":
{} }, "clientInfo": { "name": "ExampleClient", "version": "1.0.0" } }
}'
```

Note that you need to send `Accept` headers and content type. Make a note of the session ID returned, as you will use it for all remaining calls.

Create a second terminal window and then run the following command, but replace the `mcp-session-id` value with the session ID you got back in the previous step:

```
curl -X POST "http://127.0.0.1:8000/mcp" -H "Content-Type: application/
json" -H "Accept: text/event-stream, application/json" -H "mcp-session-id:
39a0b504364140ce97d8eded79b1c244" -d '{
    "jsonrpc": "2.0",
    "method": "notifications/initialized"
}'
```

Note how the session ID isn't a query parameter called `session_id` anymore, but a header value called `mcp-session-id`. The message you sent was a notification of the `notifications/initialized` type, meaning it's the last message of the handshake process. After this message, we can now do more normal things, such as listing tools, calling them, and so on, so let's do that next.

Replace the value for `mcp-session-id` and keep using the second terminal window, and then run the following command:

```
curl -X POST "http://127.0.0.1:8000/mcp" -H "Content-Type: application/
json" -H "Accept: text/event-stream, application/json" -H "mcp-session-id:
39a0b504364140ce97d8eded79b1c244" -d '{
    "jsonrpc": "2.0",
    "id": 1,
    "method": "tools/call",
    "params": {
      "name": "echo",
      "arguments": { "message": "chris" }
    }
}'
```

In this message of the `tools/call` type, we call a specific tool, `echo`, with the `chris` argument, and we should see a tool response similar to the following:

```
event: message
data: {"method":"notifications/
message","params":{"level":"info","data":"Processing file
1/3:"},"jsonrpc":"2.0"}

event: message
```

```
data: {"method":"notifications/
message","params":{"level":"info","data":"Processing file
2/3:"},"jsonrpc":"2.0"}

event: message
data: {"method":"notifications/
message","params":{"level":"info","data":"Processing file
3/3:"},"jsonrpc":"2.0"}

event: message
data:
{"jsonrpc":"2.0","id":1,"result":{"content":[{"type":"text","text":"Here's
the file content: chris"}],"structuredContent":{"result":"Here's the file
content: chris"},"isError":false}}
```

This response, in the second terminal window, says we got three notifications and a final tool response, which shows that our MCP server works as intended.

As you can see, both Inspector and cURL are good tools to use for testing out your server. Building a client, however, might be how we end up integrating our MCP server in a working solution, so let's look at that in our next section.

Creating a client to handle notifications

Let's talk about the client. Clients generally need to be instructed to also handle notifications. This is something that's seen as an extra thing needed in addition to the normal features. Let's work out an implementation plan next.

Here's what we're going to need to do:

1. Create a Streamable HTTP transport and client.

2. Import the correct schema.

3. Set up a notification handler.

For our first step, let's create the transport and the client instance like so:

```
import { Client } from "@modelcontextprotocol/sdk/client/index.js";
import { StreamableHTTPClientTransport } from
  "@modelcontextprotocol/sdk/client/streamableHttp.js";

let sessionId: string | undefined = undefined;
```

```
// 1. creating transport
const transport = new StreamableHTTPClientTransport(
  new URL(serverUrl),
  {
      sessionId: sessionId
  }
);

// creating client
const client = new Client({
  name: "example-client",
  version: "1.0.0"
});

// connect the client to the server
await client.connect(transport);
sessionId = transport.sessionId;
console.log("Connected to MCP server with session ID:", sessionId);
```

At this point, you can call the features as you please, such as in the following, where we call the process-files tool:

```
const result = await client.callTool({
  name: "process-files",
  arguments: {
      message: "Process files"
  }
});
```

To support notifications, we need to set up a notification handler. Let's import our schema called LoggingMessageNotificationSchema like so:

```
// 2. Import the logging message notification schema
import {
  LoggingMessageNotificationSchema,
} from '@modelcontextprotocol/sdk/types.js';
```

Now, let's set up the notification handler by calling setNotificationHandler:

```
// 2. Set up the notification handler
client.setNotificationHandler(LoggingMessageNotificationSchema,
  (notification) => {
    console.log(`\nNotification: ${notification.params.level} -
      ${notification.params.data}`);
    // Re-display the prompt
    process.stdout.write('> ');
});
```

That's it, you're ready to receive notifications from the server.

A complete client can look like this:

```
import { Client } from "@modelcontextprotocol/sdk/client/index.js";
import { StreamableHTTPClientTransport } from
  "@modelcontextprotocol/sdk/client/streamableHttp.js";

import { LoggingMessageNotificationSchema,
} from '@modelcontextprotocol/sdk/types.js';


const serverUrl = "http://localhost:8000/mcp";
let sessionId: string | undefined = undefined;


async function main() {
  // creating a streaming client transport
  const transport = new StreamableHTTPClientTransport(
    new URL(serverUrl),
    {
      sessionId: sessionId
    }
  );

  const client = new Client({
    name: "example-client",
```

```
      version: "1.0.0"
  });

  client.setNotificationHandler(LoggingMessageNotificationSchema,
    (notification) => {
    console.log(`\nNotification: ${notification.params.level} -
      ${notification.params.data}`);
    // Re-display the prompt
    process.stdout.write('> ');
  });

  await client.connect(transport);
  sessionId = transport.sessionId;
  console.log("Connected to MCP server with session ID:", sessionId);

  // List tools
  const tools = await client.listTools();
  console.log("Available tools:", tools);

  const result = await client.callTool({
    name: "process-files",
    arguments: {
      message: "Process files"
    }
  });

  console.log("Tool call result:", result);
}

main()
  .then(() => {
    console.log("Client is ready to use.");
  })
  .catch((error) => {
    console.error("Error initializing client:", error);
  })
```

Running the client toward a server can then look like this:

```
Connected to MCP server with session ID: 370eef25-d43c-43e2-ba3f-
d2e28a4bb60b
Available tools: { tools: [ { name: 'process-files', inputSchema: [Object]
} ] }


Notification: info - File 1 processed
>
Notification: info - File 2 processed
>
Notification: info - File 3 processed
> Tool call result: {
  content: [ { type: 'text', text: 'All files processed: Process files' }
]
}
Client is ready to use.
```

As you can see, you're getting both notifications and tool results back.

Testing out resumability

There's actually an example implementation in the SDK for resumability. Let's try that code out and see how it differs. You can find a simplified version of it at https://github.com/ PacktPublishing/Learn-Model-Context-Protocol-with-TypeScript/blob/main/Chapter05/ solutions/resumability/README.md.

What the code does is define a server with one tool, process-files. Upon calling the tool, you get three notifications and one final response. The easiest way to test the server out is by using cURL. With cURL, we can perform the handshake process, call a tool, and even do the needed bespoke request so it replays events. Let's take it step by step:

1. Start the server first.

2. Start a second terminal and call curl with the following payload to exchange what features the client and the server both have:

```
curl -X POST "http://127.0.0.1:8000/mcp" -H "Accept: text/event-
stream, application/json" -H "Content-Type: application/json" -d '{
  "jsonrpc": "2.0",
  "id": 1,
  "method": "initialize",
```

```
    "params": { "protocolVersion": "2025-03-26", "capabilities":
{ "tools": {}, "logging": {} }, "clientInfo": { "name":
"ExampleClient", "version": "1.0.0" } }
}'
```

Check the terminal response in the first terminal window. You should see the server display Session Id; copy that field for later use.

3. End the server-client handshake by sending an initialized notification; replace the mcp-session-id value with the value you just copied in the previous step:

```
curl -X POST "http://127.0.0.1:8000/mcp" -H "Content-Type:
application/json" -H "Accept: text/event-stream, application/json"
-H "mcp-session-id: 957f11af-4766-4c1c-a1f2-5bd6776cca6a" -d '{
    "jsonrpc": "2.0",
    "method": "notifications/initialized"
}'
```

4. Call the tool by pasting the following command in the second terminal window, making sure to replace the mcp-session-id value first:

```
 curl -X POST "http://127.0.0.1:8000/mcp" -H "Content-Type:
application/json" -H "Accept: text/event-stream, application/json"
-H "mcp-session-id: 957f11af-4766-4c1c-a1f2-5bd6776cca6a" -d '{
    "jsonrpc": "2.0",
    "id": 1,
    "method": "tools/call",
    "params": {
      "name": "process-files",
      "arguments": { "message": "chris" }
    }
}'
```

At this point, you should see a bunch of notifications and the final result in the second terminal window, like so:

```
event: message
id: 3a9d76c3-36d8-45f3-bd6e-8b9c82826de8_1757284976937_z6m5xbyc
data: {"method":"notifications/
message","params":{"level":"info","data":"sales1.csv
processed"},"jsonrpc":"2.0"}
```

```
event: message
id: 3a9d76c3-36d8-45f3-bd6e-8b9c82826de8_1757284976940_meh2n52f
data: {"method":"notifications/
message","params":{"level":"info","data":"sales2.csv
processed"},"jsonrpc":"2.0"}

event: message
id: 3a9d76c3-36d8-45f3-bd6e-8b9c82826de8_1757284976943_e3v55tmn
data: {"method":"notifications/
message","params":{"level":"info","data":"sales3.csv
processed"},"jsonrpc":"2.0"}

event: message
id: 3a9d76c3-36d8-45f3-bd6e-8b9c82826de8_1757284976946_sgpvardt
data: {"result":{"content":[{"type":"text","text":"Files processed:
3"}]},"jsonrpc":"2.0","id":1}
```

Let's focus on the following message, a notification that says we're on file 2/3. Imagine we went into a tunnel and lost network connection. Make note of the ID, as this ID is the last you saw before losing connection:

```
event: message
id: 3a9d76c3-36d8-45f3-bd6e-8b9c82826de8_1757284976940_meh2n52f
data: {"method":"notifications/
message","params":{"level":"info","data":"sales2.csv
processed"},"jsonrpc":"2.0"}
```

5. In our final step, we need to send a GET request to the /mcp endpoint with the session ID and last event ID passed in the headers. That should lead to the server replaying all messages that we missed out on, which should be the sales3.csv file notification and the final tool result. Remember to replace both mcp-session-id and last-event-id before you paste the following in the second terminal window:

```
curl "http://127.0.0.1:8000/mcp" -H "Content-Type: application/json"
-H "Accept: text/event-stream, application/json" -H "mcp-session-id:
957f11af-4766-4c1c-a1f2-5bd6776cca6a" -H "last-event-id: 3a9d76c3-
36d8-45f3-bd6e-8b9c82826de8_1757284976940_meh2n52f"
```

Pasting this result means you should see the following in the second terminal window:

```
event: message
id: 3a9d76c3-36d8-45f3-bd6e-8b9c82826de8_1757284976943_e3v55tmn
data: {"method":"notifications/
message","params":{"level":"info","data":"sales3.csv
processed"},"jsonrpc":"2.0"}

event: message
id: 3a9d76c3-36d8-45f3-bd6e-8b9c82826de8_1757284976946_sgpvardt
data: {"result":{"content":[{"type":"text","text":"Files processed:
3"}]},"jsonrpc":"2.0","id":1}
```

Our one missing notification and the tool result! Isn't that great? We didn't lose any messages.

It should be said, though, that if you write code that can leverage replayability, you should listen to browser events when you lose network connection, so you have a chance to save the session ID and last event ID, and remember to call the server with GET /mcp rather than POST /mcp, as the latter would start a new session.

Also, if you use the event store I'm using, remember it's not good for production and that it would need to persist the message in a database or similar to be deemed production-ready.

Summary

In this chapter, we explored the concept of Streamable HTTP and how it differs from SSE. We learned that streaming allows for real-time data transmission, which is beneficial for applications that require immediate access to data, such as live events or large files.

Additionally, we implemented an MCP server that supports Streamable HTTP and demonstrated how to consume streaming data using the MCP SDK. We also discussed the importance of notifications in providing real-time updates to clients and how to handle them effectively.

In the next chapter, we'll explain how you can use a low-level server API, as there are some use cases where you might want to do that.

Assignment

For this assignment, we'll again focus on e-commerce. Imagine you have CSV files on the server that need processing. Processing happens when all CSV files on a server are sent one by one as input to a web API. The idea is that this process will be kicked off by calling a tool. Imagine the following program output:

```
Type command> process-files
Notification: info - sales.csv processed
Notification: info - sales.csv processed
Notification: info - sales.csv processed
Files processed: 3
Type command> process-files
Files processed: 0
```

> The point of this assignment is to learn how to use notifications. The files can be a list of in-memory entries that get removed as they're processed. You will need to create both a server, where the files to process are, and a client that can process input commands.

Solution

You can access the solution at https://github.com/PacktPublishing/Learn-Model-Context-Protocol-with-TypeScript/blob/main/Chapter05/solutions/README.md.

Quiz

1. What is the primary benefit of using Streamable HTTP?

    - A: It allows for faster access to data
    - B: It requires fewer server resources
    - C: It is more secure than other protocols

2. How does Streamable HTTP differ from SSE?

    - A: Streamable HTTP uses a text-based format, while SSE uses JSON.
    - B: Streamable HTTP can send binary data, while SSE is limited to text.
    - C: Streamable HTTP is unidirectional, while SSE is bidirectional.

You can access the solution at `https://github.com/PacktPublishing/Learn-Model-Context-Protocol-with-TypeScript/blob/main/Chapter05/solutions/solution-quiz.md`.

References

- **Streaming transport:** `https://mcp-framework.com/docs/Transports/http-stream-transport/`

6

Maintaining Clean Architecture with an Advanced Server Approach

In *Chapter 3*, you saw how you can build MCP servers. However, there's another way to build these servers – namely, by using a more advanced approach. The reason for using this more advanced approach is that you want to be more in control.

In this chapter, you will learn how to do the following:

- Use context managers to manage the lifecycle of your server
- Improve the architecture of your server
- Understand low-level access to MCP servers

The chapter covers the following topics:

- Why this low-level approach?
- Context managers
- Context managers in MCP servers
- Low-level access
- Organizing your architecture

Why this low-level approach?

At this point, you might be thinking, *Why would I want to do that? The previous approach was so easy!* Well, there are a few reasons why you might want to use this approach. You may want to do the following:

- **Use context managers to manage the lifecycle of your server**: Here, you can do things such as connecting to a database or other services that are connected to your server. By having more control over the lifecycle of your server, you can ensure that your server is properly initialized and cleaned up when it's no longer needed.

- **Improve the architecture of your server**: Having more control over how the server is built allows for more freedom in how tools and resources are registered, but also how incoming requests are handled. This increased control allows you to organize your code in a way that is more maintainable and scalable. This chapter shows you how you can organize your code with both a low-level server and a normal MCP server. It's possible to create a clean architecture in both cases. However, it could be argued that the low-level server approach is a bit cleaner, as you don't have to pass the server instance around. You'll see more about what's meant by that last statement later in this chapter.

- **The only way forward in some cases**: There are cases when you deal with certain features where there simply is no other way forward than a low-level approach. This is true for using *Chapter 9*, on sampling, and *Chapter 10*, on elicitation.

Let's dive into a more low-level approach, so you know what it looks like, so you can choose the approach that suits your project the best.

Context managers

So, what's a context manager to begin with? A **context manager** is a construct that allows you to allocate and release resources precisely when you want to. The most common way to use a context manager is with the `with` statement, which ensures that resources are properly cleaned up after use, even if an error occurs. By using a context manager, your code becomes cleaner and more readable. Let's look at a simple example:

```
With(new DBManager(), () => {
    console.log("inside context");
    throw Error("💔");
})
```

In this case, we use the With function to create a context manager that manages the lifecycle of a database connection. The DBManager class is responsible for connecting to the database, and the With function ensures that the connection is properly closed when the block is exited, even if an error occurs.

Using contextlib to create context managers

Another way to use context managers is to create a custom context manager using the contextlib (there's a corresponding NPM library called contextlib) module. This allows you to create context managers without defining a class. Here's an example:

Let's now use a library called contextlib so we don't have to type as much code. Here's how you can use it:

```
const { With } = require("contextlib");

class Manager {
    enter() {
        console.log("setting up...");
    }
    exit() {
        console.log("cleaning up...")
    }
}

With(new Manager(), () => {
    console.log("inside context");
    throw Error(" 💔 ");
})
```

Here, you can see how the class DatabaseConnection is replaced with a function database_ connection() that uses the contextlib.contextmanager decorator. The yield statement provides the resource to the block, and the code after the yield statement is executed when the block is exited, ensuring proper cleanup. Is this better than the previous example? Well, at least you type less code.

Implementing a context manager

If you're interested in knowing how to implement a context manager, because you're curious or because you don't want yet another dependency, here's how you can do that:

Let's look at how we will use the code first and figure out from that how to build it:

```
With(new DBManager(), (assets) => {
    console.log("assets:", assets); // assets you get from the context
                                     // manager
});
```

Here, we call With, which takes a context manager and a function.

- **The context manager** is responsible for setting up and tearing down the resources.
- **The function** is where you use those resources. The assets parameter in the function is an object that contains the resources provided by the context manager. Based on that, we can build the following code:

```
function With(manager: ContextManager, fn: (assets: {
  [key: string]: any }) => void) {
  // TODO: implementation
}
```

What should happen next then? Well, in the With function, we need to do the following:

1. Call the enter method of the context manager to set up the resources.
2. Execute the fn function, passing the resources to it.
3. Finally, call the exit method of the context manager to clean up the resources.

How come we need to do all that, you might wonder? The reason is that the enter method is a generator function that yields the resources, so we need to iterate over it to get the resources. We wanted it to be a generator function because it allows for a more flexible way to manage resources, especially when dealing with asynchronous operations or multiple resources. What kind of resources, though? Well, it could be all kinds, but a database connection is a common example.

Let's update our code to reflect that:

```
function With(manager: ContextManager, fn: (assets: {
  [key: string]: any }) => void) {
    const iterator = manager.enter();
```

```
        const { value } = iterator.next();

    try {
        fn(value);
    } catch (e) {
        console.error("Error occurred:", e);
    } finally {
        iterator.return?.();
        manager.exit();
    }
}
```

What does a context manager look like then? Based on the preceding code, we can define a ContextManager interface that has enter and exit methods. The enter method is a generator function that yields the resources, and the exit method is called to clean up the resources. Here's an example of a context manager that manages a database connection:

```
interface ContextManager {
    enter(): Generator<any, void, unknown>;
    exit(): void;
}

class DBManager implements ContextManager {
    *enter () {
        console.log("setting up Database");
        yield { "db" : new DB() }
        // TODO: set up DB
    }
    exit() {
        console.log("cleaning up Database")
    }
}

class DB {
    name: string;
    constructor() {
```

```typescript
        this.name = "I'm a database";
    }
}


function With(manager: ContextManager, fn: (assets: {
  [key: string]: any }) => void) {
    const iterator = manager.enter();
    const { value } = iterator.next();

    try {
        fn(value);
    } catch (e) {
        console.error("Error occurred:", e);
    } finally {
        iterator.return?.();
        manager.exit();
    }
}



With(new DBManager(), (assets) => {
    console.log("assets:", assets); // assets you get from the context
                                    // manager
    if (assets.db) {
        if (assets.db instanceof DB) {
            console.log("db is an instance of DB");
        }
    }

    console.log("inside context");

    throw Error("throw error");
})
```

In the preceding code, we've done the following:

- Defined a ContextManager interface with enter and exit methods.
- Created a DBManager class that implements the ContextManager interface.
- The enter method is a generator function that sets up the database connection and yields an object containing the database instance.
- The exit method is called to clean up the database connection.
- The With function takes a context manager and a function, executes the function within the context of the manager, and ensures proper cleanup. It also passes the assets to the function, which can be used within the context.

This implementation is a bit simple, but hopefully you get the idea of why a context manager is useful. It allows you to manage resources in a clean and efficient way, ensuring that they are properly initialized and cleaned up.

Imagine what would happen if you forgot to close the connection in the finally block? You might be a very disciplined programmer and always remember to close the connection, but in a larger code base, it's easy to forget. Context managers help you avoid such pitfalls by ensuring that resources are always cleaned up properly.

Let's look at how context managers are used in the context of MCP servers next.

Context managers in MCP servers

Context managers aren't used in the TypeScript SDK at the moment but is used in other SDKs like Python. Nothing is stopping you from using it in TypeScript per se; it's just not built in. Refer to the previous section to see how you can implement it yourself.

MCP allows you to control lifecycle management of your resources, which can be hugely beneficial when you have resources that need to be initialized and cleaned up properly, e.g., database connections, external API clients, and so on.

Great – now we have an understanding of context management and why it exists. Let's look more at low-level access in the next section.

Low-level access

Let's recap how we first build a server so we can easily compare it to how low-level access is different. Here's how you build a simple MCP server with a high-level API.

In this implementation, we import the necessary classes and functions from the MCP SDK. We create an instance of McpServer, add a tool, and connect it to a transport that uses standard input and output for communication. Additionally, the zod library is used for schema validation to ensure that the input to the tool is of the correct type. You will see zod used a lot more as we progress through this chapter.

```js
import { McpServer, ResourceTemplate } from
  "@modelcontextprotocol/sdk/server/mcp.js";
import { StdioServerTransport } from
  "@modelcontextprotocol/sdk/server/stdio.js";
import { z } from "zod";

// Create an MCP server
const server = new McpServer({
  name: "Demo",
  version: "1.0.0"
});

// Add an addition tool
server.tool("add",
  { a: z.number(), b: z.number() },
  async ({ a, b }) => ({
    content: [{ type: "text", text: String(a + b) }]
  })
);

// Start receiving messages on stdin and sending messages on stdout
const transport = new StdioServerTransport();
await server.connect(transport);
```

This is a high-level way of building a server, but what if you want more control over how the server is built? Here's how you can do that using low-level access.

Let's look at how registering features is different. In the past, you would have been used to using decorators associated with specific tools or resources, and so on. What's different in a low-level server is that you need to handle all requests yourself. Instead of handling one tool or resource at a time, you handle all requests related to tools, resources, and prompts in one place.

First, we import the Server class from the `@modelcontextprotocol/sdk/server/index.js` module.

```javascript
import { Server } from "@modelcontextprotocol/sdk/server/index.js";
```

Next, we create a server instance and call `setRequestHandler` to handle requests. This method takes a schema and a function that handles the request. This is different from a high-level server, as we can deal with all calls to a tool or all listings of tools in one place. Here's an example of how you can handle requests to list all prompts and get a specific prompt:

```javascript
import { Server } from "@modelcontextprotocol/sdk/server/index.js";
import { StdioServerTransport } from
  "@modelcontextprotocol/sdk/server/stdio.js";
import {
  ListPromptsRequestSchema,
  GetPromptRequestSchema
} from "@modelcontextprotocol/sdk/types.js";

// creation of the server
const server = new Server({
  name: "Demo",
  version: "1.0.0"
}, {
    capabilities: {
        "tools": {},
        "resources": {},
    }
});

server.setRequestHandler(ListPromptsRequestSchema, async () => {
  return {
    prompts: [{
```

```
        name: "example-prompt",
        description: "An example prompt template",
        arguments: [{
          name: "arg1",
          description: "Example argument",
          required: true
        }]
      }]
    };
});


server.setRequestHandler(GetPromptRequestSchema, async (request) => {
  if (request.params.name !== "example-prompt") {
    throw new Error("Unknown prompt");
  }
  return {
    description: "Example prompt",
    messages: [{
      role: "user",
      content: {
        type: "text",
        text: "Example prompt text"
      }
    }]
  };
});
```

In the preceding code, we've done the following:

- Imported the `Server` class, our low-level server class. We've also import-ed `StdioServerTransport` as a transport, but additionally, we've imported the `ListPromptsRequestSchema` and `GetPromptRequestSchema` schemas from the @ `modelcontextprotocol/sdk/types.js` module. These schemas are used to define the structure of the requests to return all prompts and to get a specific prompt.

- Note also how we use `server.setRequestHandler()` to handle requests. It takes a sche-ma and an asynchronous function that handles the request. This is different from the high-level server, as we said before, where all requests are handled for you, and we instead define handlers for each specific feature.

Isn't this more work? Well, actually, let's explore in the next section how this could be a great way to organize your code.

Organizing your architecture

A huge advantage of using a low-level server is that you can control the architecture of your server. You can organize your code in a way that makes sense for your project. For example, you can define all your tools in a folder called `tools/`. Tools also don't need to know about the server instance. Sounds promising, right? Let's see how next.

> You can organize your code well with a high-level server too, but it's usually a bit messier as you need to pass the server instance around, as we said initially in this chapter.

Here's how you have defined MCP server features so far in a high-level server:

```
import { McpServer, ResourceTemplate } from
  "@modelcontextprotocol/sdk/server/mcp.js";
import { StdioServerTransport } from
  "@modelcontextprotocol/sdk/server/stdio.js";
import { z } from "zod";

// Create an MCP server
export const server = new McpServer({
  name: "Demo",
  version: "1.0.0"
});

// Add an addition tool
server.tool("add",
  { a: z.number(), b: z.number() },
  async ({ a, b }) => ({
    content: [{ type: "text", text: String(a + b) }]
  })
);
```

The preceding code can be rewritten to a low-level server like so:

```javascript
import { Server } from "@modelcontextprotocol/sdk/server/index.js";

import { StdioServerTransport } from
  "@modelcontextprotocol/sdk/server/stdio.js";

import {
  CallToolRequestSchema,
  ListToolsRequestSchema
} from "@modelcontextprotocol/sdk/types.js";

const server = new Server({
  name: "Demo",
  version: "1.0.0"
},
{
  capabilities: {
    "tools": {}
  }
}
);

server.setRequestHandler(ListToolsRequestSchema, async () => {
  return {
    tools: [{
      name: "add",
      description: "Add two numbers",
      inputSchema: { a: { type: "number" }, b: { type: "number" } }
    }]
  };
});
```

In the preceding code, we've done the following:

- Imported the `Server` class from the `@modelcontextprotocol/sdk/server/index.js` module.

- Created a server instance using the `Server` class.

- Used the `setRequestHandler` method to handle requests to list all tools. This method takes a schema and a function that handles the request. In this case, it returns a list of tools with their names, descriptions, and input schemas.

Right now, it looks a bit hardcoded, but if we can move the list of tools into a variable, you will see that it gets easier to add more tools. So, let's do that next.

```typescript
import { zodToJsonSchema } from "zod-to-json-schema";
import { z } from "zod";
export const MathInputSchema = z.object({ a: z.number(), b: z.number() });

let tools = {
  "add": {
    name: "add",
    description: "Add two numbers",
    rawSchema: MathInputSchema,
    inputSchema: zodToJsonSchema(MathInputSchema),
    callback: async ({ a, b }: { a: number; b: number }) => ({
      content: [{ type: "text", text: String(a + b) }]
    })
  }
};
```

Now you see how a tool is defined in a variable. Also note that the `inputSchema` is converted from a zod schema to a JSON schema using the `zodToJsonSchema` function. This is because the low-level server expects the schema to be in JSON format and to conform to the MCP specification. Thanks to the `zod-to-json-schema` utility library, this is easy to do.

In fact, we can move this into a separate file called `tools/add.ts` and import it. Let's do that next, and while we're at it, let's also create a `tools/subtract.ts` tool.

Here's what your folder can end up looking like:

```
project/
|— app.ts
├— server.ts
├— tools/
|    ├— index.ts
|    ├— add.ts
```

```
|    └── subtract.ts
|    └── schema.ts
|    └── tool.ts
```

In the preceding file structure, we've created the following:

- A tools/ folder that contains all the tools
- An index.ts file that will be used to register all the tools
- An add.ts file that contains the add tool
- A subtract.ts file that contains the subtract tool
- A schema.ts file that contains the schemas for the tools

Let's take a look at how we implement the files:

tools/index.ts

```typescript
import { z } from "zod";
import { ToolCallback } from "@modelcontextprotocol/sdk/server/mcp.js";

import addTool from "./add.js";
import subtractTool from "./subtract.js";
import {server} from "../server.js";

export let tools = [];
tools.push(addTool);
tools.push(subtractTool);
```

tools/add.ts

```typescript
import { Tool } from "./tool.js";
import { MathInputSchema } from "./schema.js";
import { zodToJsonSchema } from "zod-to-json-schema";

export default {
    name: "add",
    description: "Add two numbers",
    rawSchema: MathInputSchema,
    inputSchema: zodToJsonSchema(MathInputSchema),
    callback: async ({ a, b }) => {
        return {
```

```
                content: [{ type: "text", text: String(a + b) }]
        };
    }
} as Tool;
```

Here, you see how we did the following:

- Defined a `Tool` interface in `tools/tool.ts` that contains the name, input schema, and callback function.

- Provided `MathInputSchema` as input to `inputSchema`, which contains the input schema for this and potentially other tools, depending on whether they take the same input.

This is pretty nice as we don't have any framework dependencies where we define the tool; it's just plain TypeScript. This makes it easy to test and reason about.

tools/tool.ts

```
import { z } from 'zod';

export interface Tool {
    name: string;
    description?: string;
    rawSchema: z.ZodTypeAny;
    inputSchema: any;
    callback: (args: z.infer<z.ZodTypeAny>) =>
        Promise<{ content: { type: string; text: string }[] }>;
}
```

This schema is used to define the input schema for the tools. By using this schema, we ensure that registering a tool is consistent and easy to understand.

tools/schema.ts

```
import { z } from 'zod';


export const MathInputSchema = z.object({ a: z.number(), b: z.number() });
```

This looks pretty empty right now but will fill up as we register more tools. It gives us one place to look for all schemas. Let's have a look at the server next.

server.ts

```typescript
import { Server } from "@modelcontextprotocol/sdk/server/index.js";
import { StdioServerTransport } from
  "@modelcontextprotocol/sdk/server/stdio.js";
import { ListToolsRequestSchema } from
  "@modelcontextprotocol/sdk/types.js";

import { tools } from './tools/index.js';
console.log("Registering tools...");

// Create an MCP server
export const server = new Server({
  name: "Demo",
  version: "1.0.0"
}, {
    capabilities: {
        "tools": {}
    }
});

// TODO register tool list handler

const transport = new StdioServerTransport();

export async function start() {
    console.log("Starting server...");
    await server.connect(transport);
}```
```

This file is responsible for creating the server instance and connecting it to the transport. The `start` function is exported so it can be called from the entry point of the application. Calling `start()` will start the server and listen for incoming requests.

```
**app.ts**

```typescript
import {start} from './server.js';
```
```

```
start();

process.on('SIGINT', () => {
  console.log('\nShutting down...');
  process.exit(0);
});
```

This is the entry point of the app. It does the following:

- Imports the tools from tools/index.js to register them with the server
- Calls the start() function from server.ts to start the server

This structure allows you to easily add new tools by creating a new file in the tools/ folder and updating the tools/index.ts file. The code is well organized and only the files that really need it refer to the framework; the rest is plain TypeScript.

How can we improve this further? Well, let's look at low-level access next.

Constructing a list tools response in a low-level server

So, let's see whether low-level access can help improve our architecture further. The goal is to have a server that can register tools, resources, and prompts in a way that is easy to maintain and extend.

First, let's recap our low-level server code:

```
import { Server } from "@modelcontextprotocol/sdk/server/index.js";
import { StdioServerTransport } from
  "@modelcontextprotocol/sdk/server/stdio.js";
import {
  ListPromptsRequestSchema,
  GetPromptRequestSchema
} from "@modelcontextprotocol/sdk/types.js";

const server = new Server(
  {
    name: "example-server",
    version: "1.0.0"
  },
  {
    capabilities: {
```

```
      prompts: {}
    }
  }
);


// TODO, register tool list handler
```

In the preceding code, we've done the following:

- Imported the Server class, our low-level server class
- Defined a server instance called server with a name and version

Let's focus on the request handler; it should return a list of tools. Previously, we worked on creating a nice architecture for dealing with many tools, so let's have a look at what a request handler looks like for listing all tools:

```
server.setRequestHandler(ListToolsRequestSchema, async () => {
  return {
    tools: [{
      name: "example-tool",
      description: "An example tool",
      inputSchema: {
        type: "object",
        properties: {
          arg1: { type: "string" }
        },
        required: ["arg1"]
      }
    }]
  };
});
```

As you can see, there's only one tool in there, and the architecture we've been defining has a tools directory with tools in it. So, we need to iterate over all of those tools and add them. Let's see how we can do that.

Okay, so here's the plan – we need to accomplish the following things:

- Retrieve tools: we need to fetch a list of tools
- Return our tools list as part of the handler response

Let's start by retrieving the tools using code like so:

```
import tools from "./tools/index.js";

server.setRequestHandler(ListToolsRequestSchema, async (request) => {
  // Return the list of registered tools
  return {
    tools: tools
  };
});
```

In the preceding code, we've done the following:

- Imported the tools from `tools/index.js` to register them with the server
- Used `server.setRequestHandler()` to handle requests to list all tools

Organizing your code and creating tools and schemas

Now that we know how to register tools, let's see how we can organize the code a bit. The goal is to achieve the following:

- A file for each tool, so we can easily manage the code
- Register all the tools in one place

Sounds like a great goal, right? Who doesn't want maintainability?

Let's create a folder structure that's easy to maintain, like so:

```
server.ts
app.ts
tools/
├── add.ts
├── echo.ts
├── schema.ts
├── subtract.ts
├── index.ts
├── tool.ts
```

The following files are tools: add.ts, subtract.ts, and echo.ts. Let's have a closer look at index.ts:

index.ts

```
import addTool from "./add.js";
import subtractTool from "./subtract.js";
import {server} from "../server.js";
import { Tool } from "./tool.js";

export let tools: Array<Tool> = [];
tools.push(addTool);
tools.push(subtractTool);
```

This file is quite simple; it just imports the tools into an array. Simple is good. Next, schema.ts is interesting, as it shows how we can define a schema for what the input looks like for a tool:

schema ts

```
import { z } from 'zod';

export const MathInputSchema = z.object({ a: z.number(), b: z.number() });
```

Note how we call z.object to create Zod objects. **Zod objects** can be used later to parse incoming data – more on that later in this section. For now, let's check how a tool leverages this schema:

add.ts

```
// add.ts
import { Tool } from "./tool.js";
import { MathInputSchema } from "./schema.js";
import { zodToJsonSchema } from "zod-to-json-schema";

export default {
    name: "add",
    description: "Add two numbers",
    rawSchema: MathInputSchema,
    inputSchema: zodToJsonSchema(MathInputSchema),
    callback: async ({ a, b }) => {
        return {
            content: [{ type: "text", text: String(a + b) }]
```

```
        };
    }
} as Tool;
```

Here, you can see how `MathInputSchema` is imported and set as `inputSchema`. You might recall how we earlier used `inputSchema` when registering the tool with the MCP server. However, in that case, we had to convert it to a JSON representation.

Handling a tool being called

So far, you've seen how we're able to take care of a call asking us to list all the tools. But there's another case we need to handle, namely when a client is trying to call a tool. For that, we need to do the following with the incoming tool calling request:

- Identify which tool to call.
- Parse out the arguments and, in doing so, also validate them. This is where our Pydantic schemas will come in handy to help us with this.

Let's start with the request to the server:

```
server.setRequestHandler(CallToolRequestSchema, async (request) => {
    const { params: { name } } = request;

    // TODO: implement the rest, i.e locate the tool and
    // call it with the args provided and return result
});
```

In the preceding code, we've done the following:

- Created a request handler for when a tool is called. We do that by referencing `CallToolRequestSchema`.
- Provided a callback with the `request` object that we will use to locate the tool's name and provided arguments.

Next, let's add some code to identify the correct tool and throw an error if there's no match:

```
// get tools by name,
let tool = tools.find(t => t.name === name);
if (!tool) {
    return {
        error: {
```

```
                code: "tool_not_found",
                message: `Tool ${name} not found.`
            }
        };
    }
```

Great – let's move on to parsing the arguments next:

```
const Schema = tool.inputSchema;

try {
    const input = Schema.parse(request.params.arguments);

    // @ts-ignore
    const result = await tool.callback(input);

    return {
        content: [{ type: "text", text: `Tool ${name} called with
            arguments: ${JSON.stringify(input)}, result:
                ${JSON.stringify(result)}` }]
    };
} catch (error) {
    return {
        error: {
            code: "invalid_arguments",
            message: `Invalid arguments for tool ${name}: ${error
                instanceof Error ? error.message : String(error)}`
        }
    };
}
```

In the preceding code, we've done the following:

- Parsed the input arguments by first reading the input schema for the tool, const Schema
  = tool.inputSchema;, and then sending in the request arguments to a parse() function:
  const input = Schema.parse(request.params.arguments);. Now we have input ready
  to use. If the parsing failed, that means that whatever arguments were sent did not match
  the tools required input.

- Called the callback on the tool: `const result = await tool.callback(input);`.
- Constructed a response back to the calling client:

```
return {
    content: [{ type: "text", text: `Tool ${name} called with
        arguments: ${JSON.stringify(input)}, result:
            ${JSON.stringify(result)}` }]
};
```

Great – we've now managed to implement both listing all tools and calling a specific tool.

See the full code at `https://github.com/PacktPublishing/Learn-Model-Context-Protocol-with-TypeScript/blob/main/Chapter06/code/typescript/README.md`.

I'm sure you could improve this setup further, but this is a lot better than what we started with.

Summary

In this chapter, you learned how to use the low-level server to create a more maintainable architecture for your MCP server. You saw how to register tools, handle requests, and validate input using schemas. This approach allows you to easily add new tools and manage existing ones, making your server more flexible and easier to maintain.

In our next chapter, we'll cover how to build clients that can interact with our MCP servers.

Assignment

Let's see if we can organize the e-commerce server that we created in *Chapter 3*. Here's the code for reference. Create a tools directory – use Pydantic and a low-level API.

```typescript
// index.ts
import { McpServer, ResourceTemplate } from
  "@modelcontextprotocol/sdk/server/mcp.js";
import { StdioServerTransport } from
  "@modelcontextprotocol/sdk/server/stdio.js";
import { z } from "zod";
import { v4 as uuidv4 } from "uuid";

class Customer {
  id: number;
  name: string;
```

```
    email: string;

    constructor(id: number, name: string, email: string) {
      this.id = id;
      this.name = name;
      this.email = email;
    }
}

class Category {
  id: string;
  name: string;
  description: string;

  constructor(name: string, description: string) {
    this.id = uuidv4();
    this.name = name;
    this.description = description;
  }
}

class Product {
  name: string;
  price: number;
  description: string;

  constructor(name: string, price: number, description: string) {
    this.name = name;
    this.price = price;
    this.description = description;
  }
}

class CartItem {
  cartId: string;
  productId: number;
  quantity: number;
```

```typescript
  constructor(cartId: string | 0, productId: number, quantity: number) {
    this.cartId = cartId !== 0 ? cartId : uuidv4();
    this.productId = productId;
    this.quantity = quantity;
  }
}

class Cart {
  cartId: string;
  customerId: number;

  constructor(cartId: string | 0, customerId: number) {
    this.cartId = cartId !== 0 ? cartId : uuidv4();
    this.customerId = customerId;
  }
}

class Order {
  orderId: string;
  customerId: number;

  constructor(orderId: string | 0, customerId: number) {
    this.orderId = orderId !== 0 ? orderId : uuidv4();
    this.customerId = customerId;
  }
}

// adding static data
const products: Product[] = [
  new Product("Product 1", 10.0, "Description of Product 1"),
  new Product("Product 2", 20.0, "Description of Product 2"),
  new Product("Product 3", 30.0, "Description of Product 3")
];

const orders: Order[] = [
  new Order("1", 1),
```

```
  new Order("0", 1),
  new Order("0", 2)
];

const carts: Cart[] = [];

const customers: Customer[] = [
  new Customer(1, "Customer 1", "email@example.com"),
  new Customer(2, "Customer 2", "email@example.com")
];

const categories: Category[] = [
  new Category("Category 1", "Description of Category 1"),
  new Category("Category 2", "Description of Category 2"),
  new Category("Category 3", "Description of Category 3")
];

const productCatalog = [
  {
    name: "Product 1",
    price: 10.0,
    description: "Description of Product 1",
    categoryId: 1
  },
  {
    name: "Product 2",
    price: 20.0,
    description: "Description of Product 2",
    categoryId: 2
  },
  {
    name: "Product 3",
    price: 30.0,
    description: "Description of Product 3",
    categoryId: 3
  }
];
```

```
const cartItems = [
  new CartItem("1", 1, 2),
  new CartItem("1", 2, 1)
];


// Create an MCP server
const server = new McpServer({
  name: "Demo",
  version: "1.0.0"
});

type Result = {
  type: "text";
  text: string;
}[];

// Add a tool to get orders
server.tool(
  "get_orders",
  {
    customer_id: z.number().optional()
  },
  async ({ customer_id = 0 }) => {
    if (customer_id !== 0 && !customers.some(customer =>
      customer.id === customer_id)) {
      throw new Error(`Invalid customer_id: ${customer_id}`);
    }

    const filteredOrders = customer_id !== 0
      ? orders.filter(order => order.customerId === customer_id)
      : orders;
```

```
    const mapped = filteredOrders.map(order => {
      const customer = customers.find(c => c.id === order.customerId);
      return {
        type: "text",
        text: `ID: ${order.orderId}, customer:
          ${customer ? customer.name : "Unknown"}`
      };
    }) as Result;

    return {
      content: mapped
    };
  }
);

server.tool(
  "get_order",
  {
    orderId: z.string()
  },
  async ({ orderId }) => {
    const order = orders.find(order => order.orderId === orderId);

    if (!order) {
      throw new Error(`Order not found: ${orderId}`);
    }

    const customer = customers.find(c => c.id === order.customerId);

    return {
      content: [{
        type: "text",
        text: `ID: ${order.orderId},
          customer: ${customer ? customer.name : "Unknown"}`
      }]
    };
});
```

```javascript
// Place order
server.tool(
  "place_order",
  {
    customer_id: z.number()
  },
  async ({ customer_id }) => {
    if (customer_id !== 0 && !customers.some(customer => customer.id ===
      customer_id)) {
      throw new Error(`Invalid customer_id: ${customer_id}`);
    }

    const newOrder = new Order("0", customer_id);
    orders.push(newOrder);

    return {
      content: [{
        type: "text",
        text: `ID: ${newOrder.orderId}, customer: ${customer_id}`
      }]
    };
  });

// Get cart
server.tool(
  "get_cart",
  {
    customer_id: z.number()
  },
  async ({ customer_id }) => {
    if (customer_id !== 0 && !customers.some(customer => customer.id ===
      customer_id)) {
      throw new Error(`Invalid customer_id: ${customer_id}`);
    }
```

```
      const cart = carts.find(cart => cart.customerId === customer_id);
      if (cart) {
        return {
          content: [{
            type: "text",
            text: `ID: ${cart.cartId}, customer: ${cart.customerId}`
          }]
        };
      } else {
        return {
          content: [{
            type: "text",
            text: `No cart found for customer ID: ${customer_id}`
          }]
        };
      }
    }
  );


  // Get cart items
  server.tool(
    "get_cart_items",
    {
      cart_id: z.string()
    },
    async ({ cart_id }) => {
      const items = cartItems.filter(item => item.cartId === cart_id);
      return {
        content: items.map(item => ({
          type: "text",
          text: `ID: ${item.cartId}, product: ${item.productId},
            quantity: ${item.quantity}`
        }))
      };
    }
  );
```

```
// Add to cart
server.tool(
  "add_to_cart",
  {
    cart_id: z.string(),
    product_id: z.number(),
    quantity: z.number()
  },
  async ({ cart_id, product_id, quantity }) => {
    const newCartItem = new CartItem(cart_id, product_id, quantity);
    cartItems.push(newCartItem);
    return {
      content: [{
        type: "text",
        text: `ID: ${newCartItem.cartId}, product:
          ${newCartItem.productId}, quantity: ${newCartItem.quantity}`
      }]
    };
  }
);


// Get all products
server.tool(
  "get_all_products",
  {},
  async () => {
    return {
      content: products.map(product => ({
        type: "text",
        text: `ID: ${product.name}, price: ${product.price},
          description: ${product.description}`
      }))
    };
  }
);
```

```
// Get product by ID
server.tool(
  "get_product",
  {
    product_id: z.string()
  },
  async ({ product_id }) => {
    const product = products.find(product => product.name === product_id);
    if (product) {
      return {
        content: [{
          type: "text",
          text: `ID: ${product.name}, price: ${product.price},
            description: ${product.description}`
        }]
      };
    } else {
      return {
        content: [{
          type: "text",
          text: `Product not found with ID: ${product_id}`
        }]
      };
    }
  }
);


// Get all categories
server.tool(
  "get_all_categories",
  {},
  async () => {
    return {
      content: categories.map(category => ({
        type: "text",
        text: `ID: ${category.name}, description: ${category.description}`
      }))
```

```
      };
    }
  );

  // Get all customers
  server.tool(
    "get_all_customers",
    {},
    async () => {
      return {
        content: customers.map(customer => ({
          type: "text",
          text: `ID: ${customer.id}, name: ${customer.name},
            email: ${customer.email}`
        }))
      };
    });

  // Start receiving messages on stdin and sending messages on stdout
  const transport = new StdioServerTransport();
  await server.connect(transport);
```

Solution

You can access the solution at https://github.com/PacktPublishing/Learn-Model-Context-Protocol-with-TypeScript/blob/main/Chapter06/solutions/README.md.

Quiz

What are some benefits of using a low-level server?

- A: You use less memory
- B: You have better control over how requests are processed
- C: You can define your own transports

You can access the solution at https://github.com/PacktPublishing/Learn-Model-Context-Protocol-with-TypeScript/blob/main/Chapter06/solutions/solution-quiz.md.

Get This Book's PDF Version and Exclusive Extras

UNLOCK NOW

Scan the QR code (or go to packtpub.com/unlock). Search for this book by name, confirm the edition, and then follow the steps on the page.

Note: Keep your invoice handy. Purchases made directly from Packt don't require an invoice.

7

Consuming Servers by Building Bespoke Clients/Agents

To consume an MCP server, you need some form of client. You could, for example, use an application such as **Claude Desktop** or **VS Code**, as they have the ability to consume MCP servers and will handle the discovery of features and be able to use them. There are also cases where you want your own written client. A good example of this situation is when you want to build in AI capabilities as part of your app. Imagine, for example, that you have an e-commerce app and want to have an AI-improved search. The MCP server would be a separate app, whereas the client would be built into the e-commerce app.

With this in mind, let's explore how we can build a client and what goes into it.

In this chapter, you will learn how to do the following:

- Build a client using both STDIO and SSE transports
- Consume an MCP server and its features
- Leverage an LLM to enhance your client experience

The chapter covers the following topics:

- Building a client
- Exercise: Building a client
- Clients with LLMs
- Working with an LLM
- Exercise: Integrating the LLM

Building a client

So, what goes into building a client? At a mile-high level, here's what we need to do:

1. Set up the client to connect to the server.
2. List features.
3. Select a feature to use.
4. Prompt the user for parameters.
5. Present the results.

Great, now that we understand the high-level steps, let's see if we can build it next in an exercise that you're welcome to code along with.

Exercise: Building a client

In this exercise, you will build a client that connects to the server and consumes its features. You will use the SDK to build the client and call the server. The client will be a simple command-line application that allows you to select a feature and provide its parameters. The client will then call the server and display the results.

Set up the client to connect to the server

Let's first create the client code needed to establish a connection to the server:

```
import { Client } from "@modelcontextprotocol/sdk/client/index.js";
import { StdioClientTransport } from
  "@modelcontextprotocol/sdk/client/stdio.js";

const transport = new StdioClientTransport({
  command: "node",
  args: ["./build/index.js"]
});

const client = new Client(
  {
    name: "example-client",
    version: "1.0.0"
  }
);
```

```
async function main() {
    await client.connect(transport);

    // List features and consume features here

main().catch((error) => {
    console.error("Error: ", error);

});
```

In the preceding code, we've done the following:

- Created a `StdioClientTransport` object that specifies the command to run the server and any optional command-line arguments. This is done as the server will be run at the same time as the client, so we need to specify how to run it.
- Defined a `Client` object that will be used to connect to the server. The `Client` object is created with a name and version, which are used to identify the client when it connects to the server.
- Written a `main` function that creates a `Client` object and initializes the connection to the server. Inside the `main` function, we will soon add the code to list and call features.

List features

So far, we've set up the client to connect to the server. Now, let's add the code to list the features available on the server. This is done differently depending on the type of feature. Let's add some code.

```
// List tools
const tools = await client.listTools();

for (let tool of tools.tools) {
    console.log("Tool: ", tool.name);
}

// List resources
const resources = await client.listResources();
```

```
for(let resource in resources.resources) {
    console.log("Resource: ", resource);
}

// List resource templates
const templates = await client.listResourceTemplates();

for(let template of templates.resourceTemplates) {
    console.log("Resource template: ", template.name);
}
```

In the preceding code, we've done the following:

- Listed the tools available on the server and printed the tool name to the console for each tool
- Added code to list the resources available on the server. We also print the resource name to the console.
- Listed the resource templates available on the server, including printing the template name to the console.

Select a feature to use

Let's show how to use our listed features by taking one of the tools and calling it. In this case, we will use the add tool that we created in the previous chapter. The add tool takes two parameters, a and b, and returns the sum of the two numbers. However, imagine now the user has been presented with a list of tools and chosen a tool. Let's now prompt the user for the parameters needed to call the tool.

```
function getInput(query: string): Promise<number> {
    const read = readline.createInterface({
        input: process.stdin,
        output: process.stdout
    });

    return new Promise(resolve => {
        read.question(query, (answer: string) => {
            readline.close();
            resolve(Number(answer));
        });
    });
```

```
    }

    // in main function
    let firstArg = await getInput("Enter first argument: ");
    let secondArg = await getInput("Enter second argument: ");

    // Call a tool
    const result = await client.callTool({
        name: "add",
        arguments: {
            a: firstArg,
            b: secondArg
        }
    });
```

In the preceding code, we've done the following:

- Created a getInput function that prompts the user for input and returns the input as a number. We use the readline module to read input from the console.
- Prompted the user for the first and second value to use as parameters for the tool.
- Called the tool using the callTool method and passed the parameters as an object. The result is printed to the console.

Great, now we have a client that can connect to the server, list the features, and call a tool. However, this is still quite programmatic and not very user-friendly. Before we move on to integrate an LLM, let's show the complete code for the client.

The full code

```
import { Client } from "@modelcontextprotocol/sdk/client/index.js";
import { StdioClientTransport } from
  "@modelcontextprotocol/sdk/client/stdio.js";

import readline from "readline";
import process from "node:process";

const transport = new StdioClientTransport({
  command: "node",
  args: ["./build/index.js"]
```

```
});

const client = new Client(
  {
    name: "example-client",
    version: "1.0.0"
  }
);

async function main() {
    await client.connect(transport);

    // List resources
    const resources = await client.listResources();

    for(let resource in resources.resources) {
        console.log("Resource: ", resource);
    }

    // List resource templates
    const templates = await client.listResourceTemplates();

    for(let template of templates.resourceTemplates) {
        console.log("Resource template: ", template.name);
    }

    // List tools
    const tools = await client.listTools();

    for(let tool of tools.tools) {
        console.log("Tool: ", tool.name);
    }

    let selectedToolName = tools.tools[0].name;
    // get input from terminal, use readline
    const readline = require("readline").createInterface({
        input: process.stdin,
```

```
            output: process.stdout
    });

    let firstArg = await getInput("Enter first argument: ");
    let secondArg = await getInput("Enter second argument: ");

    // Call a tool
    const result = await client.callTool({
        name: "add",
        arguments: {
            a: firstArg,
            b: secondArg
        }
    });

    console.log("Tool result: ", result);
}

function getInput(query: string): Promise<number> {
    const read = readline.createInterface({
        input: process.stdin,
        output: process.stdout
    });

    return new Promise(resolve => {
        read.question(query, (answer: string) => {
            readline.close();
            resolve(Number(answer));
        });
    });
}

main().catch((error) => {
    console.error("Error: ", error);
});
```

Okay, if you typed along with the code, you should now have a working client that can connect to the server and consume its features. You will get an additional chance to practice this in the assignment at the end of this chapter.

Let's improve the client next by integrating an LLM into it. You will get to see how this offers a better user experience and how it can be used to abstract away the complexity of using the server.

Clients with LLMs

So far, you've seen how you can build and test a client using STDIO and SSE. However, you might have noticed how this approach is quite programmatic and not very user-friendly. That is, for each capability you want to use, you need to know the exact name of the feature and its parameters. This is where LLMs come in. By involving an LLM in the client, you can abstract away the *knowing* part and instead focus on the *doing* part. Here's how it works.

Before using an LLM

Here's how you would build an app without an LLM and how the flow in the app would be:

1. List server features.
2. The user selects a feature and the client asks for the parameters.
3. Do something with the response.

This approach is quite rigid and requires the user to explicitly know and select one of the features listed. So, what's better?

After involving an LLM

To address clients that feel rigid, imagine instead that the user doesn't know about the features; they only communicate with prompts. With that thought in mind, now let's look at the flow of the app:

1. List server features.
2. Convert the list of features into an LLM tool.
3. The user types a natural language request.
4. The client sends the request to the LLM, which figures out which feature to use and what parameters to send, and if there's no matching feature, responds with a generic LLM response.

The difference in user experience is quite significant. This second approach means the user no longer needs to know about the features, and doesn't need to select features to use. Instead, the user can just type a natural language request, and the LLM will figure out the rest.

Let's see how this works in practice.

Working with an LLM

There are many AI providers out there that let you call an LLM. In this book, we will use **GitHub Models**, as that's a free option, and all you need to use it is a GitHub account. To use GitHub Models, you will either need to start your project in GitHub Codespaces or set up a **personal access token (PAT)** with the right permissions. The reason you need a token in the first place is that you are calling an API, and the token is used as a bearer token to authenticate the request. To use a local AI model via, for example, **Ollama**, you wouldn't need a token. You can type the token directly in the source code, but it's recommended to keep it in an environment variable for security reasons.

So, what do we need to know if we've never worked with AI before? Well, the idea is to send in a prompt and get back a response. The prompt is natural language text that describes what you want the LLM to do. The response is also natural language text that contains the answer to your prompt.

To use LLM in combination with MCP, however, the idea is to have the LLM indicate which functions to call given a specific prompt. For example, with the prompt "Add 1 and 2", the LLM should indicate that the add function should be called with the parameters a=1 and b=2, if we have defined an add function in the MCP server with that name and parameters.

Here's what the calling code looks like:

```
import OpenAI from "openai";

// get token from environment variable, we use this as
// bearer token to call GitHub Models
const token = process.env["GITHUB_TOKEN"];

export async function main() {

  // list of functions represented as JSON schema
  let functions = [
    {
      "type": "function",
      "function": {
```

```
      "name": "add",
      "description": "Add two numbers",
      "type": "function",
      "parameters": {
        "type": "object",
        "properties": {
          "a": {
            "type": "number",
            "description": "The first number to add"
          },
          "b": {
            "type": "number",
            "description": "The second number to add"
          }
        },
        "required": ["a", "b"]
      }
    }
  }
];

const client = new OpenAI({
  baseURL: "https://models.github.ai/inference",
  apiKey: token
});

const response = await client.chat.completions.create({
  messages: [
    { role:"system", content: "" },
    { role:"user", content: "What is the capital of France?" }
  ],
  model: "openai/gpt-4o-mini",
  temperature: 1,
  max_tokens: 4096,
  top_p: 1,
  tools: functions
});
```

```
    console.log(response.choices[0].message.content);
}

main().catch((err) => {
  console.error("The sample encountered an error:", err);
});
```

It's worth mentioning though that, additionally to prompts, you can also send in configuration to the LLM, such as `temperature`, `max_tokens`, and `top_p`. We won't dive into what these parameters mean – you can read more about them in the OpenAI documentation – but in short, they control the randomness and creativity of the LLM response and also the size of what's known as the context window.

Exercise: Integrating the LLM

So, let's see how we can integrate an LLM into the client. The goal is to have a much better user experience and to abstract away the complexity of using the server. To get there, we will need to take the following steps:

1. **List server features**: By listing the features, we can see what we have available to us
2. **Convert the list of features to an LLM tool**: The features from the MCP server are not directly usable by the LLM, so we need to convert them into a format that the LLM can understand
3. **Manage user input**: This will allow the user to type a natural language request and the LLM on our client will make a completion request, and in doing so, tell us which feature to use and what parameters to send.

Let's do this!

List server features

> You might be building this client as the first thing you do if you, for example, are consuming someone else's MCP server. In that case, make sure you install the MCP SDK before proceeding.

The first step is no different from what we did before. We need to list the features available on the server. This is done by a call to listing tools, like so:

```
// List tools
const tools = await client.listTools();


for(let tool of tools.tools) {
    console.log("Tool: ", tool.name);
}
```

Convert the list of features into an LLM tool

Our next step is important, as we're going to convert the list of features into a format that the LLM can understand. This will set us up for the next step, where we will use the LLM to figure out which feature to use. Here's the conversion code:

1. Let's add the conversion function:

```
function toLLMTool(tool: {
    name: string;
    description?: string;
    inputSchema: any;
      }) {
      // Create a zod schema based on the input_schema
      const schema = z.object(tool.inputSchema);

      return {
        type: "function" as const, // Explicitly set type to
                                   // "function"
        function: {
          name: tool.name,
          description: tool.description,
          parameters: {
          type: "object",
          properties: tool.inputSchema.properties,
          required: tool.inputSchema.required,
          },
        },
      };
    }
```

2. Now, to use this function, we need to add a call to it as we're iterating the tool response from the MCP server:

```
const llmTools = [];

for(let tool of tools.tools) {
    toolDescriptions += `${tool.name}, ${tool.description}\n`;

    // 1. convert this response to LLM tool
    llmTools.push(toLLMTool(tool));
}
```

Great, now we are well set up for using the LLM. The next step is to manage user input and send a completion request to the LLM. In the response from the LLM, the LLM will tell us which function to use and what parameters. In this case, the function to call will be a feature on the server.

The user types a natural language request and the LLM makes a completion request

Let's look at how we can call the LLM now that we have tools for it to use.

1. Make the LLM call:

```
// create client
const openai = new OpenAI({
    baseURL: "https://models.inference.ai.azure.com",
    apiKey: process.env.GITHUB_TOKEN,
});

// make completion call
let response = openai.chat.completions.create({
    model: "gpt-4o-mini",
    max_tokens: 1000,
    messages,
    tools: llmTools,
});
```

2. Check whether the LLM returned a function to call:

```
for (const choice of (await response).choices) {
    const message = choice.message;
    if (message.tool_calls) {
        console.log("Making tool call")
        await callTools(message.tool_calls, results);
    }
}
```

In this code, we loop through the response and check whether the response contains a tool call – that is, if tool_calls is populated. If so, we call callTools, a method that will end up calling MCP server tools for us.

Let's define that function in our next subsection.

The client figures out which server feature to use and what parameters to send

At this point, we have the LLM response, and it even returns which functions to call, if any. The next step is to check the functions to call and call the MCP server if needed.

Let's have a look at the callTools function:

```
async function callTools(
    tool_calls: OpenAI.Chat.Completions.ChatCompletionMessageToolCall[],
    toolResults: any[]
): Promise<void> {
    for (const tool_call of tool_calls) {
        const toolName = tool_call.function.name;
        const args = tool_call.function.arguments;

        console.log(`Calling tool "${toolName}" with args
          ${JSON.stringify(args)}`);


        // 2. Call the server's tool
        const toolResult = await client.callTool({
            name: toolName,
            arguments: JSON.parse(args),
```

```
    });

    console.log("\nTool result: ", toolResult);

    // 3. Do something with the result
    // TODO


  }
}
```

The preceding does the following:

- Parses out the function name and its arguments:

```
const toolName = tool_call.function.name;
const args = tool_call.function.arguments;
```

- Calls a tool on the MCP server and prints the result:

```
const toolResult = await client.callTool({
    name: toolName,
    arguments: JSON.parse(args),
});

console.log("\nTool result: ", toolResult);
```

Nice, right? The user is surely thanking you now for making their life easier, as they can use natural language to interact with the server.

Summary

In this chapter, we've explored how to build clients that can connect to an MCP server and consume its features. We started by building a simple client that could list and call features on the server. We then improved the client by integrating an LLM, which allowed us to create a much better user experience by enabling natural language interactions with the server.

In the next chapter, we will explore how to consume an MCP server using VS Code and Claude for desktop.

Assignment

For this assignment, you will once again focus on e-commerce. You will build an experience where the user can interact with an e-commerce server:

- Ask for products of a certain category
- Add products to the cart, all done using natural language

Solution

Here's a solution for a client. It covers both clients with and without an LLM.

https://github.com/PacktPublishing/Learn-Model-Context-Protocol-with-TypeScript/blob/main/Chapter07/solutions/README.md.

Quiz

1. What can a client access on an MCP server?

   - A: Prompts, tools, and resources
   - B: Tools, prompts, and services
   - C: Tools and prompts

2. What's the benefit of adding an LLM to your client?

   - A: It's better to place the LLM on the server
   - B: It makes the client faster
   - C: An LLM on the client allows the end user to use prompts to interact with the server, which makes for a much better user experience

You can access the solution at https://github.com/PacktPublishing/Learn-Model-Context-Protocol-with-TypeScript/blob/main/Chapter07/solutions/solution-quiz.md.

References

- **Model Context Protocol:** https://modelcontextprotocol.io/introduction
- **Build clients:** https://modelcontextprotocol.io/quickstart/client
- **TypeScript SDK:** https://github.com/modelcontextprotocol/typescript-sdk

Get This Book's PDF Version and Exclusive Extras

UNLOCK NOW

Scan the QR code (or go to packtpub.com/unlock). Search for this book by name, confirm the edition, and then follow the steps on the page.

Note: Keep your invoice handy. Purchases made directly from Packt don't require an invoice.

8

Consuming Servers Using an IDE

So far, we have looked at how to create servers, but also at consuming them via bespoke clients that you have to write yourself. In this section, we will look at how to consume servers using existing software, such as **VS Code** or **Claude Desktop**. When we say *consume*, what we mean is installing servers, configuring them, and then using them to run tools or interact with the server in some way.

In this chapter, you will learn how to do the following:

- Understand how to consume servers using existing tools
- Install and configure servers in VS Code
- Work with the mcp.json file for server management
- Manage secrets and configuration for servers
- Use VS Code to test and interact with servers
- Apply security best practices when consuming servers

The chapter covers the following topics:

- Consuming with hosts such as Claude Desktop and VS Code
- Installation process
- Adding a server
- Local and global install
- Security aspects
- Suggestion for servers

Consuming with hosts such as Claude Desktop and VS Code

Consuming servers, okay, what does that mean? So to use an MCP server and its features, you need a way to interact with it. You've seen in *Chapter 7* how to create a server and how to write a client that can interact with it. That's a perfectly valid way to consume a server, but it requires you to write code.

Another approach is to use existing software such as Claude Desktop or VS Code. These tools are designed to work with MCP servers, and they also provide a large language model that ensures that you can interact with the server in a more user-friendly way via prompts.

We think of these two pieces of software as hosts, as they have a built-in MCP client, but they also use configuration files to keep track of the servers that are installed, the tools that are available, and so on.

How do they work? Well, they work in the following way:

- Initiate a connection to the MCP server through a selected transport type, such as STDIO, SSE, or Streamable HTTP
- Provide a user interface to interact with the server and let you type prompts, interact with tools, configuration, and more
- Use configuration files to keep track of installed servers, available tools, and other settings

Here's an example of the user interface in VS Code, which is representative of how these hosts work:

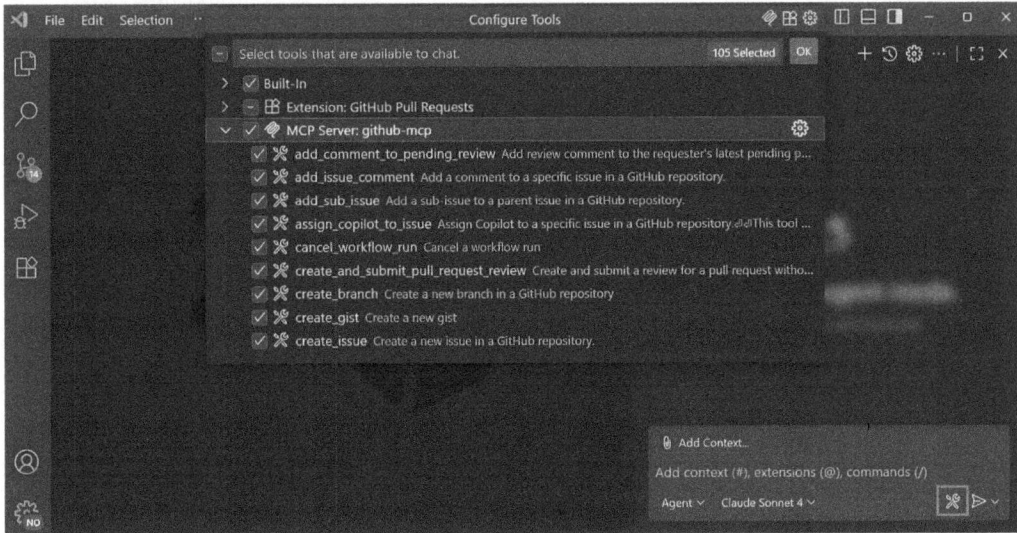

Figure 8.1 – VS Code interface

In the preceding figure, you can see the following:

- A list of tools currently available via servers that are installed
- A chat interface where you can type prompts

Let's talk about specific hosts next and their features.

MCP support in VS Code

VS Code, together with GitHub Copilot, has extensive support for MCP servers. There are a variety of features that help you to install, configure, and secure servers. It supports use cases such as trying out servers you are building, as well as turning VS Code into an agentic app that can run tools through your prompts.

Here's a list of features that VS Code provides for MCP servers:

- **Installing servers**: VS Code lets you install servers both on a global level and on a work-space level. It supports the three transport types: STDIO, SSE, and Streamable HTTP.
- **Managing tools**: You can enable and disable tools for a server, which is useful to ensure that the client has the context it needs.

- **Interacting with features**: In addition to tools, it also supports features such as user prompts and resources.
- **Managing servers**: You can add and remove servers and configure them.
- **Sampling**: It supports sampling, which means that when a server sends a sample request, you can interact with it and tweak the request before sending back a response.
- **Elicitations**: It also supports elicitation requests, which are scenarios when the server needs more information from the user to proceed with a request.
- **Logging and debugging**: There's also support for logging and debugging, which is useful when you are developing servers or clients.

Additional features are being made available all the time, and you're recommended to use **VS Code Insiders** if you want to try these features as early as possible, as they're shipped there first.

Claude Desktop

You can also use Claude Desktop to consume MCP servers. Head over to the download page (`https://claude.ai/download`) to install a client for your operating system. Just like VS Code, it provides a user interface and a whole set of features to interact with MCP servers.

Claude does a lot more than just work with MCP servers; it's a fully-fledged AI assistant and is perhaps best compared with similar products such as ChatGPT or Copilot. For a full set of features, head over to this page: `https://claude.ai/login?returnTo=%2F%3F#features`.

Installation process

To install servers, there's a central concept for both Claude and VS Code, namely, the `mcp.json` file. This file is your main configuration file where you add information on where the servers are and additional configuration needed. In fact, this JSON file acts like a manifest file for what servers are installed. The act of installing a file means adding an entry to this file. Here's an example of an `mcp.json` file:

```
{
    "inputs": [

    ],
    "servers": {
        "docs": {
            "type": "http",
```

```
        "url": "https://learn.microsoft.com/api/mcp"
      }
    }
  }
```

In this file, we have a `servers` attribute with one server entry to `https://learn.microsoft.com/api/mcp`; this MCP server is now considered installed.

The full installation process for installing and running a feature on a server looks like so:

1. Install a server by adding an entry `mcp.json` file in the `servers` attribute.

2. Start the server.

3. Use the server by typing a prompt matching a tool in the server.

We'll explore such a scenario later in this chapter, but now you have a mile-high understanding of it. Let's go into more depth on the `mcp.json` file.

The mcp.json file

The `mcp.json` file has two primary attributes:

*   **inputs**: This is used for defining placeholders for sensitive information, such as API keys or tokens. The idea is that you define that you want an input prompt to appear, and the answer should be stored in a variable that you can later refer to. Here's an example of this:

    ```
    [
        {
        "id": "my_api_key",
        "description": "The API key that my MCP server needs",
        "type": "promptString",
        "password": true
        }
    ]
    ```

    By the preceding definition, the user interface in VS Code will start an input prompt asking you to fill in this information. This then needs to be paired with a server entry, like so:

    ```
    "my_mcp_server": {
      "type": "http",
      "url": "http://localhost:8000/mcp",
      "headers": {
    ```

```
      "Authorization": "Bearer ${my_api_key}"
   }
}
```

Note how my_api_key is now passed in as a header property so that every time we call http://localhost:8000/mcp, it will also pass the API key, ensuring that we can access our MCP server securely. Setting things up this way ensures that secrets stay out of mcp.json.

- **servers**: This property takes a JSON object with server entries. What you need to know is that these entries look different depending on which transport is being used by the server. Let's show examples for each transport type:

  - **Using Streamable HTTP**:

    ```
    "my_mcp_server": {
      "type": "http",
      "url": "http://localhost:8000/mcp"
    }
    ```

    In this case, it's using Streamable HTTP; we can see that as the type value is http and a url value is specified. Let's look at SSE next.

  - **SSE**:

    ```
    "my_mcp_server": {
      "type": "sse",
      "url": "http://localhost:8000/sse"
    }
    ```

    SSE, just like Streamable HTTP, is a transport meant for servers that are accessed remotely. Therefore, a url value is used in both cases to point out where these servers live.

  - **STDIO**:

    ```
    "playwright": {
        "command": "npx",
        "args": ["-y", "@executeautomation/playwright-mcp-
            server"]
    }
    ```

STDIO, or **standard I/O**, needs to specify a command and args property as it needs to point out how to start the server in question. It's not needed for SSE or Streamable HTTP, as these servers live remotely.

Adding a server

You've already seen in the previous section how various servers can be added, but let's go through the motions of adding and using a server. Let's use **Playwright**, an **end-to-end (E2E)** testing framework, as an example. To install it as an MCP server, what you usually do for any server is to locate its GitHub repo and see what its installation instructions are. For Playwright, its repository is here: https://github.com/microsoft/playwright-mcp.

There are quite a lot of instructions as this server offers a lot of features, but let's grab the installation instructions from its *Getting started* section, which looks like so:

```
"playwright": {
    "command": "npx",
    "args": [
    "@playwright/mcp@latest"
    ]
}
```

Here, we see how it's clearly a stdio type server as its command and args properties are populated.

Step 1: Installing the server

Let's install this via VS Code. By doing so, we have a couple of different options on how to install it:

- Add the entry directly to an mcp.json file.
- Use a user interface, either with the **Add Server** button that's present when you view the mcp.json file or by running the MCP: Add Server command from the command palette. In both cases, it will trigger a user interface asking you to decide on what transport to use, and either url or command and args information, depending on the chosen transport.

As an example, let's click **Add Server**; you should be presented with the following interface:

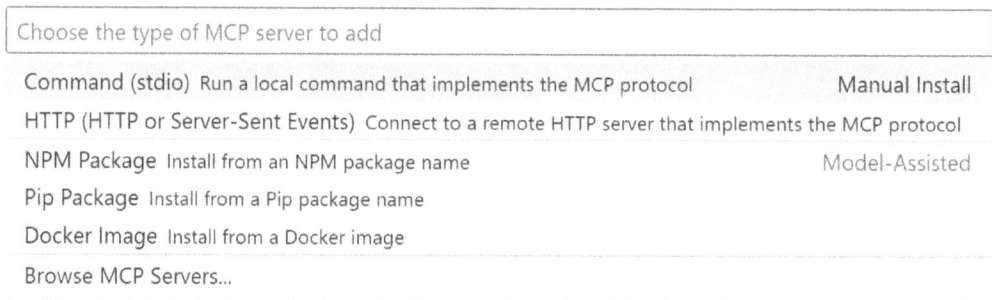

Choose the type of MCP server to add

Command (stdio) Run a local command that implements the MCP protocol   Manual Install

HTTP (HTTP or Server-Sent Events) Connect to a remote HTTP server that implements the MCP protocol

NPM Package Install from an NPM package name   Model-Assisted

Pip Package Install from a Pip package name

Docker Image Install from a Docker image

Browse MCP Servers...

Figure 8.2 – Installing the server

As you can see, there are numerous options for installing a server: different transports, some also from different package managers, and even Docker.

In fact, if you choose the **Browse MCP Servers...** option, it will take you to a list of vetted MCP servers (https://code.visualstudio.com/insider/mcp) and let you choose a server from there.

We have the complete instructions for working with Playwright from its GitHub repo, but let's install from this list of servers by selecting to install it like so, clicking **Install Playwright**:

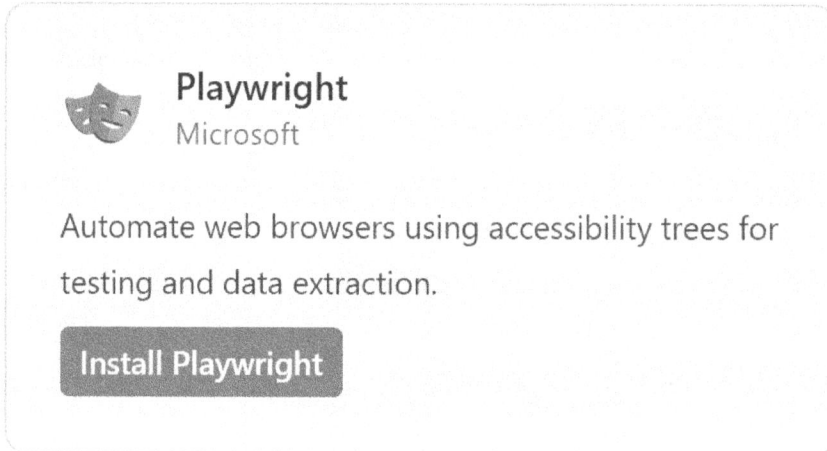

Playwright
Microsoft

Automate web browsers using accessibility trees for testing and data extraction.

Install Playwright

Figure 8.3 – Install Playwright

Now, you should see a dialog opening in your VS Code giving you more information on the server, along with installation instructions. We had previously located the installation information by going to its GitHub repo, but this is also a great way to do it.

Okay, so it seems the answer is to either manually copy-paste what you need in mcp.json or use one of the many options in VS Code.

Step 2: Managing the server

Now, you've added the server, so your mcp.json looks similar to the following JSON (note how Playwright is added):

```
{
    "servers": {
        "playwright": {
            "command": "npx",
            "args": [
            "@playwright/mcp@latest"
            ]
        }
    },
    "inputs": []
}
```

It's now time to see how the user interface supports us. One thing we can do is select **Extensions**; we should see our list of installed servers like so:

Figure 8.4 – Installed servers

From this view, we can click the cog wheel on a server to interact with it:

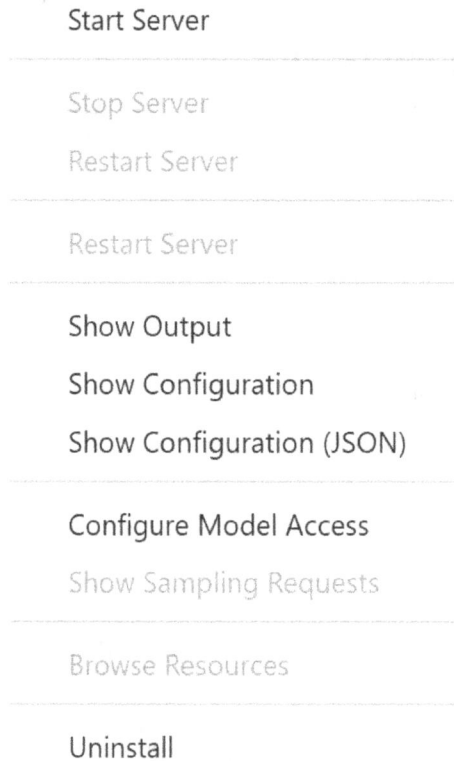

Start Server

Stop Server

Restart Server

Restart Server

Show Output

Show Configuration

Show Configuration (JSON)

Configure Model Access

Show Sampling Requests

Browse Resources

Uninstall

Figure 8.5 – Interacting with the server

As you can see, there are multiple options, from starting the server to seeing its logs, and even JSON configuration. You can take these actions from within the mcp.json file as well.

Step 3: Interacting with the server

Let's start the server, and now let's turn to the chat interface we have from installing GitHub Copilot. Make sure the agent is selected in the droplist and then type the following prompt:

```
Navigate to https://tfl.gov.uk/. I want to go from Paddington to Heathrow,
show me how to get there by underground, important use playwright tool
```

> Sometimes, VS Code is a bit unwilling to use a tool, so it's worth spending some time on the prompt to ensure it does use it. I've added `important use playwright tool` to ensure the tool is triggered.

You should see the following in the chat interface:

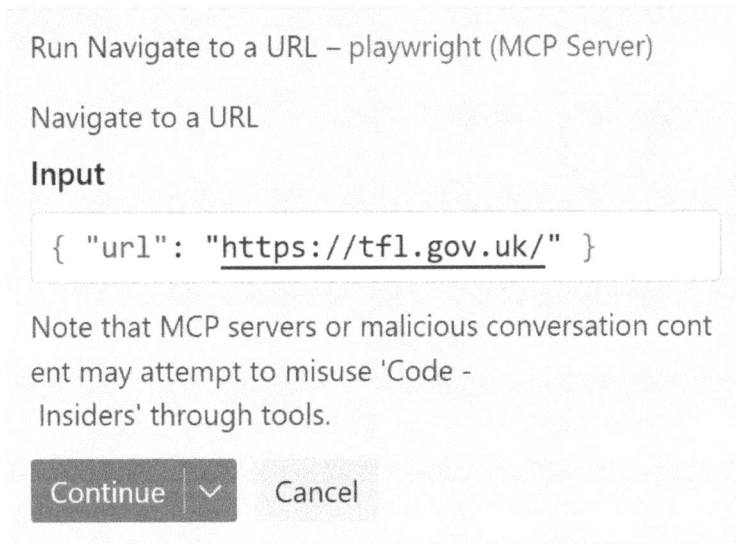

Run Navigate to a URL – playwright (MCP Server)

Navigate to a URL

Input

`{ "url": "https://tfl.gov.uk/" }`

Note that MCP servers or malicious conversation content may attempt to misuse 'Code - Insiders' through tools.

Continue ∨   Cancel

Figure 8.6 – Using the tool

This shows a tool being triggered, and you being asked to allow the tool to run as part of this. You can see how the URL is parsed out from your prompt and matched as the input to the Playwright tool. This should trigger a whole series of tool calls as Playwright will go through the website, locate the input field, and try to complete the mission set out by the prompt.

You might need to restart the chat sometimes, but once it works as it should, you should see something like the following figure, indicating that Playwright has started to navigate the site properly and is trying to get you from Paddington to Heathrow:

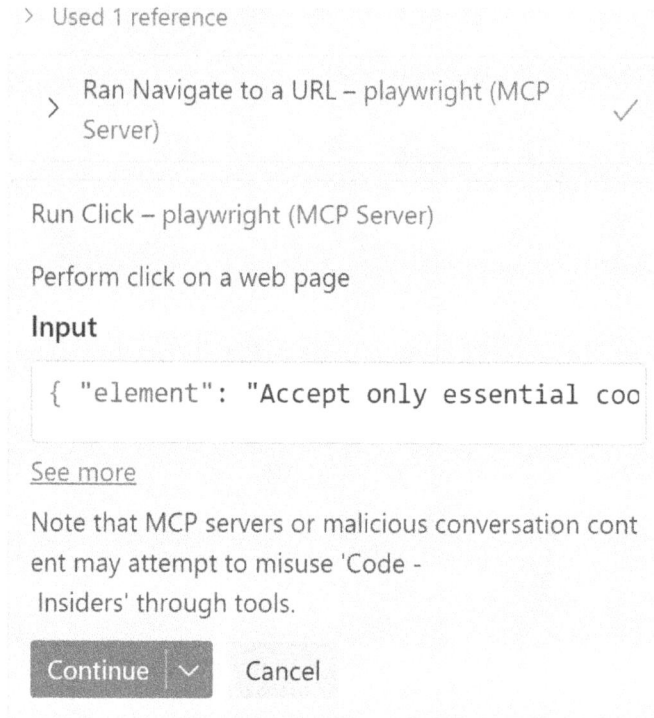

Figure 8.7 – Playwright query

Once it's done, you can interact with it in various ways to get what you need and even ask it to generate the Playwright tests from this interaction, which is where the real value lies.

Local and global install

So far, we've installed servers in .vscode/mcp.json, which means they are installed into this workspace only. You can install servers globally on your machine as well. To choose that instead, let's use MCP: Add Server from the command palette. At the last step, choose **Global**, and it will create an mcp.json file in (Settings)/User/mcp/json, which means it has added the server entry to the user setting rather than this specific workspace instance. That means that if you open up another instance of VS Code, you will not need to install this server again.

Here's what the user-level `mcp.json` file looks like after a server has been globally installed:

```
{
    "servers": {
        "my-mcp-server-6801ea17": {
            "url": "https://learn.microsoft.com/api/mcp",
            "type": "http"
        }
    },
    "inputs": []
}
```

As you can see, there's no difference in how it's installed in the actual `mcp.json` file, but the difference is in where the `mcp.json` file is located. The general rule of thumb is, if it's a server you use often, install it globally; if not, install it in the workspace at `.vscode/mcp.json`.

> So far, we've gone through the basics, but what else is there to know? Well, there are quite a few different settings. A complete listing of features can be found at this docs page: `https://code.visualstudio.com/docs/copilot/chat/mcp-servers`.

Debugging

As a developer, knowing how to debug is a critical skill, so let's show how to do that. Currently, Node.js debugging is supported, according to the documentation (`https://code.visualstudio.com/docs/copilot/customization/mcp-servers#_debug-an-mcp-server`):

```
"server-ts": {
    "command": "node",
    "args": ["08 - consuming servers/code/build/index.js"],
    "dev": {
        "watch": "08 - consuming servers/code/build/**/*.js",
        "debug": { "type": "node" }
    }
}
```

According to the preceding configuration, what you need to do is this:

1. Set up your `command` and `args` properties to instruct how to run the server.

2. Add dev with two different attributes: `watch`, which is a **global pattern (GLOB)** that looks at your JavaScript files for changes, and debug, which is where you specify which process is debugging it. In this case, it's Node. Once it's set up and the server is running, there should be a gray **debug** text just above. Make sure you've added a breakpoint in suitable places, such as starting the server, running a tool, and so on. Here's how you can test different scenarios:

3. **Testing startup**: Here, we've just added a breakpoint to our startup code, and all we need to do is start the server from `mcp.json`. You should see how the breakpoint is hit, like so:

```
10    server.registerTool("add", {
11        title: "Addition Tool",
12        description: "Add two numbers",
13        inputSchema: { a: z.number(), b: z.number() }
14    }, async ({ a, b }) => ({
15        content: [{ type: "text", text: String(a + b) }]
16    }));
17    // Start receiving messages on stdin and sending messages on stdout
18    async function main() {
19        console. log("Starting MCP server...");
20        const transport = new StdioServerTransport();
21        await server.connect(transport);
22    }
23    main();
24
```

Figure 8.8 – Breakpoint startup

4. **Testing tools**: A good way to test the tools is to run the inspector in CLI mode. Here's a command for testing a tool, add, with input parameters, a and b. Adopt this command to match the operations and parameters on your server:

```
npx @modelcontextprotocol/inspector --cli node ./build/index.js
--method tools/call --tool-name add --tool-arg a=1 --tool-arg b=2
```

You should see a response directly in the terminal that looks similar to the following:

```
{
    "content": [
        {
            "type": "text",
            "text": "3"
```

```
        }
    ]
}
```

Troubleshooting

Sometimes, you will see an error indication on the *tools* icon in the chat area. If that happens, open the **Output** section in your terminal area, and you will see what the problem is. This area is a good place to inspect generally, as you will see every interaction between VS Code and your server, such as when it starts up and stops servers, but also when it initializes, lists tools, and more.

When we ran the debugger and it connected to the server, we got all this information written to **Output**:

```
2025-08-03 19:18:56.856 [info] Connection state: Starting
2025-08-03 19:18:56.857 [info] Connection state: Running
2025-08-03 19:18:56.857 [info] [editor -> server] {"jsonrpc":"2.0
","id":1,"method":"initialize","params":{"protocolVersion":"2025-
06-18","capabilities":{"roots":{"listChanged":true},"sampli
ng":{},"elicitation":{}},"clientInfo":{"name":"Visual Studio Code -
Insiders","version":"1.103.0-insider"}}}
2025-08-03 19:18:56.888 [warning] [server stderr] Debugger listening on
ws://127.0.0.1:9230/7b07fce3-e6cc-46c7-a0b8-7b782fbe853a
2025-08-03 19:18:56.888 [warning] [server stderr] For help, see: https://
nodejs.org/en/docs/inspector
2025-08-03 19:18:57.052 [warning] [server stderr] Debugger attached.
2025-08-03 19:19:01.960 [info] Waiting for server to respond to
`initialize` request...
2025-08-03 19:19:06.960 [info] Waiting for server to respond to
`initialize` request...
2025-08-03 19:19:10.858 [warning] Failed to parse message: "Starting MCP
server...\n"
2025-08-03 19:19:10.874 [info] [server -> editor]
{"result":{"protocolVersion":"2025-06-18","capabilities":{"tools":{"listC
hanged":true}},"serverInfo":{"name":"demo-server","version":"1.0.0"}},"j-
sonrpc":"2.0","id":1}
2025-08-03 19:19:10.874 [info] [editor -> server]
{"method":"notifications/initialized","jsonrpc":"2.0"}
2025-08-03 19:19:10.874 [info] [editor -> server]
{"jsonrpc":"2.0","id":2,"method":"tools/list","params":{}}
```

2025-08-03 19:19:10.891 [info] [server -> editor]
{"result":{"tools":[{"name":"add","title":"Addition Tool","description":
"Add two numbers","inputSchema":{"type":"object","properties":{"a":{"type":
"number"},"b":{"type":"number"}},"required":["a","b"],"additionalProperties"
:false,"$schema":"http://json-schema.org/draft-07/schema#"}}]},"jsonrpc":
"2.0","id":2}
2025-08-03 19:19:10.891 [info] Discovered 1 tools
2025-08-03 19:26:34.115 [warning] [server stderr] Debugger ending on
ws://127.0.0.1:9230/7b07fce3-e6cc-46c7-a0b8-7b782fbe853a
2025-08-03 19:26:34.115 [warning] [server stderr] For help, see: https://
nodejs.org/en/docs/inspector
```

Let's highlight some interesting parts from the preceding response:

- **Editor handshakes with server**: Here, the editor sends information to the server on what features/capabilities it supports. It says to the server that it supports roots, sampling, and elicitation:

```
2025-08-03 19:18:56.857 [info] [editor -> server] {"jsonrpc":"2.0
","id":1,"method":"initialize","params":{"protocolVersion":"2025-
06-18","capabilities":{"roots":{"listChanged":true},"sampli
ng":{},"elicitation":{}},"clientInfo":{"name":"Visual Studio Code -
Insiders","version":"1.103.0-insider"}}}
```

- **Server responds to editor handshake**: Here, the response comes back to say that tools are supported:

```
2025-08-03 19:19:10.874 [info] [server -> editor]
{"result":{"protocolVersion":"2025-06-18","capabilities":{
"tools":{"listChanged":true}},"serverInfo":{"name":"demo-
server","version":"1.0.0"}},"jsonrpc":"2.0","id":1}
```

- **Server sends initialized notification**: The last step in the handshake is sending the initialized notification. This is something the client sends to the server to say it's ready to exchange data. In this case, our client is VS Code:

```
2025-08-03 19:19:10.874 [info] [editor -> server]
{"method":"notifications/initialized","jsonrpc":"2.0"}
```
```

- **Tell me about your tools:** Now the client asks the server for its tools:

```
2025-08-03 19:19:10.874 [info] [editor -> server]
{"jsonrpc":"2.0","id":2,"method":"tools/list","params":{}}
```

- **Server responds to tools request:** Lastly, the server responds to a request to list its tools with the following:

```
2025-08-03 19:19:10.891 [info] [server -> editor] {"result":{"tools"
:[{"name":"add","title":"Addition Tool","description":"Add two
numbers","inputSchema":{"type":"object","properties":{"a":{"type":
"number"},"b":{"type":"number"}},"required":["a","b"],"additional
Properties":false,"$schema":"http://json-schema.org/draft-07/
schema#"
}}]},"jsonrpc":"2.0","id":2}
```

Tool management

Tool management is an important aspect of using VS Code. There are some interesting scenarios around tools where your editor helps:

- **Selecting and deselecting tools:** When you add servers, it might add a lot of tools at once. For both scenarios, where you use your editor as an agentic tool and also where you want to ensure the correct tool is called, you can choose which tools are active. You can make this selection by clicking the *tools* icon in the chat, which will bring up a user interface of all tools. Select/deselect the tools you want to have active or inactivate.

- **Run a specific tool:** Generally, when you want to run tools, you try to type a prompt that matches a specific tool's description as much as possible. If you want to make sure that the correct tool is chosen, you can prefix it with #, which will identify that specific tool. For example, to run a tool called add, you can craft a prompt like so:

```
#add 2 and 7
```

- **Managing the number of tools:** Some models have limitations on how many tools they can accept. To address this, there's a setting called github.copilot.chat.virtualTools. enabled, which will analyze the prompt and only submit the tools that match the prompt. This is a great way to avoid any errors as a result of using too many prompts. Make sure you're on the latest version of VS Code Insider. This feature is in active development and may change over time.

- **Handle tool approval**: When VS Code decides it wants to run a tool, it displays it as a query asking you to click **Continue**. At this point, you can choose to allow it only for this prompt session, for this workspace, or to always allow. Here's how it works:

    1. Type the following prompt:

        ```
        #add 2 and 7
        ```

        This makes VS Code ask you to click **Continue**. Now, select from the dropdown to allow for this workspace. Let's run it again.

    2. Type the following prompt:

        ```
        #add 2 and 9
        ```

        This ran the tool without asking for my consent, as I had previously given it permission to run in this workspace. To undo this consent, I can run Chat: Reset Tool Confirmations from the command palette.

Other settings

There are a lot of settings being added all the time to both Copilot and VS Code. Make sure you're in VS Code Insiders, type MCP in the command palette, and you will see many dedicated MCP settings:

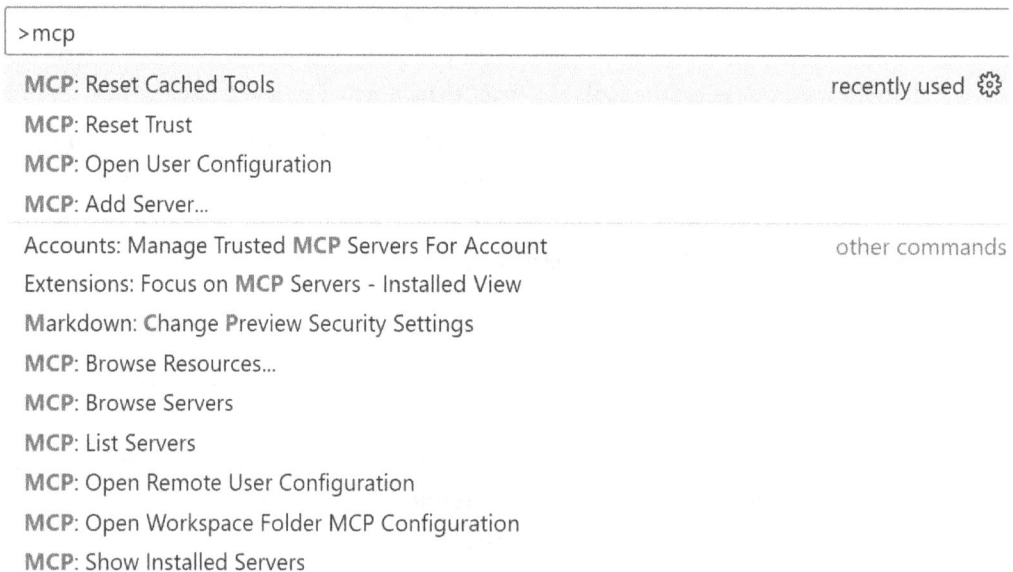

```
>mcp
```

MCP: Reset Cached Tools	recently used ⚙
MCP: Reset Trust	
MCP: Open User Configuration	
MCP: Add Server...	

Accounts: Manage Trusted MCP Servers For Account	other commands
Extensions: Focus on MCP Servers - Installed View	
Markdown: Change Preview Security Settings	
MCP: Browse Resources...	
MCP: Browse Servers	
MCP: List Servers	
MCP: Open Remote User Configuration	
MCP: Open Workspace Folder MCP Configuration	
MCP: Show Installed Servers	

Figure 8.9 – MCP commands

As you can see, there are quite a lot of commands available. Try typing Copilot as well, as it's used in conjunction with MCP. This is a changing area, though, but if you are developing MCP servers, it's part of your job to leverage your editor to the best of your ability.

Security aspects

Security is a huge topic, but let's discuss it in the context of using an editor. There are things you can do generally to stay safer, so let's try to summarize a good list of practices:

- **Keep secrets out of configuration**: Here's how you can do that by specifying the configuration in the mcp.json file:

```
{
  "mcp": {
    "inputs": [
      {
        "type": "promptString",
        "id": "my-key",
        "description": "Token for my API",
        "password": true
      }
    ],
    "servers": {
      "my-server": {
        "type": "http",
        "url": "https://my-secure-api/mcp",
        "headers" : {
          "Authorization": "Bearer ${input:my-key}"
        }
      }
    }
  }
}
```

By using the inputs element, you can ensure that secrets are kept out of the configuration file. How it works is that when the server is started, the user interface will prompt you to fill in the value for my-key, and it will be stored securely. The value can then be referenced in the server entry by using ${input:my-key}. For every request to https://my-secure-api/mcp, the Authorization header will be added with the value you provided.

- **Tool running access**: It's recommended to disallow continuous access for a tool running in a workspace. Prefer giving it access each time it's asked for. It also gives you the chance to check the parsed input.

- **Restrict what a server can do**: There are ways to restrict what a server can access. For example, there's an MCP server for file access. You should restrict it to one folder at most or folders where you're sure it can't do any harm.

- **Use trusted servers**: GitHub recently released a registry of vetted MCP servers. Using the latest version of VS Code Insiders, you can type @mcp, and it will show a list of MCP servers that you can install. You can access that same list by choosing the MCP: Add Server command and then selecting **Browse MCP Servers**. Your list of servers should look similar to this figure:

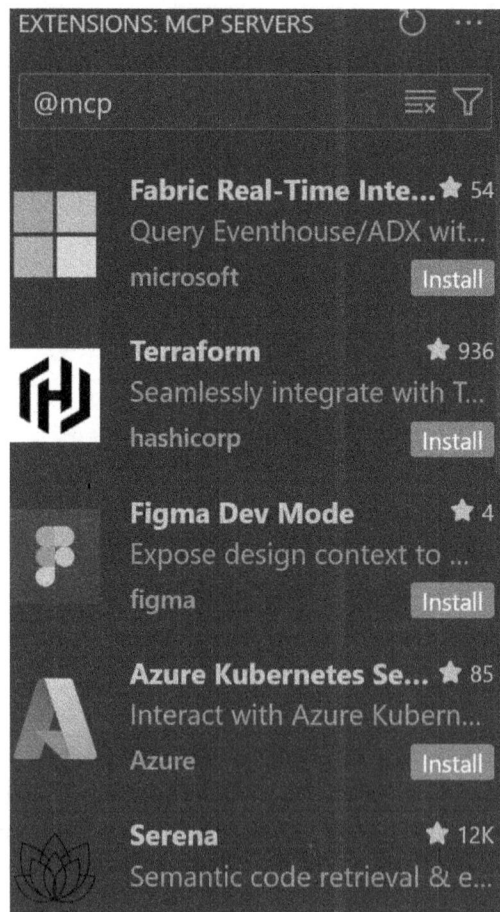

Figure 8.10 – MCP registry

In general, make sure the author behind a server is a reputable source (e.g., Stripe is behind the Stripe MCP server, and so on). Even then, resort to code scanning tools and keep track of the latest security news; breaches happen all the time. The same registry can also be found via this link (`https://code.visualstudio.com/insider/mcp`), but I prefer using the built-in experience in VS Code. Also, check out the GitHub repo for servers, as that allows you to read more on each server via their README files (`https://github.com/modelcontextprotocol/servers`).

Suggestion for servers

So what servers are recommended? Well, it depends on your needs, but I would personally use the following:

- **GitHub** (`https://github.com/github/github-mcp-server`): This server makes my life a lot easier as I can interact with issues, **pull requests (PRs)**, delegate work to agents, and more
- **Playwright** (`https://github.com/microsoft/playwright-mcp`): This is great for navigating sites, but also generates tests from that navigation, thereby saving a lot of time
- **Microsoft Learn MCP server** (`https://github.com/microsoftdocs/mcp`): This is the official Microsoft Docs and Learn server, which provides documentation directly in your editor

There are many more, but start with these and see what fits your scenario.

Summary

In this chapter, we went through how to consume an MCP server, both the ones you create and external ones. Additionally, we discussed how to manage servers once installed, their configuration, tool usage, and more.

Finally, we provided some tips on security practices. This should be seen as a bare minimum set of practices, and you should do more.

In the next chapter, we'll cover sampling, an advanced topic but very useful when the server needs to delegate work to you as the user.

Assignment

Install a server of your choice, and try it out via a prompt. Try installing a server from here: `https://code.visualstudio.com/insider/mcp`.

Quiz

How do you install an MCP server?

- A: You can install it in the same way you install extensions in VS Code.

- B: You run `mcp install <server name>` in the terminal.

- C: Servers are installed by adding text entries to `mcp.json`. You also need to specify how to start it or where the server resides.

You can access the solution at `https://github.com/PacktPublishing/Learn-Model-Context-Protocol-with-TypeScript/blob/main/Chapter08/solutions/solution-quiz.md`.

9

Delegating Tasks with Sampling

One of the most powerful features of MCP is **sampling**. What does that mean, first of all? Well, let's take a look at the definition of the word and deduce from there. Merriam-Webster defines sampling as follows:

"the action or process of taking samples of something for analysis"

Okay, so we need a sample, and we end up analyzing said sample, understood. With this definition in mind, let's talk about it in the context of MCP. In MCP, sampling means the server is sending a sampling request, a *sample* for analysis, to the client. Why does the server do that? It's simple; the server needs the client's help with some things. Because the client is the one with the LLM (even though a server can have an LLM sometimes), the server delegates tasks to the client, where an LLM can help.

Makes sense so far, right? But I bet you're asking why a server would do that.

In this chapter, we'll do the following:

- Understand the topic of sampling and when to use it
- Build a server implementation using sampling and consume it with VS Code
- Connect the server implementation to a client implementation for the occasions when we want to integrate this functionality into our app.

The chapter covers the following topics:

- Why sampling?
- Implementing sampling

Why sampling?

As we said at the beginning, the server wants to delegate some problems to the client and, specifically, to the client's LLM. So, what problems can an LLM help with that the server can't? There are lots of examples if you think about it: generating product descriptions, abstracts, tags, and more.

Let's look into the sample flow first so we understand how the interaction happens at a high level.

Sampling flow

When performing sampling, the following participants are involved:

- **User**: The user is usually involved in two places, as the originator of the initial action, and even as the *human in the loop*, accepting or modifying the sample request.
- **Server**: The server is the participant sending out a sample request. This request is usually sent out from a server feature, such as a tool call, reading of a resource, or a request from a prompt template.
- **Client**: The client's job is to receive the sample request and show it to the user, so the user can decide what to do with it. A user treats a sampling request as a recommendation for what to do. If the request asks for a specific model, number of tokens, and so on, then this is something the user can take under advisement, and either accept or change to their liking.
- **LLM**: The LLM on the client plays the part of completing the sampling request and takes a prompt originating from the server, and produces a response using its generative capabilities.

Here's a diagram depicting the overall flow:

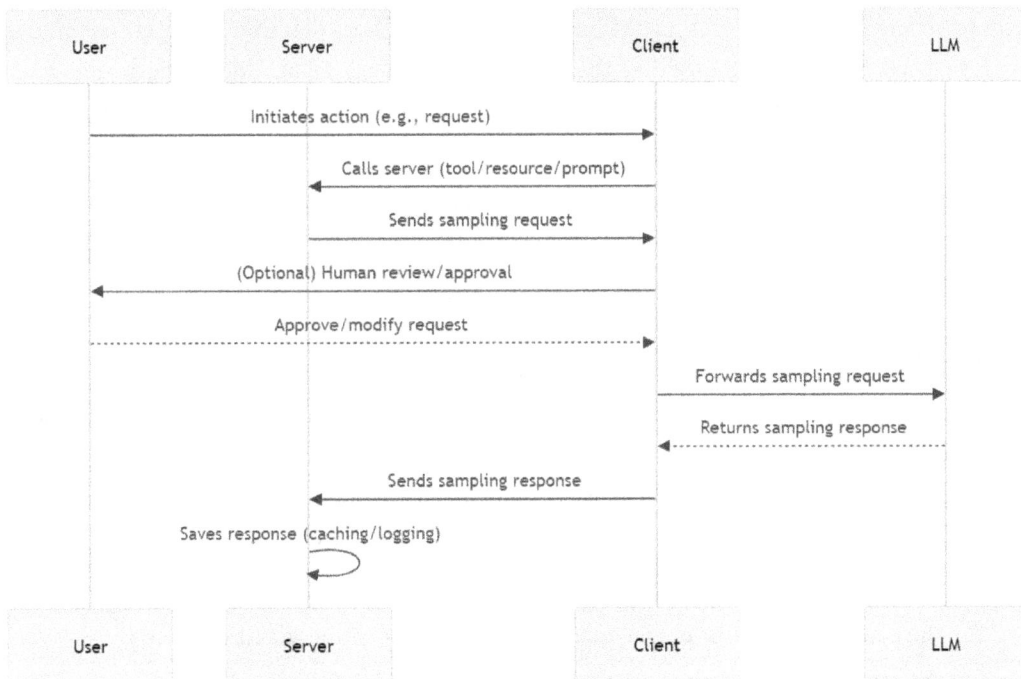

Figure 9.1 – Sampling flow

It's worth clarifying that a sampling request doesn't happen for no reason, but rather, there's an initial action that ends up triggering it. For example, the user wants to create a product, or needs help with a blog post, and so on, and that in turn leads to the server delegating part of that task back to the client.

Let's look at some specific scenarios next to understand it better.

Scenarios

We've mentioned some scenarios briefly up to this point, but let's discuss them in detail.

Writing a blog post

The act of writing a blog post is a good case, as there are aspects of it that definitely fall on the user, such as writing a draft. However, there are parts of it when an LLM does a better job, such as summarizing it for an abstract or even generating keywords (thank you, Kent Dodds, for the inspiration for this use case):

1. The user submits a draft blog post to the server.
2. The server stores the draft but asks for help with producing tags, so a sample request is sent.
3. The client uses its LLM to analyze the draft and produce a response.

Back office e-commerce

A common task for someone working in a back office as part of e-commerce is the management of products. Usually, you start off registering the product by title and capture other properties that might make sense. However, writing a compelling description might be a time-consuming task and something an LLM does better than a human. Here's how this use case could look as a sampling scenario:

1. The admin user, via the client, adds a new product with a title and keywords.
2. The server asks the client for help with creating a compelling product description with keywords as context.
3. The client produces such a description, and the server updates the product with a better description.

Mystery game

Many times, when playing games, you encounter characters in the game you want to have a conversation with; some of these characters are known as **NPCs** or **non-player characters**. Usually, these characters are limited in what they can say, as this is how they're programmed. This limitation takes away from the gaming experience, and this is where an LLM can step in and do a better job. See the following flow for how this could work:

1. The user asks to talk to a character.
2. The server retrieves character information such as name, description, motive, clues, and so on, and sends it as a sample request.
3. The client retrieves the character information from the prompt request and uses that as a system message to produce a nice conversation response.

Now that we understand more about suitable scenarios, let's discuss what the actual messages look like, as it's important to understand what is being sent back and forth. More importantly, it's important to understand what information you can configure upon sending a sample request to a client.

Messages

If you're using an SDK, you will almost never encounter a JSON-RPC, but what is interesting to know is what can be sent as part of a sampling request, so you know what type of guidance you can send to the client. Let's have a look at the following message:

Request

```
{
  "jsonrpc": "2.0",
  "id": 1,
  "method": "sampling/createMessage",
  "params": {
    "messages": [
      {
        "role": "user",
        "content": {
          "type": "text",
          "text": "Write a compelling description of this product:
            tomato, here's some keywords: red, vegetable, fresh"
        }
      }
    ],
    "modelPreferences": {
      "hints": [
        {
          "name": "claude-3-sonnet"
        }
      ],
      "intelligencePriority": 0.8,
      "speedPriority": 0.5
    },
```

```
    "systemPrompt": "You're a professional writing assistant and
      tends to want to write descriptions in a poetic way",
    "maxTokens": 100
  }
 }
}
```

In the preceding message, the following are of special interest:

- messages: Here's where you're sending the messages that get fed to the LLM.

- modelPreferences: This property is just a *preference* for which model should ideally be used. The user is the one ultimately deciding, but this should be seen as a recommendation. Also, make note of other properties we can set, such as intelligencePriority and speedPriority.

- systemPrompt: This is an important one, as this is the *personality* of the LLM and can greatly affect the outcome of the message.

- maxTokens: This property decides how many tokens will be used for this task.

Now that we have had a good look at what the server is sending to the client, let's look at what the client sends back:

Response

```
{
  "jsonrpc": "2.0",
  "id": 1,
  "result": {
    "role": "assistant",
    "content": {
      "type": "text",
      "text": "The capital of France is Paris."
    },
    "model": "claude-3-sonnet-20240307",
    "stopReason": "endTurn"
  }
}
```

Here, we can see how the LLM response comes back in the content property, and it also lets us know which model was ultimately used, among other details.

Implementing sampling

Now, we've come to the extra exciting part of this chapter, namely, how to implement sampling.

We'll cover the following parts of the implementation:

- **Server side**: How to add this to the MCP server
- **Client side**: How to enable it and what the code looks like, both to receive a request and send a response

Server implementation

To implement sampling on the server side, we need to consider when the sampling request should take place. Usually, a sampling request doesn't happen out of nowhere, but it happens in the context of an action. Imagine the following scenario. A user working in the back office of an e-commerce site adds new products for sale. They need help with the description, and it should be as compelling as possible. For the description, they will therefore use the help of a client and its LLM. Here's how it will play out:

1. The user's client calls a tool on the server that asks to create a new product.
2. The server's tool then dispatches a sample request with instructions on what to do, which is a prompt.
3. The client then takes said prompt from the sample request, calls their LLM, and returns the answer.

```ts
// index.ts, i.e the server

import { McpServer, ResourceTemplate } from
  "@modelcontextprotocol/sdk/server/mcp.js";
import { StdioServerTransport } from
  "@modelcontextprotocol/sdk/server/stdio.js";
import { z } from "zod";

// Create an MCP server
const server = new McpServer({
  name: "Demo",
  version: "1.0.0"
});
```

```
let products = [];

// create product
server.tool("create_product",
  { name: z.string(), keywords: z.string() },
  async ({ name, keywords }) => {

    // 1. Create a product
    let products = {
      id: products.length + 1,
      name: name,
      keywords: keywords,
      description: ""
    };


    let prompt = `Generate a compelling product description,
      with name: ${name} and keywords: ${keywords}`;

    // 2. Create a prompt request and run it
    const response = await server.server.createMessage({
      messages: [
        {
          role: "user",
          content: {
            type: "text",
            text: prompt,
          },
        },
      ],
      maxTokens: 500,
      model: "gpt-4o",
      systemPrompt: "You're an assistant"
    });

    // 3. Assign result to the product and construct tool response
```

```
        product.description = response.content.text;
        products.push(product);

        return {
            content: [
                { type: "text", text: `Client response:
                   ${response.content.text}` },
                { type: "text", text: `Created product:
                   ${name}, ${keywords}` }
            ]
        }
    }
);

// Start receiving messages on stdin and sending messages on stdout
const transport = new StdioServerTransport();
await server.connect(transport);
```

Let's break down what's happening:

- **Create a product:** First, we create a product and populate all the fields except `description`, which we will populate later using the sampling response.

- **Create a prompt request and run it:** Next, we send a sampling request that's passed to the client. We can specify a lot of things here, from the model, system prompt, and of course, the prompt we need help with.

- **Assign result to the product and construct tool response:** Then, we take the result from the client and its LLM and end up producing a tool response, that is, a product with a description where the latter is generated from the LLM:

```
    const response = await server.server.createMessage({
        messages: [
            {
                role: "user",
                content: {
                    type: "text",
                    text: prompt,
                },
            },
```

```
    ],
    maxTokens: 500,
    model = "gpt-4o",
    systemPrompt = "You're an assistant"
});
```

Let's test this out in VS Code. Ensure you do the following:

1. Create a server entry in mcp.json like so:

    ```
    "sample-server": {
        "command": "python",
        "args": ["path/to/server/sample-server.py"]
    }
    ```

    Make sure the server is running by clicking the **Start Server** link at the top of the server entry.

2. You also need to select which models are allowed to be used with sampling. To make the selection, open the extension view and notice the **MCP Servers – installed** section at the bottom. Click the gear icon and **Configure Model Access** for the installed server, and select the allowed models for sampling, such as **Claude Sonnet**.

3. Open the GitHub Copilot Chat window in VS Code and ensure the **Agent** mode is selected in the chat (select the icon for it at the top or run the **Chat: Open Chat** command in the command palette). Now, type the following prompt:

    ```
    "create product called tomato with keywords red and vegetable and
    delicious"
    ```

You should see a dialog asking for your permission to run that, once allowed, produces a tooling response from create_product. Here's what happened under the hood:

1. The prompt was parsed. Here's what was sent to the tool:

    ```
    {
       "keywords": "red, vegetable, delicious",
       "product_name": "tomato"
    }
    ```

2. The create_product tool was invoked.

3. The sample request was sent to the client. Because the client in VS Code has its own LLM, it produces a response to the sample request like so:

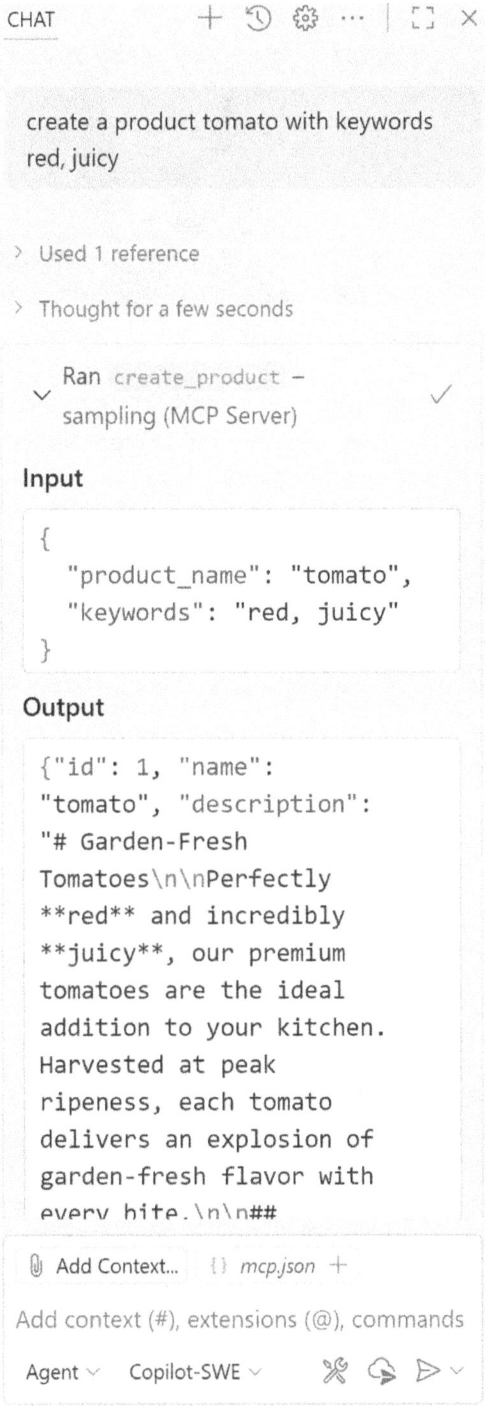

CHAT $+$ 🕑 ⚙️ ⋯ | 🔲 ✕

create a product tomato with keywords
red, juicy

> Used 1 reference

> Thought for a few seconds

⌄   Ran `create_product` –
    sampling (MCP Server)   ✓

Input

```
{
  "product_name": "tomato",
  "keywords": "red, juicy"
}
```

Output

```
{"id": 1, "name":
"tomato", "description":
"# Garden-Fresh
Tomatoes\n\nPerfectly
**red** and incredibly
**juicy**, our premium
tomatoes are the ideal
addition to your kitchen.
Harvested at peak
ripeness, each tomato
delivers an explosion of
garden-fresh flavor with
every bite.\n\n##
```

📎 Add Context...   {} *mcp.json* +

Add context (#), extensions (@), commands

Agent ⌄   Copilot-SWE ⌄   ✂️ ⟳ ▷ ⌄

Figure 9.2 – Sampling in VS Code

Let's have a look at the generated description:

```
Introducing our **Red Garden Medley**—a vibrant selection of the freshest,
most delicious red vegetables nature has to offer! Each hand-picked
assortment features juicy tomatoes, crisp red bell peppers, and sweet red
radishes, bursting with flavor and color. Perfect for salads, roasting, or
snacking, these vegetables not only brighten your plate but also deliver a
powerhouse of vitamins and antioxidants. Enjoy the taste of freshness with
every bite—delicious, nutritious, and naturally red!
```

Wouldn't you buy that tomato? :)

Okay, that's great. We got sampling to work on an MCP server, and VS Code was acting as a client, ensuring that it worked. How do we actually build a client for this in a scenario where we want to integrate this into a real solution? That's a great question and something we will cover in the next section.

Client implementation

First off, you need to let the server know that you support sampling as a feature. To do that, you need to pass the configuration when creating the client instance, like so:

```
{
  "capabilities": {
    "sampling": {}
  }
}
```

Okay, what do we need to know? For one, sampling is outside of your normal flow of calling tools, resources, and prompts. What does that mean, you wonder. Well, let's see how we listen for incoming sampling requests.

Let's have a look at what the client looks like:

```
const client = new Client(
  {
    name: "example-client",
    version: "1.0.0"
  },
  {
```

```
      capabilities: {
        sampling: {},
      }
    },
  );
```

In the preceding code, we first state that we support sampling via:

```
      capabilities: {
        sampling: {},
      }
```

Then, you need to set up a request handler to support incoming sampling messages. You use a method called setRequestHandler that takes a schema and a callback. This method is normally used for low-level implementations, so expect there to be a more convenient method developed in the future. Let's see what it looks like:

```
client.setRequestHandler(CreateMessageRequestSchema, async (request) => {
    // log the request
    console.log("[CLIENT]: ", request);

    // 1. create a prompt
    let prompt = request.params.messages[0].content.text;

    // 2. call the LLM
    let llmResponse = await callLLM(prompt as string, "You are a
      helpful assistant that generates product descriptions.");

    // 3. return the response to the server
    return {
      model: "gpt-4o-mini",
      role: "assistant",
      content: {
        type: "text",
        text: `Client LLM: ${llmResponse}`,
      },
    };
  });
```

Here's what the code is doing:

- **Parsing the incoming sample request**: Here, we parse out the incoming prompt. We could also parse out more things here, such as model, system message, and so on, if we want to make this more dynamic.

- **Query the LLM**: Here, we pass the prompt to the LLM and get our product description.

- **Send response**: Now, we have a response, but we need to create a sample response and send that to the server.

That's it, if you test running the client at this point: `https://github.com/PacktPublishing/Learn-Model-Context-Protocol-with-TypeScript/blob/main/Chapter09/code/typescript/README.md`

You should see a response similar to the following:

```
[08/16/25 19:31:40] INFO      Processing request of type CallToolRequest
server.py:624
Sampling request: [SamplingMessage(role='user',
content=TextContent(type='text', text='Create a product description
about paprika described by as red, juicy, vegetable', annotations=None,
meta=None))]
[08/16/25 19:31:43] INFO      Processing request of type ListToolsRequest
server.py:624
result: {"id": 1, "name": "paprika", "description": "**Product
Description: Paprika \u2013 The Vibrant Touch of Flavor**\n\nElevate your
culinary creations with our premium Paprika, a stunning red spice derived
from the most luscious, juicy peppers. This vibrant addition is more than
just a seasoning; it\u2019s a burst of color and taste that brings warmth
and depth to every dish.\n\nOur Paprika is sourced from high-quality, sun-
ripened vegetables, meticulously harvested at their peak to ensure maximum
flavor. With its rich, sweet notes and subtle smokiness, this natural
spice delivers a delightful punch that enhances everything from savory
stews and roasted meats to vibrant vegetable dishes and sauces.\n\nNot
only is our Paprika a feast for the eyes with its brilliant red hue, but
it's also packed with antioxidants and vitamins, making it a nutritious
choice for health-conscious cooks. Whether you sprinkle it onto a beloved
family recipe or use it to create something intentionally new, our Paprika
is versatile enough to brighten any meal.\n\nTransform everyday cooking
into an extraordinary experience with the irresistible"}
                    INFO      Processing request of type CallToolRequest
server.py:624
```

```
result: {
  "id": 1,
  "name": "paprika",
  "description": "**Product Description: Paprika – The Vibrant Touch of
Flavor**\n\nElevate your culinary creations with our premium Paprika, a
stunning red spice derived from the most luscious, juicy peppers. This
vibrant addition is more than just a seasoning; it's a burst of color
and taste that brings warmth and depth to every dish.\n\nOur Paprika is
sourced from high-quality, sun-ripened vegetables, meticulously harvested
at their peak to ensure maximum flavor. With its rich, sweet notes and
subtle smokiness, this natural spice delivers a delightful punch that
enhances everything from savory stews and roasted meats to vibrant
vegetable dishes and sauces.\n\nNot only is our Paprika a feast for the
eyes with its brilliant red hue, but it's also packed with antioxidants
and vitamins, making it a nutritious choice for health-conscious cooks.
Whether you sprinkle it onto a beloved family recipe or use it to create
something intentionally new, our Paprika is versatile enough to brighten
any meal.\n\nTransform everyday cooking into an extraordinary experience
with the irresistible"
}
```

The client does two things:

- It calls the `create_product` tool with a product name and keyword, and it ends up producing a product with an LLM-generated description like so:

```
Product Description: Paprika – The Vibrant Touch of Flavor**\n\
nElevate your culinary creations with our premium Paprika, a
stunning red spice derived from the most luscious, juicy peppers.
This vibrant addition is more than just a seasoning; it's a burst
of color and taste that brings warmth and depth to every dish.\n\
nOur Paprika is sourced from high-quality, sun-ripened vegetables,
meticulously harvested at their peak to ensure maximum flavor. With
its rich, sweet notes and subtle smokiness, this natural spice
delivers a delightful punch that enhances everything from savory
stews and roasted meats to vibrant vegetable dishes and sauces.\n\
nNot only is our Paprika a feast for the eyes with its brilliant red
hue, but it's also packed with antioxidants and vitamins, making it
a nutritious choice for health-conscious cooks. Whether you sprinkle
it onto a beloved family recipe or use it to create something
intentionally new, our Paprika is versatile enough to brighten any
```

```
meal.\n\nTransform everyday cooking into an extraordinary experience
with the irresistible
```

Doesn't that sound like paprika you would buy? Imagine sending this to an LLM and asking it to generate a photo (optional homework). What an image that would be.

- It calls the get_products tool, which lists the newly added product.

As you can see, this is a great way to delegate tasks to the client that it's better equipped to handle.

Summary

The idea with the meaning of the word *sampling* is to analyze a small sample. In the context of MCP, this is about delegation and how the server delegates part of its work to the client.

A scenario is usually started by a user, such as authoring a blog post or wanting to create a product in a back office solution. The server ends up creating a sampling request and sends that to the client as part of a task it needs help with. The client is then able to respond to said request using an LLM response.

It should also be stated that the sample request contains recommendations on model, token usage, system prompt, and much more, and that it should involve a human who either accepts these recommendations or changes them to their liking.

This is a great functionality, where an LLM on the client can be called in to help.

In our next chapter, we'll dive into yet another powerful feature of MCP, namely, elicitation, which is about improving the user experience by setting up a flow where the user is asked to pick another choice or provide more information to help the server do its job better.

Assignment

In this assignment, we'll take all our knowledge of adding sampling implementations to the client and server and apply it to a fun area, namely, a mystery game, and the conversational part. The idea is to create a character that's interesting to talk to over pre-programmed responses.

Here's how it should work:

- **User:** Talk to character *N*
- **Server:** Retrieve character info
- **Server:** Send sampling request with character info
- **Client:** Receive sampling request and produce a response using the LLM
- **Server:** Store response for caching and logging

To help you, imagine that a character is defined in a JSON file like so:

```json
[
  {
    "id": "1",
    "name": "Monsieur Lestrange",
    "description": "a 600 year old vampire",
    "personality": "very polite and will tell you a great deal of
      what it's like paying the electricity bill of a 1200 year old
        castle with bad insulation. In fact, he's quite boring and
          would rather talk about that over what you would expect
            like vampire hunters, stakes etc"

  }
]
```

Solution

You can access the solution at https://github.com/PacktPublishing/Learn-Model-Context-Protocol-with-TypeScript/blob/main/Chapter09/solution/README.md.

Quiz

1. What's the reason for using sampling?

    - A: You want to sample a smaller piece of information from a large dataset
    - B: The server needs help with a generative AI-type task, and the client can use its LLM to generate a response
    - C: The client needs the server's help with a task

2. What party initiates the sampling request?

    - A: Either of them
    - B: The client
    - C: The server

You can access the solution at https://github.com/PacktPublishing/Learn-Model-Context-Protocol-with-TypeScript/blob/main/Chapter09/solution/solution-quiz.md.

Get This Book's PDF Version and Exclusive Extras

UNLOCK NOW

Scan the QR code (or go to packtpub.com/unlock). Search for this book by name, confirm the edition, and then follow the steps on the page.

Note: Keep your invoice handy. Purchases made directly from Packt don't require an invoice.

10

Improving Interactive Workflows with Elicitation

Elicitation means the process of getting or producing something, especially information or a reaction.

Why does that matter for MCP then? The official docs have the following to say:

> The **Model Context Protocol (MCP)** *provides a standardized way for servers to request additional information from users through the client during interactions. This flow allows clients to maintain control over user interactions and data sharing while enabling servers to gather necessary information dynamically.*

So, what does that mean? It means, for some reason, the server finds it needs to involve the client additionally to ask the user for more information. Now the purpose is clearer, right?

Okay, imagine the following: as a user, you're trying to book a holiday trip, and the date you searched for isn't available. There's a way to improve that situation through using elicitation – namely, instead of just saying as a server that said trip isn't available, you make an effort to ask additional questions and perhaps suggest dates around this date that are available. Now you'll see, hopefully, how this could be a very useful technique in lots of contexts, to increase the chance of something being sold or booked, and so on.

In this chapter, we'll learn how to do the following:

- Explain what elicitation is
- Learn when to use it
- Build an elicitation integration

The chapter covers the following topics:

- Why elicitation?
- Implementing elicitation
- Elicitation flow
- JSON-RPC messages
- Implementing the server-side functionality
- Testing elicitation with VS Code
- Implementing elicitation in the client

Why elicitation?

Okay, we've already tried describing, at the beginning of this chapter, what situations might motivate the use of elicitation in MCP, but let's try to summarize some main motivating factors:

- **Task complexity**: For some tasks, it's simply not possible to provide all the information needed up front. This might be scenarios where the user needs to make selections through a workflow. For example, the user might need to make multiple choices as they purchase a ticket to the movies. They start with wanting to book a certain film on a given day, but then need to be asked whether they need a premium seat or other customizations available. Or, take a scenario such as booking a train ticket, where you need to make choices such as a ticket with a numbered seat, whether the ticket is physical or an e-ticket, and so on. You could ask for all this information up front, but it might make for a tedious user experience, and it might be better to start off asking for less input.

- **Increase the conversion rate on a website**: Another angle is for companies to ensure they have a better *conversion rate*, meaning that more users on the website become actual customers. For example, if a user wants a red sweater and you don't have it in stock at the moment, then you might want to ask the user if they're okay with a different color or want to sign up on a waitlist to order it automatically when it comes in. This type of behavior is more likely to improve your sales as a company.

- **Improved user experience**: As a logical conclusion of the preceding angle, the overall user experience is likely to improve if the user can be met with something else than just a *no*, and instead be faced with reasonable choices.

All in all, elicitation can be a great way to improve your app. Let's try to look at the implementation side of things next.

Implementing elicitation

So, we want to use elicitation – great. But first, there's a set of guidelines we should know about. Here's what the official docs have to say:

For trust, safety, and security:

- Servers MUST NOT use elicitation to request sensitive information
- Applications SHOULD:

    - Provide a UI that makes it clear which server is requesting information
    - Allow users to review and modify their responses before sending
    - Respect user privacy and provide clear decline and cancel options

Elicitation flow

In general, what happens during elicitation is that the server decides it doesn't have enough information to complete a call to a tool, resource, or prompt.

What's important to understand is that this happens as a two-step process:

1. The server asks the client if it's okay to initiate an elicitation request towards the user.
2. The client asks the user to submit information.

The user can both accept or decline in both 1) and 2); see the following sequence diagram explaining this process. To hopefully make it easier to understand, we've chosen a trip-booking process:

Figure 10.1 – JSON-RPC messages

Now that we've explained the overall flow, let's see what the JSON-RPC messages look like.

Like with most MCP features, there are specific messages in JSON-RPC that need to be sent and received:

Request message

```
{
  "jsonrpc": "2.0",
  "id": 1,
  "method": "elicitation/create",
  "params": {
    "message": "Please provide your GitHub username",
    "requestedSchema": {
      "type": "object",
      "properties": {
        "name": {
          "type": "string"
        }
      },
      "required": ["name"]
    }
  }
}
```

In the preceding message, we can see how `message` contains the payload for what we're asking for – a user choice to be made or some explanation of what we're asking for. `requestedSchema` is a schema that defines what information you need as a server, so here it's important you specify both the name of what you need, its type, and any other rules you want to impose. See this example schema, where the server asks for `name`, `email`, and age. For each parameter, we specify both type and description, and in some places, we specify format and even validation rules, such as you should be at least 18 years of age:

```
"requestedSchema": {
  "type": "object",
  "properties": {
    "name": {
      "type": "string",
      "description": "Your full name"
    },
    "email": {
```

```
        "type": "string",
        "format": "email",
        "description": "Your email address"
      },
      "age": {
        "type": "number",
        "minimum": 18,
        "description": "Your age"
      }
    },
    "required": ["name", "email"]
  }
```

Let's have a look at a response. Specifically, this is an *accept*-type response where the user has agreed to submit the information requested of them.

Response message

```
{
  "jsonrpc": "2.0",
  "id": 2,
  "result": {
    "action": "accept",
    "content": {
      "name": "Monalisa Octocat",
      "email": "octocat@github.com",
      "age": 30
    }
  }
}
```

It's actually possible for the user to say, *"I don't want to provide this information"*. If that happens, then a reject type message is sent as a response instead, and looks like so:

Reject message

```
{
  "jsonrpc": "2.0",
  "id": 2,
  "result": {
```

```
        "action": "decline"
    }
}
```

Here, it's clear that the user declines to submit the requested information.

A third type of response is cancellation. It's very similar to decline, but it's more like the user dismisses the elicitation dialog by typing *Escape*, clicking to close a dialog, so it's more like the user ignores interacting, rather than saying an explicit *No*.

Request schema types

We've mentioned the general request schema and an example. However, there are quite a few supported types, and it's important to know they exist so you use them correctly. These types are presented to the user as part of the elicitation process, and it means the user either uses a drop list, a text input field, or some other UI element to provide the information.

- `string`: This one is about asking for a string. You can add quite a few checks. Here's what the schema looks like:

```
{
    "type": "string",
    "title": "Display Name",
    "description": "Description text",
    "minLength": 3,
    "maxLength": 50,
    "pattern": "^[A-Za-z]+$",
    "format": "email"
}
```

  Here, you can see that you can limit both `minLength` and `maxLength` and even set patterns, which can be highly useful in case you're asking for a specific allowed structure, such as an address, telephone number, social security number, and so on.

- `number`: This one is slightly less complex, but by setting a minimum and maximum value, it helps the user understand what's allowed and not. See this schema:

```
{
    "type": "number", // or "integer"
    "title": "Display Name",
    "description": "Description text",
```

```
        "minimum": 0,
        "maximum": 100
    }
```

See the `minimum` and `maximum` values, which you can specify.

- `boolean`: For this type, the idea is to get the user to answer *yes* or *no*. You can also specify whether there should be a default value:

```
    {
        "type": "boolean",
        "title": "Display Name",
        "description": "Description text",
        "default": false
    }
```

- `enum`: This one should be thought of as a list of options, which can be useful if you want the user to choose between trips on different dates, for example:

```
    {
        "type": "string",
        "title": "Display Name",
        "description": "Description text",
        "enum": ["option1", "option2", "option3"],
        "enumNames": ["Option 1", "Option 2", "Option 3"]
    }
```

With that in mind, let's see if we can use several of these types, as we will show the implementation parts in the next section.

Implementing the server-side functionality

Let's start with the server. What we need to know is that a server feature, tool, resource, or prompt should run its course, and if it detects that more information is needed, it should produce an elicitation message.

First, let's see how we produce such a message. What we need to do is call a function called `elicitInput`. Said function needs an object with a message and a `requestedSchema`. The message is what's shown to the user and the schema defines the structure of the data we expect back. Here's an example:

```
const result = await server.server.elicitInput({
    message: `No trip available at on ${date}. Would you like to
      check alternative dates?`,
    requestedSchema: {
      type: "object",
      properties: {
        checkAlternatives: {
          type: "Boolean",
          title: "Alternate date",
          description: "Fill in other date"
        },
        newDate: {
          type: "string",
          title: "New Date",
          description: "Please provide a new date"
        }
      },
      required: ["checkAlternatives"]
    }
});
```

In this code, we define the message to be shown to the user – namely, No trip available at on
${date}. Would you like to check alternative dates? and the input we expect the client
to provide: checkAlternatives and newDate. The first value is a boolean indicating whether the
user wants to check for alternative dates, and the second value is a string representing the new
date they would like to try.

We can now place this call to elicitInput in, for example, a tool call like so:

```
server.tool(
  "book-trip",
  {
    date: z.string()
  },
  async ({ date }) => {
    // 1. Check availability
    const available = await checkAvailability(date);
```

```
    if (!available) {
      // 2. Ask user if they want to try alternative dates
      const result = await server.server.elicitInput({ /**/ })
      // TODO, read the response and act accordingly


    }
  }
);
```

In this code, we declare a tool called book-trip that takes a date as input and checks its availability. If the date is not available, it prompts the user to provide alternative dates by starting an elicitation process.

In fact, let's see how we can handle the response that comes from the client.

```
    // 3. Check if user provided a new date
      if (result.action === "accept" && result.content?.checkAlternatives) {
        let ok = await checkAvailability(result.content?.newDate as string);
        if(ok) {
          return {
            content: [
              {
                type: "text",
                text: `Trip booked on alternate date:
                  ${result.content?.newDate}`
              }
            ]
          };
        } else {
          // 3b. No trip available on new date
          return {
            content: [
              {
                type: "text",
                text: `No trip available on ${result.content?.newDate}.`
              }
            ]
          };
        }
```

```
    }

    // 4. User didn't provide a new date
    return {
      content: [{
        type: "text",
        text: "No booking made. Original date not available."
      }]
    };
```

What's important to highlight in this code is how we read the result object to check first what the user opted to do. If result.action === "accept", that means the user said okay to starting an elicitation process. However, we also need to check if the user thereafter said okay to providing data, which means our check looks like the following code, where we also check if checkAlternatives is true:

```
if(result.action === "accept" && result.content?.checkAlternatives) {
    // check if user said ok to start elicitation process AND chose to say
    yes to submitting data in a drop list.

}
```

Now, the next step is to check if data was actually submitted by the user, and if so, take appropriate action and book them, as in this scenario:

```
if (result.action === "accept" && result.content?.checkAlternatives) {
    let ok = await checkAvailability(result.content?.newDate as string);
    if(ok) {
      return {
        content: [
          {
            type: "text",
            text: `Trip booked on alternate date:
              ${result.content?.newDate}`
          }
        ]
      };
    }
```

Now, let's move on to testing elicitation features with VS Code.

Testing elicitation with VS Code

To test elicitation features with VS Code, you will need to add the MCP server as an entry to the `mcp.json` file like so:

```
"server": {
    "type": "sse",
    "url": "http://localhost:8000/sse"
}
```

Then, ensure you're in *Agent* mode before you type the following prompt:

```
Book trip on 2025-02-01
```

You should see the following play out in the user interface:

1. **Typing a prompt and tool invocation**: Here, you type your request to book a trip, and the system recognizes it as a tool invocation. You need to approve the tool invocation for it to proceed:

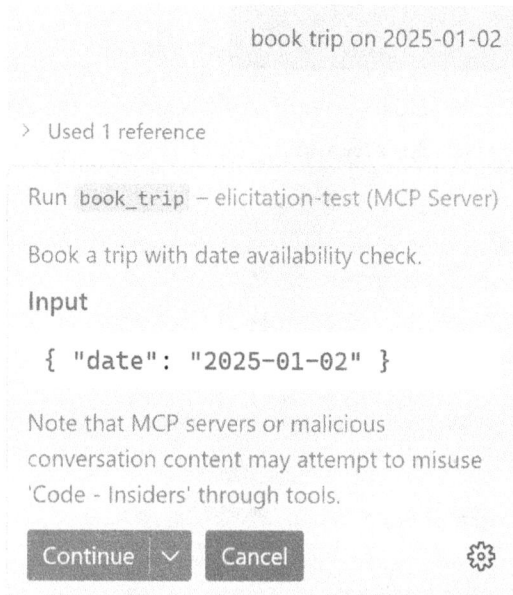

Figure 10.2 – Typing a prompt and seeing a tool invocation

2. **Approving the tool invocation**: Once you approve the tool invocation, you should see the interface telling you the selected data is busy, and you'll be asked to respond, meaning now it will take you into crafting an elicitation response:

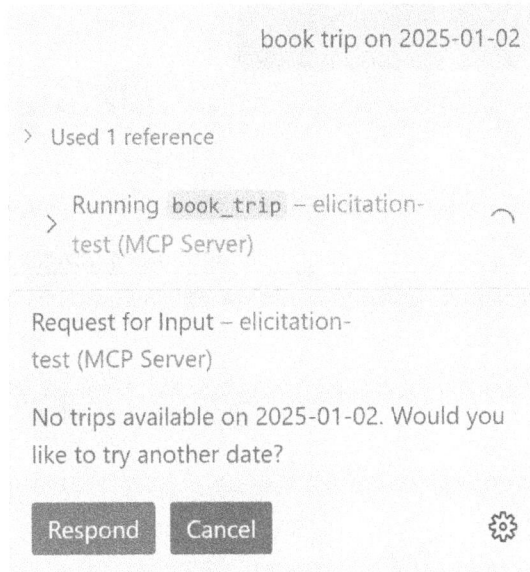

book trip on 2025-01-02

> Used 1 reference

> Running `book_trip` – elicitation-test (MCP Server)

Request for Input – elicitation-test (MCP Server)

No trips available on 2025-01-02. Would you like to try another date?

Respond   Cancel

Figure 10.3 – Approving the tool invocation

3. **Crafting an elicitation response**: Now you will need to craft a response based on the user's input and the system's requirements. This involves using the elicitation schema you defined earlier to gather any additional information needed. Here's how that looks in the user interface. In the following screenshot, you're asked whether you want to respond or not. If you choose **true**, it will continue to ask you for another date; if not, it will stop the elicitation process:

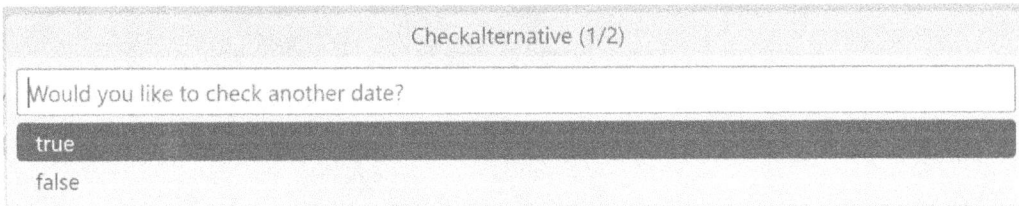

Checkalternative (1/2)

Would you like to check another date?

true
false

Figure 10.4 – Crafting an elicitation response

4. **Responding to the elicitation**: Once you've selected to continue, you need to fill in the alternate date like so:

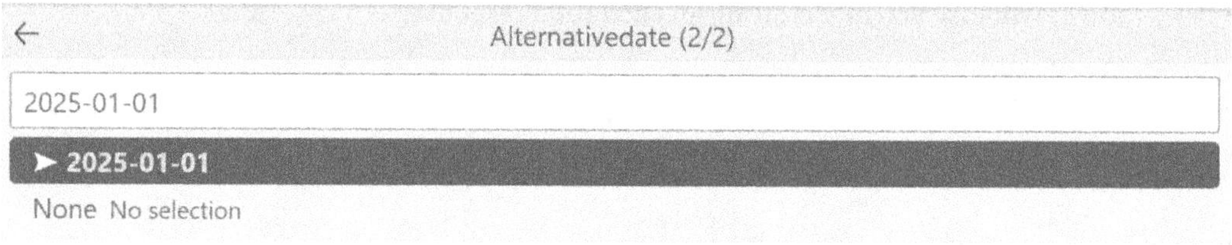

Figure 10.5 – Responding to the elicitation

5. **The final result**: Because you've now submitted an alternative date, the server will check to see if this response is okay. In the following screenshot, you can see that that's the case and you receive a confirmation for your booking:

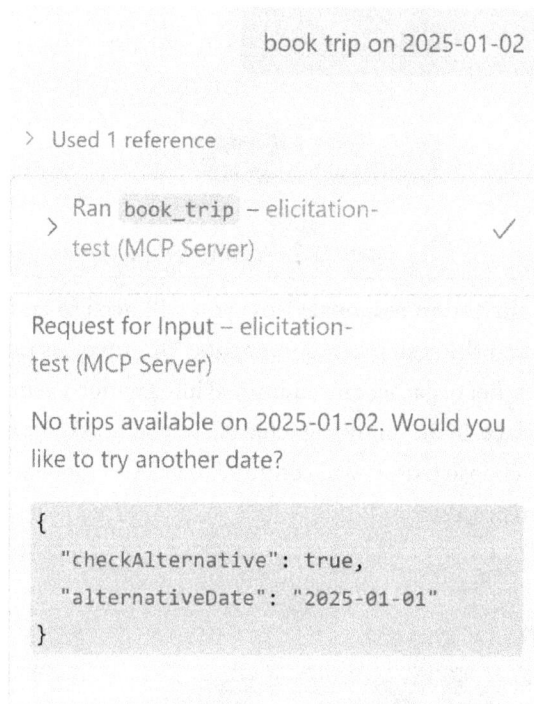

Figure 10.6 – The final result

That completes elicitation on the server side.

Implementing elicitation in the client

Great – now we have a good understanding of the server side of things, and even how to test it with VS Code. Let's proceed to implement the client side.

To implement elicitation in the TypeScript client, you need to set up a request handler that takes `ElicitRequestSchema` as a parameter and returns an `ElicitResult`. Here's what that looks like in the following code:

```
client.setRequestHandler(ElicitRequestSchema, (params) => {
    // Handle elicitation request here
    return {
        action: "accept",
        content: {
            checkAlternative: true,
            alternativeDate: "2025-01-01"
        }
    };
});
```

What you see is the client calling `setRequestHandler` to register the elicitation request handler. The second parameter, `params`, contains the message and the request input schema sent from the server. You also see how we return an object with two parameters: `action` and `content`. The `action` parameter can be either `accept` or `decline`. If you choose `accept`, you should also provide a `content` object that conforms to the schema defined by the server.

Let's look at how to call `params` next and see what the server actually sends us:

```
console.log(`${params.params.message}`);
console.log("\nProvide the following information:");
let schema = params.params.requestedSchema.properties;
for (let key in schema) {
    console.log(`[INPUT]: '${key}' of type ${schema[key].type}`);
}
```

In the preceding code, we can see how the message or title we should display to the user is accessible through `params.params.message`. The parameters we should show to the user can be found under `params.params.requestedSchema.properties`. By iterating through these properties, we can dynamically construct the input prompts for the user.

Our code so far looks like so:

```
client.setRequestHandler(ElicitRequestSchema, (params) => {
    console.log(`${params.params.message}`);
    console.log("\nProvide the following information:");
    let schema = params.params.requestedSchema.properties;
    for (let key in schema) {
        console.log(`[INPUT]: '${key}' of type ${schema[key].type}`);
    }

    // TODO, ask for this input instead of faking the response like below

    return {
      action: "accept",
      content: {
        checkAlternatives: true,
        newDate: "2025-01-01"
      },
    };
});
```

We can change it to a reject message by changing the return object to this:

```
return {
  action: "reject"
}
```

Here, you can see how we don't even provide a content object since the user has declined to provide any information.

A third choice, as a user, is to say we *accepted* to provide input data but then changed our minds, which would look like so:

```
return {
  action: "accept",
  content: {
    checkAlternatives: false,
    newDate: ""
  },
};
```

As you can see, checkAlternatives is set to false, and newDate contains an empty string.

How is client.setRequestHandler even triggered in the first place? Great question – it happens like so, with a tool call in the client:

```
async function main() {
  await client.connect(sseTransport);
  const result = await client.callTool({
    name: "book-trip",
    arguments: {
        date: "2025-01-02"
    }
  });

    console.log("Tool result: ", result);
}
```

See the call to client.callTool? This is what triggers the elicitation process. The server responds with an elicitation request, providing the data we submit isn't a valid date. Then the client handles this request using the setRequestHandler we defined earlier.

In fact, let's summarize our learning with this sequence diagram:

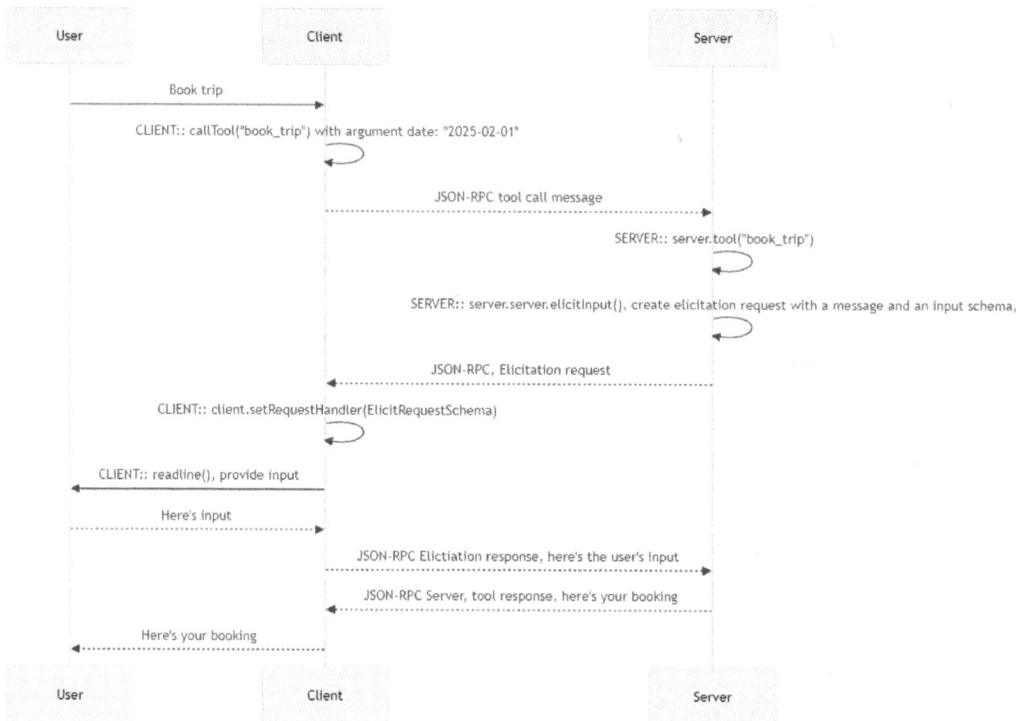

Figure 10.7 – Flow for implementing elicitation in the client in Typescript

As you can see, generally, there are a few permutations to keep track of where the user can cancel at different stages, but the key is to ensure that the client is able to handle these different scenarios gracefully.

Summary

In this chapter, we've covered the elicitation process in detail, including how it is initiated and the different scenarios in which it can occur. We've also explored the various responses that can be sent back to the server during this process. Elicitation is when the system actively seeks to gather more information from the user in order to fulfill a request or clarify intent.

We've also seen how the user can accept as well as abort at different stages of the process.

Finally, elicitation can be a powerful tool for improving user interactions and ensuring that the system is able to meet user needs effectively.

In the next chapter, we'll explore how to secure your MCP server and client using various authentication methods such as Basic Auth, JWT, and OAuth2.1.

Assignment

So far, you've seen code that handles a booking scenario. Now your task is to implement a scenario where the user finishes a booking process but is asked whether they want to be a member or not to receive a discount for future bookings. Use the code at https://github.com/PacktPublishing/Learn-Model-Context-Protocol-with-TypeScript/blob/main/Chapter10/code/README.md.

Solution

You can access the solution at https://github.com/PacktPublishing/Learn-Model-Context-Protocol-with-TypeScript/blob/main/Chapter10/solution/README.md.

Quiz

An elicitation process is technically initiated when:

- A: The server determines that it needs more information from the user to complete a request.
- B: The user provides input that requires further clarification or details.
- C: The system needs to confirm user intent before proceeding.

You can access the solution at https://github.com/PacktPublishing/Learn-Model-Context-Protocol-with-TypeScript/blob/main/Chapter10/solution/solution-quiz.md.

11

Securing Your Application

In many cases, a prerequisite for a web application is to secure it before you put it in production. There are definitely cases where you don't need to do that, but in most cases, you want to make sure that your application is secure and that only authorized users can access certain parts of it.

Let's look at some scenarios and what security measures you should consider for each of them:

Scenario	Sensitivity level	Security measures	Rationale
Public data that anyone can access	Minimal risk of exposure	Basic security or none	If you want to prevent bots or similar from using your API excessively, opt for having users sign up for an API key
Some public data and some protected data	Moderate risk of exposure	Basic security with HTTPS and API keys	Protect sensitive data while allowing public access to non-sensitive data
Sensitive personal data (e.g., health records and financial information)	High risk of exposure	Advanced security with HTTPS, OAuth 2.0/2.1, encryption, and RBAC	Comply with regulations such as **General Data Protection Regulation (GDPR)** and **Health Insurance Portability and Accountability Act (HIPAA)**, and ensure data privacy and integrity

Table 11.1 – Security measures scenarios

With that in mind, let's look at some common security measures you can implement in your web application.

In this chapter, you will learn how to do the following:

- Add basic authentication to your application
- Secure your application with a **JSON Web Token (JWT)**
- Use OAuth2 to secure your application for an even better security posture

The chapter covers the following topics:

- Basic authentication
- Hardening security with JWT
- How does JWT work?
- Creating a JWT
- Integrating JWT in our middleware (and MCP server)
- OAuth2

Basic authentication

Basic authentication is the simplest way to secure your application. It involves sending a username and password with each request to the server. This is definitely not the most secure way to do it. If it's not that secure, why would you use it? Well, there are scenarios where it's better to have at least *some* security than no security at all. For example, if you have an API and it's generally open to the public but you want to restrict access to certain endpoints, basic authentication can be a good option.

How does it work under the hood? The client sends an `Authorization` header with each request. The value of this header is the word `Basic` followed by a space and a Base64-encoded string of the format `username:password`. The server then decodes this string and checks whether the username and password are valid. Here's the flow of how it works:

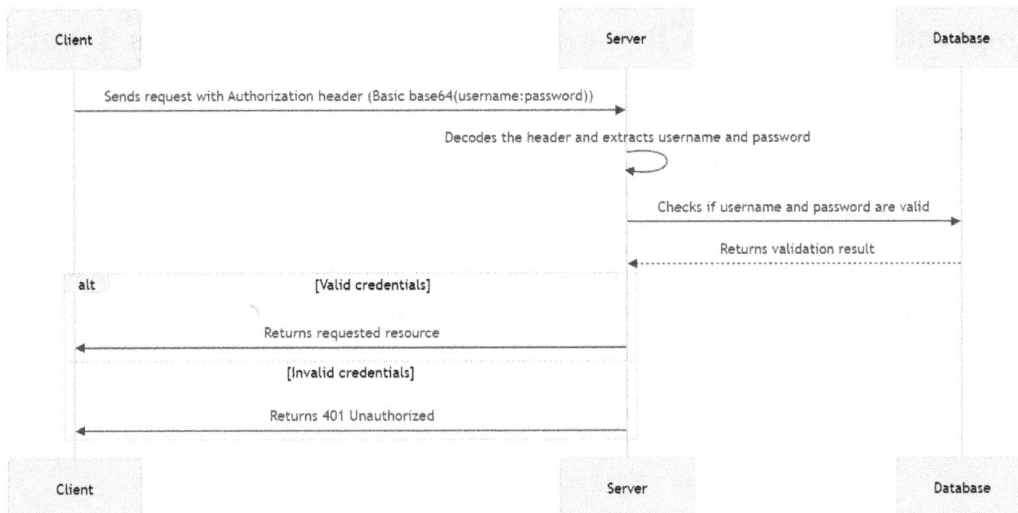

Figure 11.1 – Basic authentication flow

Sometimes the basic authentication consists of an API key instead of a username and password. The API key is sent in the same way as the username and password, but it's just a single string that identifies the client. The server then checks whether the API key is valid.

From a code viewpoint, here's what it can look like when the client sends a request with basic authentication:

```
// send api key
const apiKey = 'your_api_key';
const encodedApiKey = btoa(apiKey);
const headers = new Headers();
headers.append('Authorization', `Basic ${encodedApiKey}`);
fetch('https://api.example.com/endpoint', { headers })
    .then(response => response.json())
    .then(data => console.log(data));
```

Using basic authentication for our MCP server

Let's leverage this technique to secure our MCP server. After all, we don't want just anyone to be able to access our server and potentially misuse it. To get this to work, we need two things:

- A server middleware that checks for the Authorization header and validates the credentials
- The client that sends the Authorization header with each request

Implementing the MCP server and bootstrapping it as a web app

First things first, we need to implement the MCP server and bootstrap it as a web app. In doing so, we will have a web server that can handle MCP requests and responses. Once we're done with this, we can add the middleware to the server that will add the security layer.

For TypeScript, we can use Express.js. Bootstrapping an Express server is quite straightforward, but we need to remember to set up a route for the MCP endpoint:

```typescript
import express from "express";
import { randomUUID } from "node:crypto";
import { McpServer } from "@modelcontextprotocol/sdk/server/mcp.js";
import { StreamableHTTPServerTransport } from
  "@modelcontextprotocol/sdk/server/streamableHttp.js";
import { isInitializeRequest } from "@modelcontextprotocol/sdk/types.js"


const app = express();
app.use(express.json());


// Map to store transports by session ID
const transports: { [sessionId: string]: StreamableHTTPServerTransport } =
  {};


// Handle POST requests for client-to-server communication
app.post('/mcp', async (req, res) => {
  // Check for existing session ID
  const sessionId = req.headers['mcp-session-id'] as string | undefined;
  let transport: StreamableHTTPServerTransport;

  if (sessionId && transports[sessionId]) {
    // Reuse existing transport
    transport = transports[sessionId];
  } else if (!sessionId && isInitializeRequest(req.body)) {
    // New initialization request
    transport = new StreamableHTTPServerTransport({
      sessionIdGenerator: () => randomUUID(),
      onsessioninitialized: (sessionId) => {
```

```
      // Store the transport by session ID
      transports[sessionId] = transport;
    }
  });


  // Clean up transport when closed
  transport.onclose = () => {
    if (transport.sessionId) {
      delete transports[transport.sessionId];
    }
  };
  const server = new McpServer({
    name: "example-server",
    version: "1.0.0"
  });


  // ... set up server resources, tools, and prompts ...


  // Connect to the MCP server
  await server.connect(transport);
} else {
  // Invalid request
  res.status(400).json({
    jsonrpc: '2.0',
    error: {
      code: -32000,
      message: 'Bad Request: No valid session ID provided',
    },
    id: null,
  });
  return;
}


// Handle the request
await transport.handleRequest(req, res, req.body);
});
```

```
// Reusable handler for GET and DELETE requests
const handleSessionRequest = async (req: express.Request,
  res: express.Response) => {
  const sessionId = req.headers['mcp-session-id'] as string | undefined;
  if (!sessionId || !transports[sessionId]) {
    res.status(400).send('Invalid or missing session ID');
    return;
  }

  const transport = transports[sessionId];
  await transport.handleRequest(req, res);
};

// Handle GET requests for server-to-client notifications via SSE
app.get('/mcp', handleSessionRequest);

// Handle DELETE requests for session termination
app.delete('/mcp', handleSessionRequest);

app.listen(3000);
```

Creating the middleware

To create our middleware, we need to remember how it should work. The middleware should check for the Authorization header, validate the credentials, and either allow the request to proceed or return an error response.

With that in mind, here's what the middleware can look like:

```
app.use((req, res, next) => {
    console.log('Request received:', req.method, req.url, req.headers);
    console.log('Headers:', req.headers["authorization"]);
    if(!req.headers["authorization"]) {
        res.status(401).send('Unauthorized');
        return;
    }

    let token = req.headers["authorization"];
```

```
    if(!isValid(token)) {
        res.status(403).send('Forbidden');
        return;
    }


    console.log('Middleware executed');
    next();
});
```

The logic of the middleware is as follows:

- Check whether the Authorization header is present. If not, return a 401 Unauthorized response.
- Validate the token; if the token is invalid, return a 403 Forbidden response.
- If the token is valid, proceed with the request and add a custom header to the response. We proceed with the request by calling call_next(request), which will pass the request to the next middleware or the actual endpoint handler.

To add a middleware in TypeScript, you can either use app.use() or you can add it per route. Let's show both ways in Express.js:

```
// Middleware function
function middleware(req, res, next) {
    console.log('Request received:', req.method, req.url, req.headers);
    console.log('Headers:', req.headers["authorization"]);
    if(!req.headers["authorization"]) {
        res.status(401).send('Unauthorized');
        return;
    }


    let token = req.headers["authorization"];


    if(!isValid(token)) {
        res.status(403).send('Forbidden');
        return;
    }


    console.log('Middleware executed');
    next();
```

```
};

// alt1: global middleware, this will apply to all routes
app.use(middleware);

// alt2: per-route middleware
app.post('/protected', middleware, (req, res) => {
    res.send('Protected resource');
});
```

Testing the middleware

To test the middleware, we can use the same client code as before, but this time, we need to include the `Authorization` header with a valid token.

Here's how the client code can look:

```
const apiKey = 'my_api_key';
const token = btoa(apiKey);
const headers = {'Authorization': `Bearer ${token}`};
const response = await fetch('http://127.0.0.1:8000/protected',
    {headers});
console.log(response.status);
console.log(await response.text());
```

To test it with an MCP client, it's the same idea, but we need to know how to pass custom headers with the MCP client. Here's how you can do it.

To pass custom headers with the MCP client in TypeScript, you need to do two things:

- Define a client transport option object that includes the headers. Here's what that looks like:

    ```
    let options: StreamableHTTPClientTransportOptions = {
        sessionId: sessionId,
        requestInit: {
          headers: {
              "Authorization": "secret123"
          }
        }
    };
    ```

- Pass the options object to the transport when creating it:

```
const transport = new StreamableHTTPClientTransport(
    new URL(serverUrl),
    options
);
```

Here's the complete example:

```
import { Client } from "@modelcontextprotocol/sdk/client/index.js";
import { StreamableHTTPClientTransport,
  StreamableHTTPClientTransportOptions } from
    "@modelcontextprotocol/sdk/client/streamableHttp.js";


let sessionId: string | undefined = undefined;

// define a client transport option object
let options: StreamableHTTPClientTransportOptions = {
  sessionId: sessionId,
  requestInit: {
    headers: {
      "Authorization": "secret123"
    }
  }
};


// pass the options object to the transport
async function main() {
    const transport = new StreamableHTTPClientTransport(
        new URL(serverUrl),
        options
    );

    const client = new Client({
        name: "example-client",
        version: "1.0.0"
    });
```

```
    await client.connect(transport);
    sessionId = transport.sessionId;
    console.log("Connected to MCP server with session ID:", sessionId);

    let toolsResult = await client.listTools();

    console.log("Available tools:", toolsResult);
}
```

Let's look at JWT next.

Hardening security with JWT

What's the benefit of JWT rather than basic authentication? Well, with JWT, you can have more granular control over what the client can do. You can include claims in the token that specify what the client is allowed to do. For example, you can include a claim that specifies that the client is only allowed to read data, but not write data. This would look like something like this:

```
{
  "sub": "1234567890",
  "name": "User Userson",
  "admin": true,
  "iat": 1516239022,
  "exp": 1516242622,
 "scopes": ["User.Read"]
}
```

This token payload specifies that the client is allowed to read user data. The server can then check the token and see whether the client has the required scope to perform the requested action. There are a lot of other benefits as well, such as the following:

- **Stateless:** The server doesn't need to store any session information. The token contains all the information needed to authenticate the client.

- **Scalability:** Since the server doesn't need to store any session information, it can easily scale horizontally.

- **Security:** The token can be signed and/or encrypted to ensure its integrity and confidentiality.

- **Flexibility:** The token can include any number of custom claims, allowing for a wide range of use cases.

- **Interoperability**: JWT is a widely adopted standard, making it easy to integrate with other systems and services.

Okay, all of that sounds great, but let's take you through what you need to do to *upgrade* your basic authentication to JWT. First off, let's talk about how JWT works.

How does JWT work?

JWT is a compact, URL-safe means of representing claims to be transferred between two parties. The claims in a JWT are encoded as a JSON object. This JSON object has three parts separated by dots (.):

- **Header**: This typically consists of two parts: the type of the token (JWT) and the signing algorithm being used, such as HMAC SHA256 or RSA. A header typically looks like this:

```
{
  "alg": "HS256",
  "typ": "JWT"
}
```

  Here we see that the algorithm used is HMAC SHA256, and the type is JWT. This information is important for the server to know how to verify the token.

- **Payload**: This contains the claims. Claims are statements about an entity (typically, the user) and additional data. There are three types of claims: registered, public, and private claims. A payload typically looks like this:

```
{
  "sub": "1234567890",
  "name": "User Userson",
  "admin": false,
  "iat": 1516239022,
  "exp": 1516242622,
  "scopes": ["User.Write", "User.Write"]
}
```

  This payload represents a user with an ID of 1234567890, the name User Userson, who is not an admin, and the User.Write and User.Read scopes. The iat claim represents the time the token was issued, and the exp claim represents the time the token expires.

- **Signature**: This is used to verify that the sender of the JWT is who it says it is and to ensure that the message wasn't changed along the way.

Creating a JWT

Okay, so we know what parts we have, but how do we create a JWT? Well, it's actually quite simple. You can use a library to create the JWT for you. Here's how you can do it:

```
// npm install jsonwebtoken
import jwt from "jsonwebtoken";

export function createJWT(): string {
    const header = {
        alg: "HS256",
        typ: "JWT"
    };

    const payload = {
        sub: "1234567890",                // Subject (user ID)
        name: "User usersson",            // Custom claim
        admin: true,                      // Custom claim
        iat: Math.floor(Date.now() / 1000), // Issued at
        exp: Math.floor(Date.now() / 1000) + 60 * 60, // Expires in 1 hour
        scopes: ["Admin.Write", "User.Read"]
    };

    const secret = "your-256-bit-secret";
    const token = jwt.sign(payload, secret, {
        algorithm: "HS256", header: header });
    return token;
}
```

Here, we see how we construct the header and payload as JavaScript objects. We then use the jsonwebtoken library to sign the token with a secret. Currently, the token is Base64-encoded and can be used as a bearer token in the Authorization header. If you were to reverse the Base64 encoding, you would see that the token consists of three parts separated by dots (.), namely the header, payload, and signature. To decode the token, however, you would see the header and payload in JSON format.

Validating the JWT

We also need to know how to validate the JWT. What we do when we validate is ensure that the token is valid, not expired, and that the signature is correct. That's by no means all we can do, but it's a good start. Here's how you can validate a JWT:

```
import jwt from "jsonwebtoken";

export function validateJWT(token: string): boolean {
    const secret = "your-256-bit-secret";
    try {
        const decoded = jwt.verify(token, secret, {
            algorithms: ["HS256"] }) as jwt.JwtPayload;
        console.log("Decoded Payload:", decoded);
        return true;
    } catch (error) {
        if (error instanceof jwt.TokenExpiredError) {
            console.log("Token has expired");
        } else {
            console.log("Invalid token");
        }
        return false;
    }
}
```

Here, the code checks that the token is valid, not expired, and that the signature is correct. If the token is valid, it prints the decoded payload. If the token has expired or is invalid, it prints an error message.

We mentioned earlier that these structural checks are a good start. What other checks should we do? Here are some ideas of things you can check:

- The iss (issuer) claim to ensure the token was issued by a trusted authority, for example, your auth server.
- The aud (audience) claim to ensure the token is intended for your application. Valid values could be your MCP server URL.
- The nbf (not before) claim to ensure the token is not used before a certain time.

- Scopes or roles, to ensure the client has the required permissions to perform the request-ed action. Examples of scopes could be User.Read, User.Write, Admin.Read, and Admin.Write, and the roles could be User, Admin, and so on. These look similar, but scopes are typically more granular than roles.

Integrating the JWT in our middleware (and MCP server)

So far, you've seen how we perform basic authentication and check whether a credential is valid as part of our middleware. Now, let's see how we can integrate JWT validation. Our plan is as follows:

- Create a JWT for testing. We will do so with a utility script. In a real-world application, you would get the token from an **identity provider (IDP)** such as Auth0, Keycloak, or Entra ID.
- Update the middleware to validate the JWT.
- Update the client to send the JWT in the Authorization header.

Creating a JWT for testing

Here's the utility code we will use to create a JWT token for testing, including functions for gen-erating a JWT and validating it:

```
import jwt from "jsonwebtoken";
import fs from "fs";

export function createJWT(): string {
    const header = {
        alg: "HS256",
        typ: "JWT"
    };

    const payload = {
        sub: "1234567890",                  // Subject (user ID)
        name: "User usersson",               // Custom claim
        admin: true,                        // Custom claim
        iat: Math.floor(Date.now() / 1000), // Issued at
        exp: Math.floor(Date.now() / 1000) + 60 * 60, // Expires in 1 hour
        scopes: ["Admin.Write", "User.Read"]
    };

    const secret = "your-256-bit-secret";
```

```
    const token = jwt.sign(payload, secret, {
        algorithm: "HS256", header: header });
    // save to .env file
    fs.writeFileSync(".env", `JWT_TOKEN=${token}\n`);
}


export function validateJWT(token: string): jwt.JwtPayload | null {
    const secret = "your-256-bit-secret";
    try {
        const decoded = jwt.verify(token, secret, {
            algorithms: ["HS256"] }) as jwt.JwtPayload;
        return decoded;
    } catch (error) {
        if (error instanceof jwt.TokenExpiredError) {
            console.log("Token has expired");
        } else {
            console.log("Invalid token");
        }
        return null;
    }
}


if (import.meta.url === `file://${process.argv[1]}`) {
    createJWT();
}
```

In this code, we create a JWT with a header, payload, and signature. The createJWT function generates the token and writes it to a .env file. Note how the validateJWT function validates the token and returns the decoded claims if the token is valid.

Updating the client to send the JWT

Let's move on to the client. It will need to load the token from the .env file and send it in the Authorization header. Here's how you can do it:

```
import dotenv from "dotenv";


dotenv.config();
```

```
function getAuthToken(): string {
    const token = process.env.JWT_TOKEN;
    return `Bearer ${token}`;
}


const headers = { 'Authorization': getAuthToken() };


// omitted, creating and connecting the MCP client
```

Updating the server middleware to validate the JWT

Finally, we need to update the server middleware to validate the JWT. Here's how we can do it:

```
import { validateJWT } from "./your_jwt_utility"; // import the
validateJWT function


app.use((req, res, next) => {
    const authHeader = req.headers["authorization"];
    if (!authHeader || !authHeader.startsWith("Bearer ")) {
        res.status(401).send("Unauthorized");
        return;
    }

    const jwtToken = authHeader.split(" ")[1];
    const decoded = validateJWT(jwtToken);
    if (!decoded) {
        res.status(401).send("Unauthorized");
        return;
    }

    // TODO, check things like existing user, scopes etc.

    // Optionally attach user info to request object
    (req as any).user = decoded;
    next();
});
```

In this code, we've integrated JWT validation into the middleware. It checks for the `Authorization` header, validates the JWT, and either allows the request to proceed or returns a `401 Unauthorized` response. We're also leaving a `TODO` task for you to check things such as existing users, scopes, and so on.

OAuth2

We've definitely improved our security posture by moving from basic authentication to JWT. However, there's still room for improvement. **OAuth2** is a widely adopted authorization framework that provides a more robust and flexible way to secure your application.

It allows you to delegate access to your resources without sharing credentials. What that means concretely is that there are three parties involved when accessing a resource:

- **Resource server**: This is the server that hosts the protected resources, in our case, the MCP server
- **Client**: This is the application that wants to access the protected resources, in our case, the MCP client
- **Authorization server**: This is the server that issues access tokens to the client after successfully authenticating the resource owner and obtaining authorization

What about the delegation part? Well, the resource owner (typically the user) can delegate access to the client by granting it an access token. The client can then use this access token to access the protected resources on behalf of the resource owner. This way, the client doesn't need to know the resource owner's credentials, and the resource owner can revoke access at any time by invalidating the access token. This is clearly a better approach than basic authentication. JWT, however, is often used to represent the access token in OAuth2. So the real improvement with OAuth2 is that it represents a complete framework for managing access tokens, including how they are issued, validated, and revoked.

OAuth2.1 code flow

OAuth2.1 is what's supported by the MCP SDK. Or rather, the way it's supported is by providing a middleware that lets you point out the following:

- **The authorization server**: This is used to issue and validate tokens
- **The resource server**: This is where your data lives and is typically your MCP server
- **The scopes you want to request**: This is where you define what access you want to the resource server

Here's what the flow looks like:

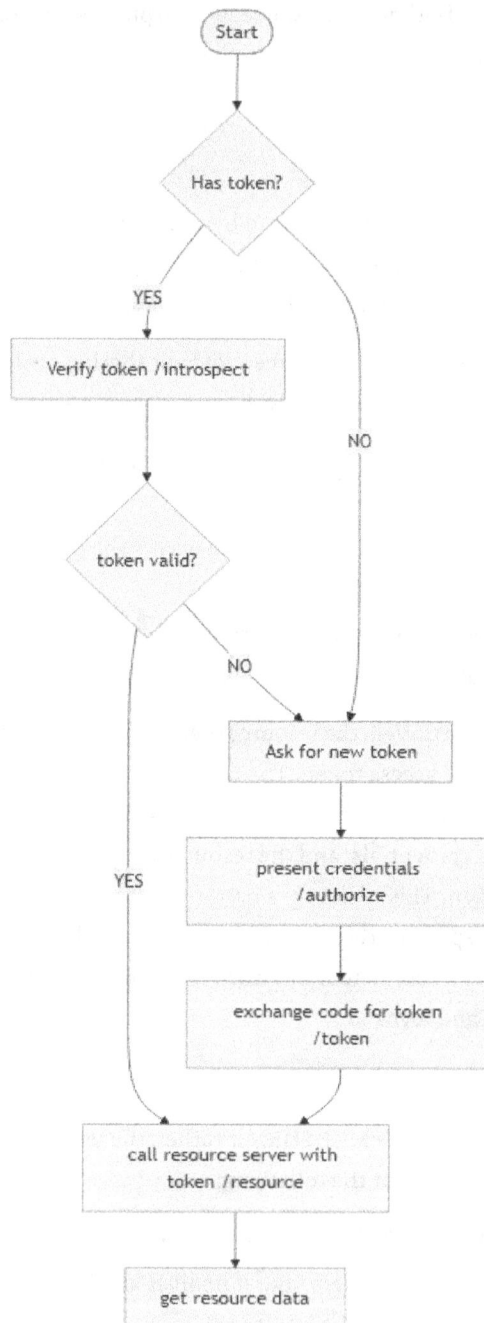

Figure 11.2 – OAuth2.1 flow

The preceding flow tells us that the client will first check whether it has a valid token. If it does, it will use it to access the resource server. If not, it will ask the user to authenticate and authorize the client to access the resource server on its behalf. Once the client has a valid token, it can use it to access the resource server.

So, what does the MCP SDK do for us then? It provides middleware that lets us easily integrate OAuth2.1 into our MCP server. All we need to do is provide the following configuration options:

```
import express from 'express';
import { ProxyOAuthServerProvider } from
  '@modelcontextprotocol/sdk/server/auth/providers/proxyProvider.js';
import { mcpAuthRouter } from
  '@modelcontextprotocol/sdk/server/auth/router.js';

const app = express();

const proxyProvider = new ProxyOAuthServerProvider({
    endpoints: {
        authorizationUrl: "https://auth.external.com/oauth2/v1/authorize",
        tokenUrl: "https://auth.external.com/oauth2/v1/token",
        revocationUrl: "https://auth.external.com/oauth2/v1/revoke",
    },
    verifyAccessToken: async (token) => {
        return {
            token,
            clientId: "123",
            scopes: ["openid", "email", "profile"],
        }
    },
    getClient: async (client_id) => {
        return {
            client_id,
            redirect_uris: ["http://localhost:3000/callback"],
        }
    }
})

app.use(mcpAuthRouter({
```

```
        provider: proxyProvider,
        issuerUrl: new URL("http://auth.external.com"), // auth server
        baseUrl: new URL("http://mcp.example.com"), // resource server
        serviceDocumentationUrl: new URL("https://docs.example.com/"),
}))
```

In the preceding code, we see how we set up the middleware. A key part is defining ProxyOAuthServerProvider, which is used to interact with the authorization server. As part of this, we define the endpoints for the authorization server, which are the following:

- authorizationUrl: This is the URL where the client will redirect the user to authenticate and authorize the client
- tokenUrl: This is the URL where the client will exchange the authorization code for an access token
- revocationUrl: This is the URL where the client can revoke the access token

These are the fields of the middleware configuration:

- issuer_url: This is the URL of the authorization server that issues the tokens. In a real-world application, this would be the URL of your IdP, such as Auth0, Keycloak, Entra ID, and so on.
- resource_server_url: This is the URL of the resource server, in our case, the MCP server. This is used to validate that the token is intended for this resource server.
- required_scopes: This is a list of scopes that the client must have to access the resource server.

This middleware takes care of validating the token, checking the scopes, and ensuring that the token is intended for the resource server. It also handles the OAuth2 flow, including redirecting the user to the authorization server to obtain an access token if needed.

OAuth 2.1 under the hood

To understand how the OAuth2.1 middleware works under the hood, let's explain the OAuth2.1 code flow in more detail. Here's how the flow works:

1. **Validate token or obtain authorization code:** The client checks whether it has a valid access token. If it does, it uses it to access the resource server. If not, it calls the /authorize endpoint on the authorization server to obtain an authorization code. This code is obtained when the client presents valid credentials and performs a login. The user is then redirected back to the client with the authorization code.

2. **Call /token to exchange authorization code for access token:** The client then calls the /token endpoint on the authorization server to exchange the authorization code for an access token. At this point, it's ready to access the resource server.

3. **Access resource server:** Accessing the resource server is done by calling the desired endpoint and providing the access token in the Authorization header as a bearer token. The resource server then validates the token, checks the scopes, and ensures that the token is intended for this resource server. If everything checks out, it allows the request to proceed.

Just to get a sense of roughly what code is involved, here's a simplified version of the OAuth2.1 middleware flow:

```js
import axios from 'axios';
import process from 'node:process';


// Configuration - use globalThis.process to avoid depending on node type
declarations in this example
const AUTH_SERVER = process.env.AUTH_SERVER || 'http://localhost:5000';
const RESOURCE_SERVER = process.env.RESOURCE_SERVER ||
  'http://localhost:5001';
const CLIENT_ID = process.env.CLIENT_ID || 'abc';
const REDIRECT_URI = process.env.REDIRECT_URI ||
  'http://localhost:3000/callback';
const STATE = 'xyz';
const CODE_CHALLENGE = '123';
const CODE_VERIFIER = '123';


// Helper to exit in Node.js if available
function exit(code = 0) {
  if (process && typeof process.exit === 'function') {
    process.exit(code);
  } else {
    // fallback for environments without process
    throw new Error(`Exit with code ${code}`);
  }
}


// TODO: add existing token use case (introspect existing token before
starting auth flow)
```

```
async function run() {
  try {
    // Step 1: Simulate browser redirect to /authorize
    const authorizeUrl =
      `${AUTH_SERVER}/authorize?client_id=${encodeURIComponent(CLIENT_ID
        )}&redirect_uri=${encodeURIComponent(REDIRECT_URI)}
          &state=${encodeURIComponent(STATE)}
            &code_challenge=${encodeURIComponent(CODE_CHALLENGE)}
              &code_challenge_method=plain`;

    console.log(`Requesting authorization: ${authorizeUrl}`);

    const authResp = await axios.get(authorizeUrl, {
      // prevent following redirects so we can inspect Location header
      maxRedirects: 0,
      // accept non-2xx statuses without throwing
      validateStatus: () => true,
    });

    const redirectLocation = (authResp.headers &&
      (authResp.headers['location'] || authResp.headers['Location'])) as
      | string
      | undefined;

    if (!redirectLocation) {
      console.error('Authorization server did not redirect.
        Is it running?');
      exit(1);
    }

    // Step 2: Extract authorization code from redirect
    const parsed = new URL(redirectLocation!);
    const authCode = parsed.searchParams.get('code');
    console.log(`Received authorization code: ${authCode}`);

    if (!authCode) {
```

```
      console.error('No authorization code found in redirect');
      exit(1);
    }


    // Step 3: Exchange code for access token
    const tokenParams = new URLSearchParams();
    tokenParams.append('grant_type', 'authorization_code');
    tokenParams.append('code', authCode!);
    tokenParams.append('redirect_uri', REDIRECT_URI);
    tokenParams.append('client_id', CLIENT_ID);
    tokenParams.append('code_verifier', CODE_VERIFIER);


    const tokenResp = await axios.post(`${AUTH_SERVER}/token`,
      tokenParams.toString(), {
      headers: { 'Content-Type': 'application/x-www-form-urlencoded' },
    });


    const accessToken = tokenResp.data && tokenResp.data.access_token;
    console.log(`Access token: ${accessToken}`);


    if (!accessToken) {
      console.error('Token response did not include access_token',
        tokenResp.data);
      exit(1);
    }


    // Step 4: Call resource server
    const resourceResp = await axios.get(`${RESOURCE_SERVER}/userinfo`, {
      headers: { Authorization: `Bearer ${accessToken}` },
    });


    console.log('User info response:');
    console.log(resourceResp.data);
  } catch (err: any) {
    if (axios.isAxiosError(err) && err.response) {
      console.error('Request failed:', err.response.status,
        err.response.data);
```

```
    } else {
      console.error('Unexpected error:', err);
    }
    exit(1);
  }
}

run();
```

Here's what the code does:

- **Step 1:** The client constructs the authorization URL and makes a GET request to the /authorize endpoint on the authorization server. The user is redirected to this URL to authenticate and authorize the client. The response contains a redirect URL with an authorization code.

- **Step 2:** The client extracts the authorization code from the redirect URL.

- **Step 3:** The client makes a POST request to the /token endpoint on the authorization server to exchange the authorization code for an access token.

- **Step 4:** The client makes a GET request to the resource server, providing the access token in the Authorization header as a bearer token. The resource server validates the token and returns the requested resource if the token is valid.

Concluding thoughts on security with OAuth2.1

In a production scenario, the only code you would write yourself would be the client and the resource server. The authorization server would be a separate component/service, for example, handled via Entra ID if you're using Azure, or Amazon Cognito if you're on AWS. Auth0 is another good choice.

You need to decide what you are putting the authorization component in front of:

- **The web server:** If so, you can use standard web server middleware approaches with your chosen IdP, such as Entra ID, Amazon Cognito, Auth0, or similar.

- **The MCP server:** If choosing this, by all means, leverage auth components in the MCP SDK. You can still use standard middleware approaches here as well, but you will use the MCP SDK's built-in authentication features.

- **A gateway (a reverse proxy)**: A gateway is a service such as Azure API Management or Gateway from AWS. Both of these services are capable of handling authentication and can simplify the architecture. Additionally, these services have features you might want to use around AI usage, such as content safety and semantic caching, and also features that help with resiliency and scaling.

Also, when it comes to authorization per tool, you might need to add extra code checks for the call to a tool to ensure that the user has the right scopes/permissions to use that tool. Different tools might require different scopes/permissions.

Summary

In this chapter, you've learned about the importance of securing your MCP server and client. You've seen how to implement basic authentication, JWT, and OAuth2.1 to enhance the security of your applications. Remember that security is an ongoing process, and it's essential to stay updated with the latest best practices and technologies to protect your applications and data. In our next and final chapter, we'll explore how to bring your MCP server to production and ensure that it's robust and scalable.

Assignment 1: Secure your MCP server with basic authentication

In this assignment, you're asked to implement basic authentication in your MCP server, which involves the creation of a middleware that checks for the Authorization header in incoming requests. The client should send the credentials in the Authorization header. This is a good first step to secure your MCP server, but remember that basic authentication has its limitations and should ideally be replaced with more secure methods.

> **Tip**
>
> Review the code snippets provided earlier in the section on basic authentication for guidance.

Solution 1

You can access the solution at `https://github.com/PacktPublishing/Learn-Model-Context-Protocol-with-TypeScript/blob/main/Chapter11/code/basic/README.md`.

Assignment 2: Secure your MCP server with JWT

In this assignment, you're asked to improve upon your previous assignment by implementing JWT authentication in your MCP server. Review the parts on JWT in this chapter for guidance.

Solution 2

You can access the solution at `https://github.com/PacktPublishing/Learn-Model-Context-Protocol-with-TypeScript/blob/main/Chapter11/solutions/README.md`.

Quiz

1. What is the most secure approach out of the following?

    - A: Basic authentication over HTTP

    - B: JWT over HTTP

    - C: OAuth 2.1

2. Which of the following best describes a *scope* in the context of authentication and authorization?

    - A: The specific permissions or access rights that a client application is requesting from a resource server.

    - B: A unique identifier for a user session

    - C: A type of encryption algorithm used to secure tokens

You can access the solution at `https://github.com/PacktPublishing/Learn-Model-Context-Protocol-with-TypeScript/blob/main/Chapter11/solutions/solution-quiz.md`.

Resources

- The whole chapter in this free curriculum tells you about problems, attacks, and how to mitigate them: `https://github.com/microsoft/mcp-for-beginners/tree/main/02-Security`

- This lesson covers Entra ID security with MCP: `https://github.com/microsoft/mcp-for-beginners/tree/main/05-AdvancedTopics/mcp-security-entra`

- This repository shows solutions for working with Azure API Management and OAuth with GitHub: `https://github.com/Azure-Samples/mcp-auth-servers/blob/main/README.md`

- This chapter covers security best practices: `https://github.com/microsoft/mcp-for-beginners/blob/main/05-AdvancedTopics/mcp-security/README.md`

Get This Book's PDF Version and Exclusive Extras

UNLOCK NOW

Scan the QR code (or go to `packtpub.com/unlock`). Search for this book by name, confirm the edition, and then follow the steps on the page.

Note: Keep your invoice handy. Purchases made directly from Packt don't require an invoice.

12

Bringing MCP Apps to Production

Welcome to the final chapter of this book. Great that you've made it this far! You've learned how to build both servers and clients and might be wondering how you take that last step toward sharing what you've built with the world.

That's a great question, and this chapter will guide you through all the things you should consider to ensure that your MCP application is well-tested, reliable, secure, and performs well in a production environment. Let's begin!

This chapter covers the following topics:

- **Architecture and design:** Here, we will go through modular design, integration patterns, and specific architectural impact due to AI
- **Packaging and distribution:** Here, we will discuss different packaging options, standalone, embedded, deployment channels, and semantic versioning
- **Testing and deployment automation:** Here, we will look at different types of testing strategies, such as unit testing, integration testing, and AI testing, and ensure that those tests are used within a CI/CD pipeline to deploy with confidence
- **Operations and observability:** Here, we will talk about scaling, resiliency patterns, observability, governance, and future proofing

Architecture and design

When designing your MCP application, there are several architectural considerations to keep in mind. These include modular design, integration patterns, and the impact of AI on architecture. In this section, we'll look at the following topics:

- **Integration patterns:** How does MCP fit into your existing architecture, and what patterns can you use to ensure seamless integration?

- **Documentation:** How do you document your architecture and design decisions to ensure clarity and maintainability?

- **Architecture review:** What are the key aspects to consider when reviewing your architecture to ensure that it meets your requirements and is scalable, maintainable, and secure?

Now that we have an overview, let's dive into each topic.

Integration patterns

MCP comes with its own set of integration patterns to facilitate seamless communication between clients and servers. However, if you use a transport such as Streamable HTTP or SSE, this server is then hosted via a web app using HTTP and most likely organized like a RESTful API. That could mean you need to develop or use specific middleware for web API-to-MCP communication for the sake of logging, security, and more. Here's how that could work. Note the middleware used in the web API. Also note how the web API is most likely a RESTful API, and the client and server use JSON-RPC, as dictated by the MCP protocol:

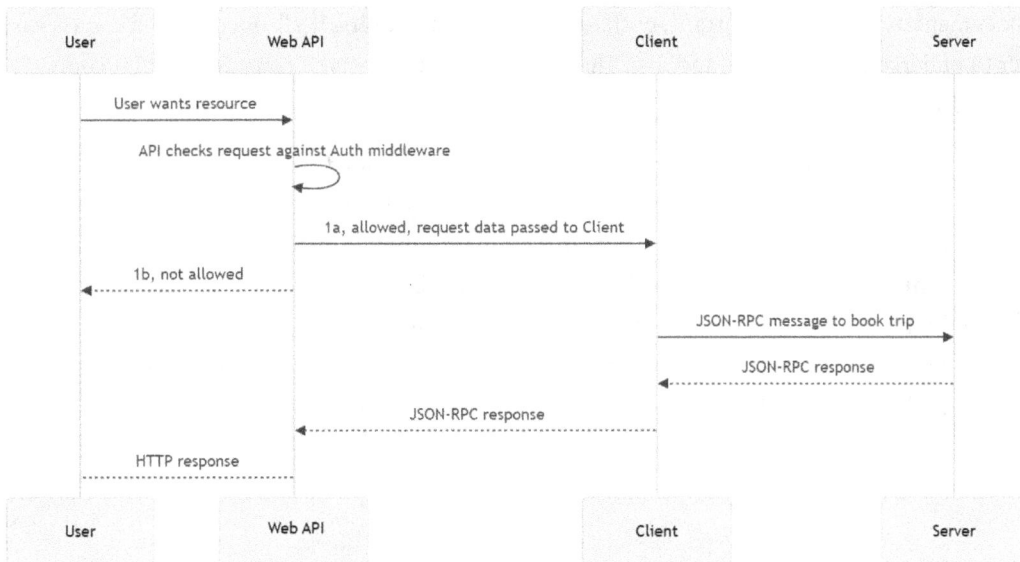

Figure 12.1 – Integration patterns flow

In this sequence diagram, you can see how the different components interact with each other. The user makes a request to the web API, which then checks the request against its authentication middleware. If the request is allowed, the web API forwards the request data to the client. The client then communicates with the server using JSON-RPC messages.

Documentation

It's important that we document our code well so we understand all the bigger parts and how they fit together. This will help both current and future developers to understand the system and make it easier to maintain and extend.

Documentation is very important, both for developers and users. Well-documented code is easier to understand, maintain, and use. There are different aspects to consider when it comes to documentation:

- **Document code and generate documentation**: All code should generally be well documented, which means we should aim to document all the operations on input and output. As developers, we know that out-of-date information is sometimes worse than no documentation, so we should strive to generate documentation from the code. What you're looking for is to have your code generate documentation in an Open API format, formerly known as Swagger. For example, this piece of code has its routes documented in a way to make it easy for the used framework to generate documentation from it:

```python
from fastapi import FastAPI
from pydantic import BaseModel
from typing import List


app = FastAPI()



class Booking(BaseModel):
    id: int
    title: str
    description: str = False
    when: str

@app.get("/booking/", response_model=Booking, tags=["bookings"],
    summary="Book a trip",  description="Lets user book a trip[]")
def book_trip():
    return Booking(id=1, title="Trip to Paris", description="A
        wonderful trip to Paris", when="2023-09-15")
```

When the code is documented like so with tags, summary, and more, this will be used to generate Open API documentation automatically. Whatever framework and runtime you go with, make sure your code is easy to document and easy to generate documentation from.

- **Tests are also documentation**: Tests are sometimes the best way to understand how a feature is supposed to work. They provide concrete examples of expected behavior and can help clarify the intent behind complex logic. Ensure that you include comprehensive tests that cover various scenarios and edge cases.

- **Include context flow diagrams and edge case handling**: Mermaid diagrams are becoming a standard and are also supported by GitHub in terms of rendering various flowcharts, sequence diagrams, and more, so consider Mermaid or another way of creating these diagrams. Seeing how something works visually can save both developers and consumers of the code countless hours.

Architecture review

Your architecture should consider the following:

- **Modular design**: Make sure all functionality is separated into logical boundaries so that all areas are in their own modules. Different runtimes do this in different ways, but a good rule of thumb is that your code should be organized in a way that makes it easy to understand and maintain. Additionally, you should aim to keep related code together and minimize dependencies between modules. Finally, there should only be one reason to change, meaning each module should have a single responsibility. For example, you wouldn't keep parsing logic in the same module as business logic.

- **Validation**: Implement robust validation mechanisms to ensure data integrity and correctness. This includes input validation, output validation, and contract validation between different components. There's also a security aspect to this, as malicious actors may try to exploit vulnerabilities in your system. TypeScript SDK uses Zod. Leverage these validation libraries for both input and output to address both correctness and security. Here's an example of using input validation:

```
import { StdioServerTransport } from
  "@modelcontextprotocol/sdk/server/stdio.js";
import { z, ZodRawShape, ZodObject } from "zod";
import { Server } from "@modelcontextprotocol/sdk/server/index.js";
import { ListToolsRequestSchema, CallToolRequestSchema } from
  "@modelcontextprotocol/sdk/types.js"
```

```
// Create an MCP server
const server = new Server({
  name: "demo-server",
  version: "1.0.0"
},{
  capabilities: {
    tools: {}
  }
});


let AddToolInputSchema = z.object({
  a: z.number(),
  b: z.number()
});


type AddInputType = z.infer<typeof AddToolInputSchema>;


let tools = [
  {
    "name": "add",
    "description": "Adds two numbers",
    "inputSchema": {
      "type": "object",
      "properties": {
        "a": { "type": "number" },
        "b": { "type": "number" }
      },
      "required": ["a", "b"]
    },
    "schema": AddToolInputSchema,
    "callback": async (input) => {
      let args = input as z.infer<typeof AddToolInputSchema>;
      const { a, b } = args;
      return a + b;
    }
```

```
    }
  ];

  server.setRequestHandler(ListToolsRequestSchema, async (request)
    => {
    return {
      tools: tools
    }
  });

  server.setRequestHandler(CallToolRequestSchema, async (request)
    => {
    const { method, params: { name }} = request;

    let tool = tools.find(t => t.name === name);

    if (tool) {
      try {
        let schema = tool.schema as ZodObject<ZodRawShape>;
        let input = schema.parse(request.params.arguments);
        let result = await tool.callback(input);
        return {
          content: [{ type: 'text', text: `Result ${result}` }]
        };
      } catch(a) {
        throw new Error(`Failed to parse input: ${a}`);
      }
    }

    throw new Error(`Unknown tool: ${name}`);
  });

  const transport = new StdioServerTransport();
  await server.connect(transport);
  console.log("MCP server is running...");
```

Let's break down the code:

1. **Server creation**: The code starts by creating an MCP server instance with a name and version.

2. **Tool definition**: It defines a tool called add with an input schema for validation:

```
let AddToolInputSchema = z.object({
    a: z.number(),
    b: z.number()
});
```

This schema, defined in Zod, is used to validate the input for the add tool to ensure that both a and b are numbers and that both are present in the input.

3. **Request handlers**: The server sets up request handlers for listing tools and calling a tool.

4. **Input validation**: When a tool is called, the input is validated against the defined schema using Zod:

```
try {
    let schema = tool.schema as ZodObject<ZodRawShape>;
    let input = schema.parse(request.params.arguments);
    let result = await tool.callback(input);
    return {
      content: [{ type: 'text', text: `Result ${result}` }]
    };
} catch(a) {
    throw new Error(`Failed to parse input: ${a}`);
}
```

The call to the parse function will fail if the user/client is providing the wrong input format or missing required fields. If it parses correctly, we end up calling callback on the tool object. This might look like a bit of code to achieve validation; however, you can easily add more tools to the tools array with their own schemas and callbacks, and you don't have to change any of the other code.

5. **Error handling**: If validation fails, an error is thrown with a descriptive message.

6. **Transport connection**: Finally, the server connects to a transport layer for communication.

In this example, you see that there's a tool called `create_user`. It takes a `User` model as input, which will immediately help with validation and serialization. The following payload would lead to a new user being created:

```
{
    "id": 0,
    "name": "chris",
    "email": "chris@example.com"
}
```

On the other hand, the following payload would lead to a validation error as `id` is missing:

```
{
    "name": "chris",
    "email": "chris@example.com"
}
```

This way, you can set up validation for all incoming data and ensure that only correct data enters your system. Of course, from a business and security standpoint, you can keep adding more validation rules as needed before you end up persisting the data.

- **AI's impact on architecture**: If you ship a client and a server, your client will most likely have access to an AI model, which means there are specific things to consider from an architectural standpoint. This includes how the client communicates with the AI model, how to manage context between the client and server, and how to handle any potential failures or timeouts:

  - **Decoupled architecture**: Ensure you decouple content management, model invocation, and the UI.

  - **Latency and reliability, and impact on UI**: Also consider the implications of latency and reliability when designing interactions with the AI model. This means, for example, if the AI model takes time to return a response, ensure that the UI remains responsive and provides feedback to the user. If the AI stops responding due to failure or rate limiting, it needs to be handled gracefully. Also, ensure you have fallback mechanisms such as retry logic and circuit breakers. We'll talk more about this later in the chapter.

- **Token budgeting:** Not only is the token budget something to consider as a running cost for the AI model, but it's also important from an architectural standpoint, as we will need to implement caching strategies and other mechanisms to optimize token usage.

- **Security:** Implement security best practices to protect your application and its data. This includes securing APIs, managing user authentication and authorization, and ensuring data privacy and compliance with regulations. Consider how you can adopt *least privilege* to minimize access rights for users and services. That means ensuring that users and services only have access to the resources they absolutely need. A consequence of this is that you may need to implement more granular access controls and continuously monitor for any unauthorized access attempts.

Packaging and distribution

Before you even type a single line of code, you need to consider what you're building. With MCP, you have different options on how to package and distribute your application.

Packaging options

Let's look at some packaging options.

- **Standalone server:** This is designed for public access or for private use. Regardless of private or public access, you need to think about authentication, authorization, and data privacy. But for private distribution within a company or organization, you need to think about discoverability, how internal teams will find and use the service, and also compliance with internal policies.

- **Embedded client/server:** Such a system probably consists of a client and a server component, and the client most likely ships with AI capabilities, so make sure you consider the implications of that, such as data privacy and security and responsible AI use, and any regulatory requirements that may apply.

Standalone server

Let's say your goal is to build an MCP server only; that means you most likely focus on building an API that wasn't there before you wrap a pre-existing API. With this being MCP, you need to decide where this server is meant to run. Here are some considerations:

- **Local machine**: In this case, the server needs to use the STDIO transport. Also, because it runs on a user's machine, from a security aspect, how can you ensure it's sandboxed and doesn't have access to resources it shouldn't? In fact, should you even allow it to access the network? That's up to you, but you should consider these aspects. See this filesystem MCP server, where the server comes with configuration that both restricts access, which directories it has access to, and it also ships instructions on how to run it in a container environment to ensure the MCP server has as little access as possible (https://github. com/modelcontextprotocol/servers/tree/main/src/filesystem).

- **Remotely via a URL**: If your server is accessed remotely, you might not need to be as much concerned about sandboxing, but you do need to think about authentication and authorization, and every aspect of securing the API endpoint. For authentication/authorization, consider using OAuth2 or API keys, and always validate incoming requests. Additionally, consider **role-based access control (RBAC)** to ensure that users don't have more access to various server features than they need. That is, consider whether you need administrator users, normal users, or guest access, and what resources and what type of permission levels everything should have.

In both of these cases, you're most likely storing the source code in something like GitHub or a similar version-controlled system.

Embedded client/server

Integrating MCP into your existing architecture requires careful planning. From a distribution standpoint, your MCP implementation will most likely deploy in the same motion as your existing services and apps it's integrating with. From a code organizational perspective, you can still create them as separate services callable as APIs or a microservices architecture; the choice is yours. What you do need to realize, though, is that shipping an MCP integration means you ship more than a server; you need to ship an MCP client as well. The client will be responsible for communicating with the MCP server, handling requests, and managing context.

Distribution channels

When it comes to distribution channels, you have a few options:

- **Package the server as a Docker container:** This is a great option if you want to ensure that the server runs in a consistent environment, regardless of where it's deployed. You can push the Docker image to a container registry such as Docker Hub or GitHub Container Registry, and users can pull and run the container easily. With this option, you should specify how to configure the container and any environment variables that need to be set, as in this example:

```
FROM node:22.12-alpine AS builder

WORKDIR /app

COPY src/filesystem /app
COPY tsconfig.json /tsconfig.json

RUN --mount=type=cache,target=/root/.npm npm install

RUN --mount=type=cache,target=/root/.npm-production npm ci --ignore-
scripts --omit-dev


FROM node:22-alpine AS release

WORKDIR /app

COPY --from=builder /app/dist /app/dist
COPY --from=builder /app/package.json /app/package.json
COPY --from=builder /app/package-lock.json /app/package-lock.json

ENV NODE_ENV=production

RUN npm ci --ignore-scripts --omit-dev

ENTRYPOINT ["node", "/app/dist/index.js"]
```

The preceding example is from the example filesystem MCP server (`https://github.com/modelcontextprotocol/servers/tree/main/src/filesystem`).

- **Distribute via a package manager**: If your server is built with Node.js or Python, you can package it as an `npm` module or a PyPI package, respectively. This allows users to easily install and manage your server as a dependency in their own projects. The corresponding package manager for .NET would be NuGet, and for Java, it would be Maven or Gradle. Different package managers have different rules for what's needed to package and distribute your code, but it usually involves the creation of a README file, a license, and compressing the code into a bundle. It's a great way for users of your MCP server to find and use what you've built.

- **Repository distribution**: You can also distribute your server by providing access to the source code repository directly. This allows users to clone the repository and build the server themselves, giving them more control over the build process and dependencies. Make sure you provide instructions on how to run it and configure it. This configuration instruction from Playwright's MCP server (`https://github.com/RBC/microsoft-playwright-mcp`) is a good example showing how to start using it from a host such as VS Code or Claude Code:

```
{
  "mcpServers": {
    "playwright": {
      "command": "npx",
      "args": [
        "@playwright/mcp@latest"
      ]
    }
  }
}
```

In this instruction, you see how to start the server using `npx` and how to provide arguments via `args`.

Adopting semantic versioning

Semantic versioning is another thing we should adopt for our code. This is because it makes it easier for both you and the consumer of your code to understand the nature of changes in each release.

It works with the following versions:

- A major version when you make incompatible API changes
- A minor version when you add functionality in a backward-compatible manner
- A patch version when you make backward-compatible bug fixes

How you encode this in your software is to version your software; for example, in version 1.3.0, 1 is the major version, 3 is the minor version, and 0 is the patch version. If you only fix the software by applying a patch, then you should increment it from 1.3.0 to 1.3.1. Adding a new feature should be seen as a minor, so you would increment it from 1.3.0 to 1.4.0. A lot of changes, including changes that make the code break, are seen as a major change, and the version should therefore increase from 1.3.0 to 2.0.0.

By encoding it this way, you create a clear and predictable versioning scheme that communicates the nature of changes to users and developers alike. Developer teams can therefore choose whether to stay on 1.3.x (in which case, they only update the software due to bug fixes and patch changes), or if they want new features but to prioritize stability, they would instead be okay with any version matching 1.x.x, which would allow them to receive new features while still being on a stable base that doesn't risk breaking changes.

Testing and deployment automation

Testing is a crucial part of software development, and it's especially important when working with AI models. Automated tests help ensure that your code behaves as expected and can catch issues early in the development process. Additionally, deploying your application should be automated to ensure consistency and reliability.

Testing strategy

We've mentioned testing already as a form of documentation. It's also a vital part to ensure the code behaves as expected. Make sure that the tests you write are comprehensive and cover various scenarios. Some tests you might consider include the following:

- **Unit tests:** These are good for ensuring that individual components work as intended. In the context of MCP, consider breaking out parsing logic into separate modules to facilitate easier testing.

- **Integration tests**: These validate the interaction between different components and ensure that they work together as expected. For MCP, if your MCP integration is part of a web application, it could be a good idea to set up end-to-end tests that simulate user interactions with the UI. Such a test would then call a web endpoint, which calls a client, and said client would then call an MCP server feature that processes the request and returns a response.

- **AI tests**: As AI models can behave unpredictably, it's crucial to have tests that specifically validate their outputs. This includes testing for various input scenarios and edge cases, and ensuring that the model's responses are within acceptable parameters. Consider using techniques such as adversarial testing to probe the model's weaknesses. Adversarial testing involves creating inputs that are specifically designed to trick the model into making mistakes. It's also a good idea to have a set of prompts to test against, where the system should work well or should invoke a tool or some other functionality.

Generally, with tests, focus on various aspects such as performance, security, and usability.

Deployment automation

Building an app, securing it, architecting well, and logging... all that is good, but without a robust process for deployment, none of that matters. So what's **robust** then? Robust in the year 2025 means that we can deploy something at the click of a button, many times a day, and that we do so with a number of guardrails in place. **Guardrails** are steps where we ensure that tests run and pass, policies are followed, and we're keeping within certain metrics, for example, we don't make the code slower, and so on.

There are many choices for how to deploy, such as GitHub Actions or Jenkins. They have one thing in common, though: to deploy, you need to define a pipeline with steps in it and make sure the final step leads to an artifact that either can be deployed or you end up with a new deployment in production.

In addition to being able to deploy, we need to ensure that the deployment process is reliable and can be repeated consistently. Also, mistakes happen, so we need to be able to roll back changes if something goes wrong.

What does all this mean for our code? Well, it usually results in a .yml file being created to represent the pipeline mentioned previously.

Then, you might need a different configuration or a different environment, so that's also something to keep in mind.

Is this different for MCP compared to normal software? Well, the difference lies in realizing that you may ship AI, and for that reason, you might need a separate deployment pipeline for your AI, looking at performance on models, context management, and more.

Operations and observability

Once your application is in production, there's a set of problems we need to address:

- **Observability**: Do you know how your app is doing? Is it under load, is it slow, is it failing, and is it secure?

- **Scalability and resilience**: Can your app handle traffic spikes? Can it scale up and down, and is it resilient to failures?

- **Monitoring and feedback**: Do you know when something goes wrong? Can you alert the right people, and do you have a feedback loop to improve the app over time?

- **Governance and compliance**: Are you compliant with regulations? Do you have the right policies in place, and are you managing data responsibly?

- **Future proofing**: Are you prepared for future changes? Can you adapt to new technologies, and are you continuously improving your app?

Observability

Do you know how your app is doing, really? If you do, that means you've been diligent in terms of adding logging, tracing, and metrics. You have probably added a dashboard so you can easily visualize all that, and you even know where to optimize if needed. Most of us aspire to have that level of knowledge of our app and how it's doing. When you develop a piece of software at a business, for a client, and so on, there's a lot at stake. We need to keep the data secure, the app needs to respond at a decent speed and use the resources it's been constrained with, and it needs to work. It doesn't sound that hard, right? But it is, especially when you start serving tens of thousands of customers, or even millions. But instead of focusing on how difficult it is to get all this correct, let's talk about the most important things we need to get in place to at least be able to observe our app:

- **Logging**: Logging is crucial for understanding the behavior of your application. It helps understand what goes in, what went out, and hopefully, how long it took through various parts of the app. Having logging at the right places can help you identify bottlenecks and optimize performance. What's important to consider is the log level (e.g., info, debug, or error) and the context you include (e.g., user ID, request ID, etc.) to make your logs more useful.

- **Tracing**: Tracing is essential for understanding the flow of requests through your system. It allows you to see how different services interact and where bottlenecks may occur. Implement distributed tracing to get a complete picture of request paths and latencies. Tracing differs from logging in that it captures the journey of a request. Therefore, it usually contains additional information such as origin, destination, and any intermediate services involved.

- **Metrics**: Metrics are about knowing the health, performance, and scalability of your server. Important metrics to capture are therefore CPU and memory usage, request throughput, response time, and even error rate. Capturing all that will provide you with a good understanding of how your system is doing.

For observability, MCP isn't vastly different from traditional applications, but there are unique aspects to consider, such as model performance and token usage. What could be of particular interest to measure for MCP specifically could be token usage per request versus when it's being cached or reused. Also, for the sake of logging, MCP has different logs built in that we should leverage to indicate errors, warnings, normal logs, and so on (`https://modelcontextprotocol.io/specification/2025-03-26/server/utilities/logging`).

Scalability and resilience

Another very important aspect of deploying MCP applications is ensuring that they can scale and remain resilient under load. The problem you're solving is to ensure the following:

- **Traffic spikes**: You can take on a sudden increase in traffic without degrading performance. This is usually business-critical if you're an e-commerce company and need to be able to handle an increase in purchases during peak shopping times.

- **Scaling up and down**: You can efficiently manage resources to handle varying loads.

- **Resilience**: You can quickly recover from failures and minimize downtime. Doing this well means the users will barely notice failures or at all. The opposite means the users will experience disruptions and degraded service, and might take their business elsewhere.

Now that we understand the major problems and why we should care about these problems, what's the solution? For traffic spikes, we need to be able to scale up and down quickly. Most cloud providers have this feature built in. What you need to decide on is how much you want to control this. For example, do you want to specify that scaling should happen on a certain CPU or memory load, or are you okay with the chosen platform to handle this?

Also, as an architect, you could also design so that you, for example, use a message queue over directly talking to a database and so on. There are several ways to go about this, and only you know what size you need to account for:

- **Load balancing**: The idea with load balancing is to distribute incoming traffic across multiple instances of your application or service to ensure no single instance is overwhelmed. This improves responsiveness and availability. For the sake of your solution, though, you might treat your application and your AI as separate entities and therefore set up different sets of load-balancing schemes for your MCP server and your AI model endpoints.

- **Rate limiting**: Rate limiting is a technique used to control the amount of incoming requests to a service within a specific time frame. This helps prevent abuse, ensures fair usage, and manages API costs. Again, just like load balancing, you might have different schemes for your web app and your AI endpoints.

- **Circuit breakers**: The idea behind circuit breakers is to detect failures and prevent the system from making requests that are likely to fail. When a certain threshold of failures is reached, the circuit breaker trips, and subsequent requests are automatically rejected for a period of time. This allows the system to recover and prevents it from being overwhelmed by failed requests. From a user experience standpoint, circuit breakers can help maintain a smooth experience by providing fallback options or graceful degradation when certain services are unavailable.

So, how do we implement these mechanisms? Well, some of them can be done at the application level, while others may require infrastructure support. Here are some strategies:

- **Load balancing**: Use a load balancer to distribute traffic across multiple instances of your application or service. This can be done using cloud provider features or dedicated load balancing solutions.

- **Rate limiting**: Implement rate limiting at the API gateway or application level to control the number of requests from users or services. This can help prevent abuse and ensure fair usage.

- **Circuit breakers**: These can be implemented using an API gateway.

If you're using a cloud provider, you should be looking into Azure API Management or Amazon API Gateway to implement these strategies effectively. These services will address security, scalability, and reliability concerns, and even have features helping you with AI concerns. What they have in common is that they use a declarative approach to define these strategies. For example, Azure API Management uses XML to define policies for rate limiting, caching, and other features. That makes it easy to apply and configure without changing any code.

So, the recommendation here is to look into your cloud provider of choice and leverage their API management solutions to implement these strategies. Check the links at the end of this chapter in the *Resources* section for more information.

Monitoring and feedback

For monitoring, we've alluded to the problems you can run into, such as performance bottlenecks, error rates, and user behavior patterns. Here are some strategies to address these issues:

- **Implement application performance monitoring (APM) tools**: Use APM tools to gain insights into performance bottlenecks and error rates.

- **Address error rates**: Implement automated error tracking and alerting to quickly identify and resolve issues.

- **User behavior analytics**: Leverage analytics tools to understand user interactions and identify potential areas for improvement.

- **AI usage**: You want to make sure your AI is used as intended and not being abused or misused, and that it produces the responses you expect. For a solution, you should sample requests and analyze them at regular intervals to ensure compliance with usage policies and performance expectations. Also, add feedback loops in the form of letting users provide input on AI-generated content. Having this in place allows you to perform prompt tuning and context refining. Things you want to set up a system for are also to mitigate prompt injection attacks, unsafe content generation, and other potential risks, such as the mentioning of competitor names and more. Whichever service you end up with should be able to tackle all these.

The major cloud providers have monitoring solutions that can help you set up dashboards, alarms, and more. Also, for AI service usage, there are specialized tools that help you analyze prompts. See more on this in the *Resources* section in this chapter.

Governance and compliance

Governance is about ensuring that your application operates within the bounds of legal and ethical standards. How much you need to adhere to these depends on the sector you work in. There's GDPR for data protection, HIPAA for health information, and other regulations that may apply. Ensure you have a robust compliance framework in place.

From a software standpoint, make it easy to comply with these policies by ensuring you log all interactions and create an *audit trail* so you know who changed what and when. You might also consider implementing access controls and data encryption to further protect sensitive information. If you are shipping AI, you will need to care about bias and fairness in your models. Therefore, you might need things such as robust system prompts and usage of content safety services that help implement the policy you need to adhere to, whether it's GDPR or other regulations.

Future-proofing

Okay, so you've managed to deploy a system that meets your current needs. But what about the future? How can you stay safe, secure, compliant, and whatever else you define as success?

MCP is a fairly young protocol, and as such, it will continue to evolve. You need to keep track of such changes; if there are no constructs you should apply, perhaps there are transports you should stop using (SSE is already deprecated in favor of Streamable HTTP). There might also be new guidance on certain feature usage. You need to stay on top of all of that.

There's also tooling associated with MCP (for example, the Inspector tool) that may change, with either more tools or how you interact with it changing.

Then, you have the SDKs, as software, which are continuously changing. Some changes are so major that they might break your code. You might consider staying on a certain major version at least for a while, but ensure you get all security updates. Combine this with recognized tools such as Dependabot, GitHub Advanced Security, and more to ensure you make informed choices and know what risks you are taking by staying on a certain SDK version or moving on to a new one.

It's hard to foresee the future, but you can have a responsible stance on heightened security. Software changes quickly, and new threats are detected regularly. Stay informed about the latest security practices and be ready to adapt your system as needed.

Summary

This has been a long chapter with much ground to cover, but hopefully you've felt helped by the guidance provided. As long as you're aware of the problems you face and actively work to address them, then the choice is yours for whether you choose to address them through a library, a cloud service, or something else. You should probably spend more time than you think on security, as it's becoming a top concern of companies worldwide.

Make sure you plan according to what you need to do before production, in production, and post-production, and prepare for the future. Stay informed. Things will break; the question is how you respond to those breaks and what measures you have in place to mitigate any potential issues.

If you read this far, it means you've learned a lot from this book, from building your first server and client, interacting with an LLM, consuming the server with a tool such as VS Code, and finally, deploying it in a responsible manner. Congratulations! I'm also always happy to connect with you on LinkedIn at `https://uk.linkedin.com/in/christoffer-noring-3257061`.

Resources

Here are some useful resources:

- *API gateway in Azure AI Management*: `https://docs.azure.cn/en-us/api-management/api-management-gateways-overview`
- This is a great repo showcasing how to add many of the features from rate limiting, monitoring, security, and more – *AI Gateway*: `https://github.com/Azure-Samples/AI-Gateway`

13

Unlock Your Exclusive Benefits

Your copy of this book includes the following exclusive benefits:

- ☁ Next-gen Packt Reader
- 🖫 DRM-free PDF/ePub downloads

Follow the guide below to unlock them. The process takes only a few minutes and needs to be completed once.

Unlock this Book's Free Benefits in 3 Easy Steps

Step 1

Keep your purchase invoice ready for *Step 3*. If you have a physical copy, scan it using your phone and save it as a PDF, JPG, or PNG.

For more help on finding your invoice, visit https://www.packtpub.com/unlock-benefits/help.

> **Note:** If you bought this book directly from Packt, no invoice is required. After *Step 2*, you can access your exclusive content right away.

Step 2

Scan the QR code or go to `https://packtpub.com/unlock`.

On the page that opens (similar to *Figure 13.1* on desktop), search for this book by name and select the correct edition.

Figure 13.1: Packt unlock landing page on desktop

Step 3

After selecting your book, sign in to your Packt account or create one for free. Then upload your invoice (PDF, PNG, or JPG, up to 10 MB). Follow the on-screen instructions to finish the process.

Need help?

If you get stuck and need help, visit `https://www.packtpub.com/unlock-benefits/help` for a detailed FAQ on how to find your invoices and more. This QR code will take you to the help page.

Note: If you are still facing issues, reach out to `customercare@packt.com`.

‹packt›

packtpub.com

Subscribe to our online digital library for full access to over 7,000 books and videos, as well as industry leading tools to help you plan your personal development and advance your career. For more information, please visit our website.

Why subscribe?

- Spend less time learning and more time coding with practical eBooks and Videos from over 4,000 industry professionals
- Improve your learning with Skill Plans built especially for you
- Get a free eBook or video every month
- Fully searchable for easy access to vital information
- Copy and paste, print, and bookmark content

At www.packtpub.com, you can also read a collection of free technical articles, sign up for a range of free newsletters, and receive exclusive discounts and offers on Packt books and eBooks.

Other Books You May Enjoy

If you enjoyed this book, you may be interested in these other books by Packt:

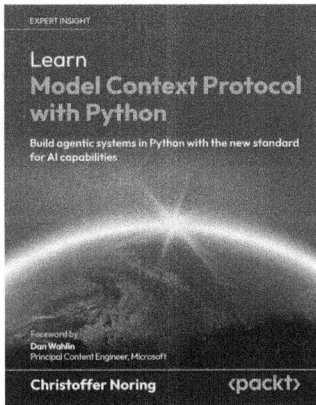

Learn Model Context Protocol with Python

Christoffer Noring

ISBN: 978-1-80610-323-2

- Understand the MCP protocol and its core components
- Build MCP servers that expose tools and resources to a variety of clients
- Test and debug servers using the interactive inspector tools
- Consume servers using Claude Desktop and Visual Studio Code Agents
- Secure MCP apps, as well as managing and mitigating common threats
- Build and deploy MCP apps using cloud-based strategies

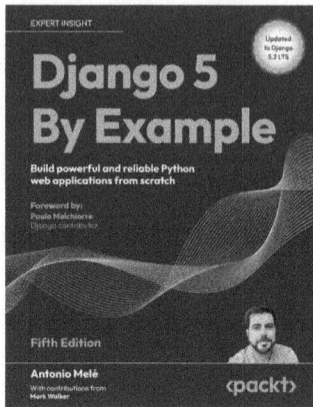

Django 5 By Example

Antonio Melé

ISBN: 978-1-80512-545-7

- Use various Django modules to solve specific problems using the latest features
- Integrate third-party Django applications into your project
- Build complex web applications using Redis, Postgres, Celery/RabbitMQ and Memcached
- Set up a production environment for your project with Docker Compose
- Build a RESTful API with Django Rest Framework (DRF)
- Implement advanced functionalities, such as full-text search engines, user activity streams, payment gateways, and recommender engines
- Build real-time asynchronous (ASGI) apps with Django Channels and WebSockets

Packt is searching for authors like you

If you're interested in becoming an author for Packt, please visit `authors.packtpub.com` and apply today. We have worked with thousands of developers and tech professionals, just like you, to help them share their insight with the global tech community. You can make a general application, apply for a specific hot topic that we are recruiting an author for, or submit your own idea.

Share your thoughts

Now you've finished *Learn Model Context Protocol with TypeScript*, we'd love to hear your thoughts! Scan the QR code below to go straight to the Amazon review page for this book and share your feedback or leave a review on the site that you purchased it from.

`https://packt.link/r/180666139X`

Your review is important to us and the tech community and will help us make sure we're delivering excellent quality content.

Index

www.ingramcontent.com/pod-product-compliance
Lightning Source LLC
Chambersburg PA
CBHW081052220326
41598CB00038B/7070